the Unofficial Guide™ to
Real Estate Investing

Martin Stone
and Spencer Strauss

Hungry Minds, Inc.
New York, NY • Cleveland, OH • Indianapolis, IN

Hungry Minds, Inc.
909 Third Avenue
New York, NY 10022

For general information on Hungry Minds' books in the United States, please call our Customer Care department at 800-762-2974. For reseller information, including discounts and previous sales, please call our Reseller Customer Care department at 800-434-3422.

ISBN: 0-02-863665-1

Manufactured in the United States of America

10 9 8

First edition

Martin Stone dedicates this book to his wife Lori for her love and encouragement and to his longtime teacher, mentor, and friend Jack Buckingham.
Spencer Strauss dedicates this book to the man who gave him an opportunity to succeed, his co-author and great friend Marty Stone.

Acknowledgments

The authors would like to thank all their fantastic editors who made this book possible including Matthew X. Kiernan, Randy Ladenheim-Gil, Jessica Faust, Jennifer Perillo, Brice Gosnell, Faunette Johnston, Georgette Blau, William Bronchick, Warren Ladenheim, Ed Stevens, and Amy Lepore. They also are grateful to everyone at Hungry Minds who had a hand in this project.

Martin Stone would like to thank Spence ("We made a great team!"), his boys Aaron, Chris, and Adam for understanding all the time he spent away from them working at the computer, Kirk and Leslie, Jim, and James Waedekin for his refresher course.

Spencer Strauss owes a debt of gratitude to Sheree Bykofsky, Blake Mitchell, Florence Fagan, Jack Buckingham, and Lori Stone. He also would like to acknowledge, and thank his mom Sandi, his sister Maria, his oldest brother Larry, and his late great father Martin L. Strauss and say, "Dad, today I am a fountain pen."

Finally, both authors would especially like to thank Glenn Bozarth, Keith Covington, Seymour Fagan, and Steven D. Strauss. They all gave their time, encouragement, and help unconditionally.

Contents

The *Unofficial Guide* Reader's Bill of Rights

We Give You More Than the Official Line

Welcome to the *Unofficial Guide* series of lifestyle titles—books that deliver critical, unbiased information that other books can't or won't reveal—*the inside scoop*. Our goal is to provide you with the *most accessible, useful* information and advice possible. The recommendations we offer in these pages are not influenced by the corporate line of any organization or industry; we give you the hard facts whether those institutions like them or not. If something is ill-advised or will cause a loss of time and/or money, we'll give you ample warning. If it is a worthwhile option, we'll let you know that, too.

Armed and Ready

Our hand-picked authors confidently and critically report on a wide range of topics that matter to smart readers like you. Our authors are passionate about their subjects, but they have distanced themselves enough from them to help you be armed and protected and to help you make educated decisions as you go through the process. It is our intent that, from having read this book, you will avoid the pitfalls everyone else falls into and get it right the first time. Don't be fooled by cheap imitations; this is the genuine *Unofficial Guide* series from IDG Books. You may be familiar with the proven track record of our travel *Unofficial Guides*, which have more than three million copies in print. Each year thousands of travelers—new and old—are armed with a brand new, fully updated edition of the flagship *Unofficial Guide to Walt Disney World* by Bob Sehlinger. It is our intention here to provide you with the same level of objective authority that Mr. Sehlinger does in his brainchild.

The Unofficial Panel of Experts

Every work in the lifestyle *Unofficial Guides* series is intensively inspected by a team of three top professionals in their fields. These experts review the manuscript for factual accuracy, comprehensiveness, and an insider's determination as to whether the manuscript fulfills the credo in this Reader's Bill of Rights. In other words, our panel ensures that you are, in fact, getting "the inside scoop."

Our Pledge

The authors, the editorial staff, and the Unofficial Panel of Experts assembled for *Unofficial Guides* are determined to lay out the most valuable alternatives available for our readers. This dictum means that our writers must be explicit, prescriptive, and above all, direct. We strive to be thorough and complete, but our goal is not necessarily to have the "most" or "all" of the information on a topic; this is not, after all, an encyclopedia. Our objective is to help you narrow down your options to the best of what is available, unbiased by affiliation with any industry or organization.

Each *Unofficial Guide* will give you:

- Comprehensive coverage of necessary and vital information

- Authoritative, rigidly fact-checked data

- The most up-to-date insights into trends

- Savvy, sophisticated writing that's also readable

- Sensible, applicable facts and secrets that only an insider would know

Special Features

Every book in our series offers the following six special sidebars in the margins. These sidebars were devised to help you get things done cheaply, efficiently, and smartly.

1. **Timesaver**—tips and shortcuts that save you time

2. **Moneysaver**—tips and shortcuts that save you money

3. **Watch out!**—more serious cautions and warnings

4. **Bright Idea**—general tips and shortcuts to help you find an easier or smarter way to do something

5. **Quote**—statements from real people that are intended to be prescriptive and valuable to you

6. **Unofficially...**—an insider's fact or anecdote

We also recognize your need to have quick information at your fingertips. Therefore, we have provided the following comprehensive sections at the back of the book:

1. **Glossary:** definitions of complicated terminology and jargon

2. **Resource Guide:** lists of relevant agencies, associations, institutions, Web sites, and so on

3. **Recommended Reading List:** suggested titles that can help you get more in-depth information about related topics

4. **Sample Real Estate Investment Plan:** provides you with the ruler to measure how well you're meeting your real estate investment goals.

5. **Sample Property Inspection Report:** familiarizes you with the scope and content of professional property inspections.

6. **Index.**

Letters, Comments, and Questions from Readers

We strive to continually improve the *Unofficial* series, and input from our readers is a valuable way for us to do that.

Many people who use the *Unofficial Guide* travel books write to the authors to ask questions, to make comments, or to share their own discoveries and lessons. For lifestyle *Unofficial Guides*, we also would appreciate all such correspondence—both positive and critical—and we will make our best efforts to incorporate appropriate reader feedback and comments in revised editions of this work.

How to write to us:

Unofficial Guides

Lifestyle Guides

IDG Books

919 E. Hillsdale Blvd. Suite 400

Foster City, CA 94404

Attention: Reader's Comments

About the Authors

Martin Stone has been an investment property broker for the last 27 years. Throughout his career, he has managed more than 1,000 units, has built more than 40 apartment and commercial buildings, and has written and lectured extensively about all areas related to real estate investing. He also is the managing broker of Buckingham Investments and Richmond Financial Services in El Segundo, California. You can reach him or receive free real estate investment advice by logging on www.buckinghaminvestments. com. Marty lives with his wife Lori and their three sons—Chris, Aaron, and Adam—in a home he built himself.

Spencer Strauss makes his living as a real estate broker at Buckingham Investments in El Segundo, California. In that capacity, Spencer has bought, sold, and managed countless buildings and has helped many investors get their start in real estate. He holds a degree from California State University at Fullerton. In addition to *The Unofficial Guide to Real Estate Investing,* he is also the author of *The Complete Idiot's Guide to Impeachment of the President.*

Spencer has been heard on radio stations KFI and KABC in Los Angeles. He has been featured also in *USA Today*, the *New York Post*, the *Chicago Tribune*, the *Long Beach Press Telegram*, and the *Los Angeles Times*. Spencer can be reached by e-mail at spence@ buckinghaminvestments.com.

The *Unofficial Guide* Panel of Experts

T he *Unofficial* editorial team recognizes that you've purchased this book with the expectation of getting the most authoritative, carefully inspected information currently available. Toward that end, on each and every title in this series, we have selected a minimum of two "official" experts comprising the Unofficial Panel who painstakingly review the manuscripts to ensure the following: factual accuracy of all data; inclusion of the most up-to-date and relevant information; and that, from an insider's perspective, the authors have armed you with all the necessary facts you need—but that the institutions don't want you to know.

For *The Unofficial Guide to Real Estate Investing*, we are proud to introduce the following panel of experts:

William Bronchick William Bronchick of Denver, Colorado, is an attorney, lecturer, and active investor in residential housing. Mr. Bronchick is the author of numerous books and home study courses, and he regularly presents real estate workshops around the country. Mr. Bronchick is the president of the Colorado

Association of Real Estate Investors and has appeared on several radio and television talk shows including "*Real Estate Roundtable.*" His articles have appeared in *The Denver Business Journal,* the *National Preventative Law Reporter, Creative Real Estate Magazine,* and most recently in a Russian legal newspaper. Mr. Bronchick is the host of the popular Internet Web site www.Legalwiz.com.

Warren Ladenheim   Warren Ladenheim is a Director at Peak Search, Inc., an executive recruitment firm in New York City. Warren specializes in accounting and financial recruitment, primarily in the real estate industry. Prior to his career in executive recruitment, Warren was a financial controller for firms in the real estate and financial services industries. He is a certified public accountant and began his career, after attending graduate school at Baruch College, City University of New York, in a national, Big-5 CPA firm. Warren lives on Long Island with his wife and two children.

Ed Stevens   Ed Stevens has been actively involved in real estate investment since 1992 including single-family rentals, "rehab and resale" projects, and vacation rentals. He is the developer and principal author of the consumer oriented real estate Web site House Clicks (www.houseclicks.com) as well as several other consumer information Web sites. Ed lives in Richmond, Virginia, with his wife (and invaluable assistant) Cathy. He is president of Smart Sense Publications as well as a licensed Realtor® associated with Century 21 Signature Realty.

Introduction

Creating wealth from real estate is a long-term proposition and, it is not realistic to think you can make a fortune in this game overnight. But fortunes can be made. The purpose of this book is to give you the proper tools, so (with a bit of patience) you can successfully create a lifetime of cash flow and value for you and your loved ones. We know that if you learn the business of real estate, believe in your abilities, enjoy the adventure, and take a risk every now and then, there's a great chance that a richer future is yours for the asking.

It comes as no secret that the global economy has seen its share of turmoil. It appears as though we have corrected our own course, however, and hopefully with the twenty-first century upon us, the rest of the world will follow suit. This economic downturn taught us a lot, specifically about the problems that come with rapid growth, business overhead, inflation, and a host of other basic business principles that somehow got lost over the years. To right our ship, we were forced to rethink our way of doing business.

One of the industries that suffered mightily in the '90s was real estate. We could devote the next

350 pages to a discussion of whether the economy caused the problems in the industry or vice versa. Instead, we choose to believe that the real estate industry fell prey to the same excesses as the rest of the economy. That is, when the tough times hit, owners who weren't invested based on sound economic principles simply couldn't stay afloat, causing a domino effect. In a short span of time, a lot of real estate owners became statistics, just as a host of other business owners did.

Today, however, we are experiencing the longest growth period in America's history. In fact, many experts are referring to this as a "golden era." Federal Reserve Chairman Alan Greenspan was quoted as saying, "I don't recall as good an underlying base for the long-term outlook … in the last two or three decades." Part of the reason for our country's success is that we have cut the fat and gone back to the basic principles of running our country like a profitable business. Energetic entrepreneurs who still believe in the American dream are opening up shop again all over the country. These new businesses are lean and mean and are ones in which everyone pulls their own weight.

Experts agree that real estate has bounced back, too. A recent article in *USA Today* said, "Not since the 1960s has the housing market been so uniformly strong across the USA." The article added that "the market is largely devoid of extremes," and "today's hot markets can be found in all regions of the country."

The goal of this guide is to highlight the legitimate business side of real estate. Because real estate is a cyclical commodity, it's possible to get caught investing with your pants down—just as a host of others did in the late 1980s. However, our unshaken belief is that if you approach real estate as a business and use sound business principles in running and investing in it, the probability of failure is minimal.

Here you will learn the differences between legitimate real estate investing versus speculative ventures. The profits generated by speculating on foreclosures and zero-money-down deals seem to get the most press, but we feel this kind of investing should be undertaken only after you have gained some good hands-on experience. Even a beginner, however, can combine the sound principles of compound interest and leverage and generate exceptional returns without taking any undue risk at all.

Here's a quick illustration: A modest 2 percent growth rate in value translates to a 20 percent return on a property purchased with just a 10 percent down payment. That's right, a 20 percent return. Most of us work 25 or 30 years at our job to receive a small retirement package and a token gift. If you were to invest $30,000 and were able to maintain a 20 percent return for that same period of time, your initial investment would be worth well over two million dollars. Two million dollars!

You see, real estate is a rare investment vehicle. For starters, it can provide you with a place to live while it's working as an investment. What's more, this investment offers several kinds of return including cash flow, equity growth from loan payoffs, equity growth from appreciation, and great tax benefits. How does $250,000 of tax-free profit sound? Probably pretty good. Well, a new twist in the tax laws allows homeowners that exact benefit. (We promise to tell you more about it in Chapter 7, "Broad Categories of Real Estate.")

How about what value appreciation can do for you? Rone Tempest wrote an article for the *Los Angeles Times* about urban renewal in Beijing. There, the Chinese were being forced to raze the old buildings because land prices had escalated to a whopping $6,000 per square meter. That translates to more than $24 million per acre. The question then is, if it can happen in Beijing, why not here? You may not live to see those kinds of prices, but you can make a fortune by simply taking advantage of the modest value appreciation that takes place in your own area. We'll show you how.

We'll also devote some of our writing to a few key economic principles that affect real estate investing. This might seem like a foreign language lesson as you try to understand how this can impact your need for a four-unit apartment building. That's understandable, but come back to these principles after a few years of ownership. Chances are they'll mean more to you then. Understanding how real estate fits into the overall picture of the economy will help your profits multiply in the long run.

A large portion of this guide is dedicated to teaching you some of the hard-earned lessons from our years of experience in this business. In Part 6, "Property Management Essentials," we have outlined many property-management techniques that will allow you to start your career head and shoulders above most of your competition. These principles should help you get your career off on the right foot and should give you the foundation to ask the important questions of the professionals you seek out for assistance.

Above all, our most important message will be to make a plan and then to simply work your plan to achieve your goals. Planning is a common principle for every successful business, but it is sorely lacking when it comes to real estate. You don't have to be Donald Trump or Ted Turner to need a plan. A plan simply gives you the opportunity to catch up to (and eventually pass) them.

Your best guarantee for success will be to:

1. Learn about the business
2. Research the market
3. Make a plan for your success
4. Purchase an investment according to plan
5. Manage your investment to meet your plan's goals

We believe so strongly in these five tenets that we have written a book around them. We're happy you chose this source as your introduction to real estate investing, and we will do our best to give you the insider's perspective of how to get rich using these techniques.

Finally, beyond reading this guide, we encourage you to continue to educate yourself about this business. A separate book could be written about every section in this guide. Some are listed in Appendix C, "Recommended Reading List." Find and read them with a keen eye. Never stop your search for knowledge. If you work it like a business, we believe that real estate investing is the best and safest field for you to make phenomenal profits.

Now, get a yellow highlighter and start reading.

Understanding Real Estate as an Investment

GET THE SCOOP ON...
Why the 2000s will require a new way of
thinking ▪ The reasons working for others will
always be a dead-end job ▪ The difference
between speculation and investing ▪ Real
estate versus other investments ▪ How the
government becomes your partner in investing
▪ The beauty of compound interest ▪ Getting
rich using "other people's money"

PART I

Basic Investment Concepts

The desire to obtain material things is a basic human quality. It's nothing we should feel bad about; it's the truth. Things make us happy. It drives our efforts from the day we are born until the day we die. If you think back, it is easy to track this collective mindset. As kids, it was toys, skates, and bicycles we wanted. As teens, it might have been a used car or some new clothes for an upcoming date. Now as adults, what is it we're after? New car, bigger house, a vacation on the beach, security for our families... How about all of the above?

As always, however, bills are due and new cars and vacations seem to be out of the question. Instead of sunning yourself on the sands of Cabo, you're working 40, 50, even 60 hours a week and can't seem to make ends meet. In fact, no matter how many hours you put in, you still manage to just scrape by. You know it's not due to an actual conspiracy, yet it is a hard fact that most of us average folk just can't seem to get ahead—no matter how hard we work.

If you were born with a silver spoon in your mouth, are an incredible athlete who has the skill of basketball superstar Michael Jordan, or happened to have won the lottery, you surely have no idea what the average person goes through. In fact, if you are in one of these categories, skip ahead a few chapters. We'll show you how to make your fortune that much larger. For everyone else, keep on reading.

A new world order

We are living in an era of rapid change. In fact, our world is changing at a faster pace than ever before in human history. This kind of comment surely has been made before, but most of us don't stop to consider the impact these changes might have on us. In the early '70s, for example, we communicated with most computers using punch-cards, and the computer itself took up an entire room that needed to be air-conditioned. Today, a computer with umpteen times the capacity of that '70s machine weighs less than two pounds and can easily fit into a small briefcase. Most of the lower-level jobs of the '70s are gone, and now, in some companies, it's those computers that handle the lion's share of the work.

But many things haven't changed. Babies are still being born, you still need to eat, bills keep piling up, and at some point, you will want to quit the rat race and retire. In the old days, you decided on a career, got an education, and then found a company to call home for the next 40 years. It was a job. It became part of your social life, and your years of loyal service were rewarded at the finish line with a gold watch and a retirement package. Not any more. With rapid change, the old ways are gone. With the new millennium upon us, the old ways of thinking need to change, too.

Take charge of your own destiny

Today, "lean and mean" is the only way companies can survive. Unfortunately, this also means that the same rules need to be applied by the average 9-to-5 worker. With the probability that we all will have to change careers several times in our lives, this sends some clear messages about what we need to do to survive financially.

One of the most difficult forces to anticipate and guard against is inflation. In the last few decades, we have seen rampant inflation, periods of minimal to negative inflation, and in the late '90s, some fairly low, stable inflation. We have been lucky; other countries have suffered double- and triple-digit inflation. It makes us wonder, "Could it happen to us?" Really, no one knows. The message is clear, however; inflation can wipe you out financially if you aren't prepared for it.

For that reason, you need to acquire some inflation-hedging assets, but you need to be careful. In past periods of inflation, investors bought property just for the increase in value they were sure would take place. Unfortunately, when the economy turned, these investments couldn't stand on their own. A prudent investor looks for sound business opportunities that also offer a hedge against inflation. Our goal is to train you to make those decisions.

The time to acquire these assets is when you are young. Like the professional athlete, we all are at our best in our youth. Maybe it's because, when we're

> **66**
> By investing in some income-producing property, my wife was able to quit her job. She now manages our properties from the house and is able to be a full-time mom for our new baby girl.
> —Tony P., investor
> **99**

young, we believe we can achieve anything to which we set our minds. We have energy, drive, and ambition. If we fall off a horse, we simply get up and try again. Somehow these skills get lost as we get older.

Therefore, the challenge facing all of us is to replace in the first 10 or 15 years of working the basic retirement package we used to expect from a lifetime career and social security. We have read enough about social security to doubt it's future. With the lifetime career also a thing of the past, this leaves the burden on you to create a financial foundation that can carry you for the rest of your life.

Trading time for dollars

In a capitalistic society such as ours, the big rewards are given to those who take the chances—the entrepreneurs. They have the vision, they take the risks, and consequently, they get the big benefits. The problem for the average person is that, rather than being a risk taker, most of us have gotten into the habit of putting in eight hours a day working for someone else. At the end of the week, we look forward to cashing our paycheck and then doing it all over again. After enough years of this routine, we've programmed ourselves to believe that trading our time for a paycheck is the way to get rich.

Think about your boss, the guy who owns the company for which you work. He's not hurting for money, is he? He knows something that you are just figuring out—working for someone else doesn't work. It certainly doesn't make you rich. Being the employee just makes you the employee. Being the boss can make you rich.

The erroneous idea that you can get ahead by trading time for dollars is the biggest barrier you can have to getting wealthy. This is true in real estate or, for that matter, in any other endeavor. Instead, the mindset you had when you went to school is the one you need to tap into again. It is the concept of investing your time for knowledge, not trading it for dollars.

Think back to your college days. Aside the fun of being away from home, school was tough. You always were broke, never ate right, and endured many a sleepless night getting term papers done on time. No one paid you a salary to go to school. You just plowed along and received one lone letter grade at a time for your efforts. After a while, the grades added up. In time you got a degree, and that degree got you the job that pays your salary. In college, you didn't trade your time for dollars; you invested it for knowledge. As you can see, the concept worked.

It is now time to go back to school. It is time to invest your effort and mental energies into learning the entrepreneurial skills necessary to take back control of your financial house. It's going to require taking chances with both your time and your money and possibly being told by your loved ones that it can't be done. But it can. The difference this time is that it will be with the wisdom of having lived and struggled in the adult world. You now know there is no free lunch. Moreover, you see that punching the time clock day in and day out is not the winning proposition you had hoped for.

This is all about taking back control of your destiny: cars, homes, vacations, security, less stress, more fun, and more time—they all are attainable and within reach.

Investing vs. speculating

Once you have mentally graduated from the ranks of a wage earner, one who previously traded time

Watch Out!

Don't walk out on your job tomorrow because you've decided to invest in real estate today. Creating wealth from real estate is a long-term proposal, and it is not practical to think you can make a fortune overnight.

for dollars, it becomes imperative that you understand the difference between the concepts of speculating and investing. The differences are subtle but
are still very important, especially when it comes to
the security of your hard-earned investment dollar.

> **Speculate:** To enter into a transaction or ven-
> ture in which the profits are conjectural or
> subject to chance; to buy or sell with the hope
> of profiting through fluctuations in price.

Speculating seems to be a natural human char-
acteristic. Think about the raffle tickets we used to
sell as fund-raisers. The prize offered for the winner
usually was pretty enticing: a new car, some money,
or perhaps a Hawaiian vacation. Because the tickets
were for a good cause (charity, schoolbooks, or
another such cause), this began a mindset that speculating is an acceptable way of getting a return.

As we get older, speculation becomes a way of
life. Who hasn't participated in a football or
Academy Awards pool at the office? These, too, are
speculative ventures. By participating, we are
"hoping" to make a profit. The outcome, in reality,
is completely out of our control. Because we so will-
ingly speculate with our money, most states have
caught on and have lured us to spend our money on
their games of chance. Not surprisingly, a vast majority of people in our country spend dollar after dollar on lottery tickets each week hoping to some day
get lucky.

What about Las Vegas? This city was founded as
the first legitimate American location for legalized
speculation. Most of the nation has caught on to
this, too. Whether it's horse racing, organized
bingo, blackjack, or slot machines, if you want to
play, it's pretty easy to find someone to take your bet.

How does investing differ from speculating?

Invest: To commit money or capital in business to earn a financial return. The outlay of money for income or profit.

When it comes to our finances, investing does not come naturally. It seems as though we understand investing when it comes to investing our time for education or investing our labors to do work around the house. Investing our money, however, needs to be learned.

Understanding the difference between speculating and investing is simple once you focus on dictionary definitions of these two concepts. The key word in the definition of speculation is "hopes." The key word in the definition of invest is "earn." As you can see, these two concepts are at the opposite ends of the money spectrum. When something is based on "hope," it implies that someone or something else is in control of the outcome. When it is based on "earning," it requires action on your part to attain success.

Our goal is to teach you how to invest your money. We're going to show you the actions needed to reach your dreams. Speculation, hope, and rolling the dice are best left for weekends away in Las Vegas or Atlantic City. On the other hand, investing, action, and earning are the keys to getting rich in real estate.

Go ahead, Columbus took a chance

Getting started always is the toughest part when taking on anything new. Investing is no different. Perhaps you will breathe easier if you look at people who have a lot of money. In fact, if you look at people who are filthy rich, you quickly will see that real

Bright Idea
Start a savings account into which a small percentage of your paycheck gets deposited automatically. In time, you can painlessly accumulate some extra money to help pay for a down payment on your first investment in income property.

estate is one common denominator many of them share. People such as Donald Trump, Jerry Buss, Marvin Davis, and Merv Griffin—all owe their fortunes to this commodity. Of course, some of them started out with a large pot to begin with, but many of them didn't. The most important thing to note is that the principles they used to gather their wealth are exactly the same ones we are teaching here. The beauty of real estate is that a small investor will earn the exact same percentage return that any large investor will earn.

Most people get their start in real estate investing by purchasing their first home. Others who understand the long-term benefits of real estate start out living in a small set of units that they own. This lowers the cost of living while giving them valuable experience in managing a property. In a few years, the savings and other benefits enable them to move into a single-family home while retaining the units as a pure investment. Others get their start by providing housing for a relative in need or a child away at college. After this need has passed, the equity is transferred into a regular rental investment. In short, the reason for the purchase is to provide a very basic human need—housing—but the result is the start of a new and profitable career.

One great advantage of an investment in real estate is that it allows you as much or as little control as you desire. You can choose to be an active manager of your property, or you can subcontract all the day-to-day operations to a management company. By using a management company, you avoid the daily hassles of being a landlord but still maintain control of your asset. If you have other types of investments, such as stock in a corporation, you know that the destiny of your capital is in the hands of someone else. These corporate managers or "experts" may do a good job, but if things go wrong, you can't jump in to help run the company like you can with a real estate investment. Just ask your stockbroker.

The roots of lending

Most people don't realize that the minute they earn some extra money and put it in the bank, they become an investor. A savings account is the simplest investment you can make. To most of us, making a deposit into our savings account is nothing more than putting money away for a rainy day. In reality, the small amounts of cash deposited by millions of people form the foundation for most lending in our country.

In the classic film *It's a Wonderful Life,* Jimmy Stewart plays a young man who takes over the family building and loan business. At their inception, building and loans, now called savings and loans, were started by the little people of a community as a safer place to put their extra money when their mattress just would not do anymore. When they were fortunate enough to do a little better financially, they went to the building and loan and borrowed enough money to buy or build a first home. Until that point, they were forced to rent a place to live from someone else.

From simple beginnings, as seen in the movie, savings and loans have grown in huge proportions. Nonetheless, they still are based on the simple economic concept of small investors banding their money together and then having that institution lending the money to others to purchase property— lending it to people like you.

Unofficially...
Former President Jimmy Carter is a firm believer in home ownership. He demonstrates this belief with his hands-on involvement in the nonprofit organization Habitat for Humanity, whose goal is to build affordable housing for Americans in need.

Unofficially...
Real estate loans usually get the lowest interest rate, the longest repayment term, and the lowest down payment requirements of any bank loan. This is because bankers are convinced that these loans have the lowest risk of loss to the bank.

Bankers know that real estate is one of the safest products to loan against. To begin with, they are aware of all the basic economic facts previously mentioned. Second, unlike a car loan, you can't drive their asset away if you quit making payments. For this reason, they can get their security back fairly quickly if something goes wrong. Finally, lenders check your credit and do an appraisal to ensure that you and the property are qualified for the loan they are making.

Great government subsidies

They say America is a great country in which to live, a true land of opportunity. One of the reasons we have it so good is that we all have an uncle that watches over us. His name is Uncle Sam. Many live in fear of him because they think he is always looking over their shoulder, but these people aren't seeing the whole picture. To the real estate investor, Uncle Sam is our best friend and our staunchest supporter.

When we're just starting out, Uncle Sam gives us quite a hand. First, he loans us the money (at great terms) to buy our first property. He then tells the guy who collects the taxes on the money we earn (the IRS) to give us as many breaks as he can. Finally, in areas where it's tough for some people to pay the fair market rent, Uncle Sam pays it for them. What a guy!

Even if you're young, energetic, and ambitious, the fact remains—you still need cash to get started investing. If money is tight and all seems lost, Uncle Sam steps in with two special programs to lend a hand to the beginning investor. These programs are the Federal Housing Administration (FHA) and the Veterans Administration (VA).

We will discuss all the specifics of the FHA and the VA in Chapter 5, "Financing your Investment," but knowing some of the basic details at this point will give you the encouragement you need now. The FHA is a government loan-insurance program that is open to any citizen who can meet some basic qualifying guidelines. These guidelines are very generous and give most of us the opportunity to buy our first property.

The most important advantage of this program is that it only requires a down payment of three percent of the purchase price of a property. So for the purchase of a $200,000 piece of property, you only need $6,000 down to get started. There usually are some other costs associated with a purchase, but the FHA requires that the seller assist you in paying most of them. In the case of the purchase of small units, the proration of the rents and security deposits can lower your actual out-of-pocket cash even more.

The second program Uncle Sam provides is Veterans Administration loans. The VA guarantees loans to people who have served in the military. Because home ownership is one of the most important tenets of our society, there is no better way to reward someone who has served their country than to help them buy their first home. An eligible veteran can purchase a qualified property with no down payment and, in most cases, with no other out-of-pocket costs. What a country!

Terrific tax benefits

Once you are a property owner, Uncle Sam steps in every year and gives you some extra help making your new business work. He does this through various tax breaks and incentives offered by the IRS.

> "
> By using an FHA loan, I bought my first home and made an investment at the same time. I bought a four-unit apartment building. It has a three-bedroom owner's unit that I use for my family, and it also has three attached rental units. The income from those units pays for almost all of my mortgage payment.
> —Brad S., investor
> "

Most of these benefits are mirrored by the states in our country that have a state income tax.

As a property owner, you now will be filing a Schedule C with your regular tax returns, wherein you will be reporting all income and expenses from your real estate business. The money you spend to run the property will be a deduction from the rental income you receive in determining your taxable profit. This then is taxable, just as any other earnings are. Any legitimate expense of running your property can be a deduction including the money you spend to upgrade the property to increase its value. Major expenses need to be deducted over several years, but they still can help decrease your taxable profit.

The tax-deferred exchange

The most important tax incentive Uncle Sam provides is the ability to sell a property and trade all your equity into another property without paying the taxes due on the profit you have made. This is called an IRS 1031 tax-deferred exchange. The number 1031 refers to the code section that contains all the rules governing such an exchange.

This deferment of the tax due enables you to trade into another property and therefore increase all the components of your return. The beauty is that, under the current code, an IRS 1031 exchange can be done over and over again. This is a major factor in your ability to trade up to ever-more-profitable properties while not paying any capital gains tax.

Let's assume you just sold a duplex that you have owned for several years. You are getting back your $20,000 initial down payment and a net profit of $30,000. Assuming you are in the 30-percent tax bracket and are going to buy another property with

Unofficially...
The IRS even offers extra benefits to people who own historical properties. Rather than a normal depreciation deduction, the IRS gives these property owners tax credits that amount to actual hard money savings come tax time.

10 percent down, the following table shows the difference in the property you can purchase:

	Tax Paid	Tax Deferred
Down Payment	$20,000	$20,000
Profit	$30,000	$30,000
Tax	$9,000	$0
Equity for Purchase	$41,000	$50,000
New Property Value	$410,000	$500,000

It is important to note that you are not escaping the payment of your tax due; you are just postponing the payment to some time in the future. In a sense, Uncle Sam now becomes your partner in the next property you purchase. This is because you are investing his money (the taxes owed) along with your own. If you do a good job with it, you actually will be increasing his investment, too.

The biggest little secret of them all: levered compound interest

Albert Einstein, when asked what the most powerful force on Earth was, answered without hesitation, "Compound interest!" Ben Franklin defined the term as "the stone that will turn lead into gold."

You all know compound interest because it is the concept the banks and savings and loans talk about when they tell you how your money will "grow" when you leave it with them. You leave the interest in the bank along with your original investment. In a short period of time, the interest earned on the interest of your original investment makes your return multiply like rabbits.

We will go over the compound interest formula in great detail in Chapter 9, "Building an Investment Plan," but we want you to get a glimpse now of the reason this works so well in real estate. The truth is, the return you get on real estate if you pay for your purchase using all cash (without getting a loan) isn't much higher than you get on most other types of investments. With real estate, however, you usually don't pay using all cash. Instead, you use "leverage" to buy properties. That is, you put down a small down payment on the property, usually 10–20 percent, and you then finance the balance.

Archimedes said, "Give me a lever and I'll move the earth." As investors, we don't want to use a lever to move the earth; we just want to use it to buy as much of it as we can. The ability to finance 80 to 90 percent of your real estate business is the rule, not the exception. With an investment in real estate, you don't need a stockbroker to sell your public offering, and you don't need a great balance sheet and 30 years of experience to talk a banker into loaning you money to start your business. Leverage allows others to buy your property for you.

Most commodities in which you can invest require that you pay all cash to purchase them. At best, you can obtain some financing that usually requires a substantial down payment and exceptional credit. Take the stock market, for example; unless you are buying on margin, you are required to pay all cash for the shares you want to purchase. This is true whether you're buying stocks, bonds, or mutual funds. This also is true for most investments in coins, stamps, art, and commodities. If you want to own it, you'll be paying for it with your own hard-earned money.

The ability to use leverage with real estate significantly increases the percentage of profit you can make, but more importantly, it allows you to purchase

Watch Out!
Leverage is a wonderful way to multiply the profit on the dollars you invest. Remember, however, that because leverage increases your potential profit, it will also increase your risk because you are obligated to pay back the entire debt on the borrowed money.

a significantly larger investment than you normally would have been able to. If you have $9,000 to invest, for example, you could buy 9,000 worth of stocks, bonds, coins, or art. With $9,000 to invest in real estate, however, you could purchase a four-unit FHA apartment building worth $300,000. You'd achieve this because $9,000 is 3 percent of $300,000. And 3 percent is all an FHA loan requires you to put down. The structure of this kind of deal could look like this:

Property	Four-unit apartment building
Property Price	$300,000
Down Payment (3% of price)	$9,000
FHA Loan	$291,000

By buying a property with a low down payment and financing the balance, you thereby significantly increase the percentage return on your money invested. To illustrate how this works, let's say you have $100,000 to invest, and you decide to use the entire $100,000 to buy a small apartment building outright. Your cash flow might look like this:

Property Price	$100,000 Investment
Gross Income	$14,000
Expenses	−$4,000
Net Cash Flow	$10,000

Your profit as a percentage of your investment would be calculated using the following formula:

$$\frac{\text{Net Income}}{\text{Investment}} = \% \text{ Profit}$$

Therefore, your profit would be:

$$\frac{\$10,000}{\$100,000} = 10\%$$

Ten percent on your money isn't bad, especially if you're used to the return you get from your savings account. But now let's use leverage. For purposes of this example, let's say you put 10 percent down and borrow 90 percent of the purchase price. The loan on the property at 7 percent interest costs you $575 per month. Your cash flow on the building is now:

Gross Income	$14,000
Expenses	-$4,000
Loan Payment	-$6,900
Net Cash Flow	$3,100

(Obviously, you will need to adjust these numbers, or any others you see in this book, to meet the interest rate you get.)

Compared to buying the property outright, you see that your cash flow drops from $10,000 to $3,100. At first glance, this doesn't seem so good. That is, until you see what it means in terms of a percentage return on your investment. Because your down payment is only $10,000 (rather than $100,000), the return now looks like this using the formula you just learned:

$$\frac{\text{Net Income}}{\text{Investment}} = \% \text{ Profit}$$

Or:

$$\frac{\$3,100}{\$10,000} = 31\%$$

You see, that's what leverage does for you. In this scenario, it would give you a 31% return on your money. If you buy 10 of these properties with your $100,000, your annual cash flow would be $31,000. As you will learn later, when you put the power of leverage together with compound interest, you can (and will) make phenomenal returns.

Just the facts

- The old "work 40 years and retire" system no longer applies to the average person.

- To get rich, you must rid yourself of the belief that trading time for dollars is the way to go.

- Because an investing mentality is not inherent in human behavior, it is a skill you will have to learn in order to grow wealthy.

- When it comes to investing in real estate, Uncle Sam is your best ally.

- The opportunity to use other people's money is the greatest advantage real estate has over all other investments.

GET THE SCOOP ON...
The profit you see in the beginning ▪ What to
expect in the middle years ▪ Retirement realities ▪ Why a systematic approach is critical ▪
Research—the key to success

Specific Real Estate Principles

In Chapter 1 we covered some of the basic reasons why an investment in real estate can work
for you. Now it is time to review some specific
principles that make real estate investing so incred-
ibly rewarding.

Because real estate is a long-term investment, it
doesn't have the same liquidity as an investment in
stocks, bonds, or mutual funds. By making this long-
term commitment, however, real estate can give you
an excellent return over your lifetime. One of the
great advantages that an investment in real estate
has over other investments is that it offers different
kinds of profits over the tenure of your ownership.
This is a feature you cannot find in other investments. The beauty is that the different types of profits in real estate all build on each other. You retain
your short-term profits into your middle years, and
you carry both of these into your retirement.

Short-term profits

You can expect to earn two types of profits in the short-term. They are:

1. Cash flow

2. Tax benefits

Either one of these by itself can give you just as good a return as most other investments. Taken together, the return they offer usually is far superior to any other investment you might choose.

Cash flow

Cash flow is probably the most sought-after return from any investment. Simply stated, cash flow is the monthly or annual cash return you receive from your investment. Take your savings account, for instance. When you deposit your excess earnings in your account, the bank pays you interest on your money; this interest is your cash flow from that investment. Generally speaking, the greater the cash flow you desire from any investment, the greater the effort and sometimes the greater the risk you will need to take to obtain your goal.

Moneysaver
Negative cash flow exists when your payments are greater than your income. One way to avoid dipping into your pocket each month to pay expenses and to repay your loan is to make sure your rents are at least at market rate.

With real estate, it is important to understand that cash flow is a direct function of how much you put down on the property. If you bought a property without the aid of a loan, for example, your cash flow would be huge. This is because all the money you take in from rent, less operating expenses, would be yours to keep. Conversely, if you buy a property with a minimal down payment and take out a loan to cover the balance, your cash flow will be adjusted accordingly. This is because paying back the loan reduces your cash flow.

To calculate cash flow, use the following formula:

Gross Income
−Operating Expenses
−Loan Payments
Net Cash Flow

Cash flow doesn't mean much unless you relate it to the amount of money you have invested. Most investors like to talk about the cash-on-cash return they get on their money. Your cash-on-cash return is calculated as follows:

$$\frac{\text{Net Cash Flow}}{\text{Cash Investment}} = \% \text{ Cash-on-Cash Return}$$

With an investment in real estate, you can structure your financing to obtain the cash flow you desire. Smart investors have the most financing on their properties when they begin their investment careers and have the least on when they retire. This is because, when you are working full-time, your steady paycheck (for the most part) will cover your current standard of living. Once you retire, however, and aren't getting paid on a regular basis, you will have a greater need for steady monthly income. Reducing the amount of your mortgage by the time you retire is the best way to achieve this result.

Tax benefits

The second short-term benefit in real estate investing relates to taxes. You should look at the tax benefits you receive from property ownership as frosting on the cake. With real estate, you can receive a nice cash-on-cash return from your property at the end of the year. This is because you are allowed to deduct your "losses" from operating expenses on your federal taxes. Most states that have state income taxes also offer a state tax benefit.

The theory behind the tax deduction for operating expenses is rooted in the costs most companies incur to replace expensive equipment needed to produce durable goods. Because machines wear out or become obsolete in just a few years, the IRS allows companies to take a deduction against profits to replace equipment. The business is allowed to deduct the cost of the machine over its useful life so that it can be replaced when it wears out. With real estate, you can produce a positive cash flow and still have a loss as far as the IRS is concerned.

Unofficially...
Ordinary and reasonable expenses connected to real estate are deductible as investment expenses including interest, utilities, insurance, property taxes, maintenance, supplies, legal fees, and more.

We'll be reviewing ongoing and capital expenses in detail in Chapters 14 and 15, but we want you to understand the benefits to the real estate investor now. As a real estate investor, you will have an opportunity to take a deduction against earnings for an expense that probably will never occur. That is, you will never have to replace your building because it wore out. This depreciation deduction, especially in the early years of ownership, usually shelters all cash-flow profits. In addition, there usually are enough extra write-offs to offset taxes on some of your earnings from your regular job.

Middle-years payoffs

The middle years of ownership should keep you both busy and happy. You will be busy because you will have the responsibility of running your real estate business each day. You will be happy because you will be making money. During the middle years, you can expect to spend most of your time on three phases of operation:

1. Running the day-to-day operation of your properties like a business.

2. Utilizing the equity in the properties like a savings account to provide for some of the finer things in life.

3. Fine-tuning your investment plan to make sure you reach your stated goals according to your set timetable.

The day-to-day operations

You will recognize that you are in the middle years of ownership when certain clues pop up time and again. For one thing, you will find yourself skipping over the front-page and sports sections of your newspaper to get to the real estate ads. You will become a bloodhound for rental rates, upcoming vacancies, and any other kinds of information that could impact your business. Additionally, in these years, you will find that your Home Depot or Orchard Supply credit card bill is consistently larger than your Macy's or Nordstrom's bill. Finally, when you travel to your favorite vacation spots, you will always be checking out rental rates and the price of small units. Your master plan will be to buy a vacation home there and let tenants pay the mortgage when you're not on holiday.

At this point, you have arrived. You're in business for yourself, and you're enjoying the challenges and the profits. This is when all the things you learn in this book will be the most meaningful to you. You will see this business as just that—a business. The profit plans you have designed will become as important as your paycheck is at your day job. Going to your property won't seem like a chore; instead, it will feel like an opportunity to check on your investment. Did the gardener do his job? Does anything need to be painted or fixed? Are the tenants happy?

> **"**
> We worked hard on our properties, and after five years, we decided to refinance. Because of the appreciation that took place in that time period, we were able to pull out enough money to help build ourselves a brand new home.
> —Jim S., 51
> **"**

You will start taking trips around the neighborhood to see what the competition looks like. Yes, you will now see all the other buildings in your neighborhood as competition. How do they look? What are they charging for rent? Which ones always seem to stay full and why? Just as grocery stores and department stores compete for customers, you will begin to compete for tenants with the other building owners in your neighborhood.

The first few days of the month will now have a new meaning for you; they will be the days you collect your rents and pay your bills. The first challenge will be getting all the rents in on the first of the month. Even in the best areas, it takes work to get your tenants trained to pay on time. After collecting rent, you will have to pay out a lot of it to cover bills. This will become a game to you, and you will constantly be asking yourself, "How can I keep the most for myself?" At your day job, your boss says, "Increase revenue and cut expenses." You do it there because it is your job; now you will do it because the money you save is yours to keep.

Use your equity to your advantage

As your real estate holdings move into the middle years, the cash flow and equity grow. This is because, by this time, you will have raised your rents and found ways to curtail expenses. Now is the time when you can use your property as you would use a savings account—to buy things you couldn't afford on your salary alone. These middle-year items should be the kind of things that will give you the extra incentive to work that much harder at this second career.

Providing an education for their children is one of the first things many people do with the money they make from real estate. Indeed, education comes with a large price tag. A recent study predicts that the cost of a public college education in the year 2018 will be more than $70,000, and the cost of a private university education will be more than $180,000. These are staggering numbers, especially when you multiply them by the number of children you have.

There are, however, some more pleasurable things you can look forward to doing with your money. The equity in your properties can be tapped to help provide for that larger home in the better neighborhood where you have always wanted to live. You also might choose to invest some of the money you're making into a vacation home in the mountains or the desert. Instead of sitting vacant while not in use, it becomes another holding in your investment portfolio. You earn income from renting it when you're not vacationing there.

Last but not least are all the other luxuries you would like if you had a few extra thousand dollars at your disposal. How about a water-ski boat like your neighbor has? What about a trip to Hawaii or Europe with the family? In short, your properties should provide you with the funds to pay for all those "if only I had the extra money" things about which most people only dream.

Of course, new cars and vacations sound great, but do you want to know how it is realistically possible? Here's how: Your real estate is going to produce income through cash flow but also through equity growth. As you know, the cash flow is the money you get to keep after you pay your bills. If you're doing you job correctly, your cash flow should grow steadily as you properly manage your expenses. Your equity in your property will grow in two ways:

Watch Out!
Avoid the idea of buying a property for your child to live in while he or she is away at college. Prices in college towns usually are pretty high, and kids are known to transfer schools.

1. Appreciation in value (inflation + demand)

2. By paying down on your mortgage

Inflation has always been a part of our economy. In the past, you weren't happy during high inflation because the cost of everything you needed to live seemed to correspondingly grow. Now, however, higher inflation will be your best friend. This is because not only will the value of your property increase because of inflation, but you also can increase your monthly income by raising rents during inflationary times. Additionally, your equity also will increase as you pay off your mortgage. This takes longer to see the big dollars, but every dollar paid off increases your net worth correspondingly.

This increased equity also gives you borrowing power at the bank. Your banker will gladly loan you money based on the appreciation that has taken place on your property as well as the increased value you have created by paying down on your loans. Any new loan you get will first be used to pay off your old loan. Then, if there is money left over, you can do with it what you choose. Even if you are pulling out actual profit from the building, your new loan will be greater than what you originally paid for the property. Finally, if you have increased your rents to keep up with the market, these increased rents usually will pay any increase in your payments because of the higher loan you now have.

Knowledge is key

You will use the middle years to fine-tune your knowledge of any and all real estate investment opportunities. The more you get involved, the more you will want to know about real estate and the business of owning it. This should lead you to seminars, books, and discussions with other investors.

Moneysaver
Be sure to contact your existing lender when it's time to refinance. Many times, you can save on loan fees, escrow fees, and other costs by using the same lender the second time around. They want your business, so don't be afraid to try and negotiate their fees down.

Through the years, you probably will be following in your mind various types of properties you might consider buying. There are single houses, small units, commercials, and developable land that you might try your hand at. Additionally, you might consider buying distressed properties. Situations such as fixer-uppers, mismanaged properties, bank repossessions, use conversions, and development all provide opportunities to make money (See Chapters 7 and 8). All of these properties may become opportunities after you gain the proper knowledge and experience.

At some point, you will make a decision whether real estate will remain a secondary career to you or whether you will quit working for someone else and hire yourself to manage your real estate holdings full-time. Whatever your choice may be, you will find that the middle years of property ownership will provide you with plenty of flexibility.

The retirement years

As you make your decisions about your future in real estate, you also will be setting the stage for your retirement. For some people, real estate will be one part of a diverse retirement portfolio, a true passive investment. Many investors choose to purchase only one property in their careers and to manage the financing so that it is paid off by the time they retire. By that time, there is no mortgage to worry about, and there is plenty of positive cash flow.

Other investors purchase many properties in their careers and decide that they just want to be "gone fishin'" or playing golf when they retire. At that point, the properties can be sold. They can settle up with Uncle Sam, bank the remaining cash, and then fish and golf to their heart's content.

Another option is to sell the properties and become the banker by carrying notes against the property. This strategy will be discussed in detail later in this book, but in short, carrying paper offers two distinct advantages over an outright sale:

1. You don't pay your taxes until you receive your profit. Therefore, you can earn interest on all your equity including the money you eventually will give to the IRS for taxes.

2. You will find out that you will earn a greater interest rate on your money by being the banker rather than by letting the banks pay you interest. Remember, early on we learned that the banks pay you interest when you give them your money and then they lend it to others to buy property. By carrying the financing yourself, you cut out the middleman (the bank) and keep the profit all for yourself.

Many people find that their real estate holdings make a great part-time retirement business. Managing the properties is just enough to keep them busy, but it doesn't require a daily 9 to 5 commitment. For others, real estate might grow into a family business, with the kids learning at a young age the lessons you had to learn while working two jobs.

A last option is to relinquish all the operations of your business to a property management company. At this point, your new job will be to supervise them rather than your properties. The management company will have all the duties of running the properties and paying the bills. They will then send you a check each month for your profit. Even better, they can easily deposit your funds to the bank of your choice, and you can draw on them from anywhere in the world.

A systematic approach to investing

Once you understand the kinds of profits you might expect, you need a plan for attaining the biggest return. We believe a systematic approach to investing is the best way to maximize your profits. This approach has five phases. They are:

1. Learn about real estate investing in general.
2. Research the market in your area.
3. Plan your investment strategy.
4. Invest in a property.
5. Manage your investments according to your plan.

Go back to school

The first and most important thing to do when you decide to invest in anything is to learn about the commodity in which you are investing. Real estate investing requires a fairly large commitment of both time and capital, so the homework and planning you do before you make your first purchase is critical.

Remember, there is an element of risk associated with any type of investment. The profit you earn on your investment usually is directly related to the amount of risk the investment has compared to other investments. For example, a United States Government Savings Bond is the safest investment you can make based on risk. Generally speaking, rates of return start increasing from about that point. The theory is that the day our government can't pay the debt is the day none of your investments count anyway.

Your education process should start with gaining knowledge about the actual ownership of real

Watch Out!
Make sure to do
some stringent
checking before
you attend some
of the "get rich
quick" real
estate seminars.
Be especially
wary of the ones
that are free;
often they are
designed to just
get you in the
door so they can
sell you some
expensive books,
tapes, or addi-
tional training.

estate. You started that process when you bought this book but don't stop there. Our goal is to give you a strong foundation of knowledge about real estate investing. Once you have this foundation, you need to keep educating yourself about the business and do more specific reading and studying on topics such as property management and taxation.

Most colleges offer courses covering a wide range of real estate investment topics. What's great is that they usually don't cost much, especially at the community college level. The biggest advantage is that people who have hands-on knowledge of the subject matter usually teach the classes. In addition, if you have an apartment owners association in your community, it might offer property-management seminars where you can learn management skills and the latest rules and regulations for your local area. Finally, many authors and lecturers offer weekend seminars covering a range of real estate–related subjects. Often held only in larger cities, these courses can be a good source of information.

Research your market area

While you are learning about real estate in general and real estate investing specifically, you need to begin educating yourself about the actual market for property in your area. Our book, and most books, can only provide a broad overview of real estate investing. Markets can change drastically within a few miles, let alone across the entire country. Therefore, it is important for you to understand your market and how it performs before you start buying.

You should start by finding a real estate agent who is willing to help. Don't worry; you won't have to pay him anything because he will earn a commission paid by the seller if (and when) you buy. Your goal at this stage is to get a basic understanding of the pricing of properties in the area where you expect to buy. You won't be calculating returns or looking for something to actually buy at this point. Your goal is simply to get a basic understanding of what properties sell for. If you can answer the question "What would a duplex cost in my neighborhood?" or "What is the price per unit for a four-plex?" you're well on your way to a solid foundation. If, when asked that question, you said, "I need to know whether the units are one or two bedrooms and how many bathrooms they each have," you probably have an excellent handle on value.

While you are researching value, it also is important to become familiar with rental rates in your market area. Working with an agent, you will be able to see what current properties rent for, but this is only part of the picture because all of those rents are based on units that have rented at some time in the past. You also will want to find out what owners are asking for units currently on the market. You need to discover what the trend is. Are rental rates in the area going up or down over a period of time? Is the area stable, improving, or declining?

Historical data

Once you have a current understanding of property values, you will want to research the historical value in your area. Again, the help of a good real estate agent will be invaluable because most have access to this information through their local Board of Realtors®. If you can find an agent who specializes in investment property, he may have the data you want readily available for the asking.

Unofficially...
Keep in mind that many small property owners don't do a very good job of keeping up on rental rates. It's not unusual for some owners to rent a vacancy at the last rate they were getting without checking the current market rate.

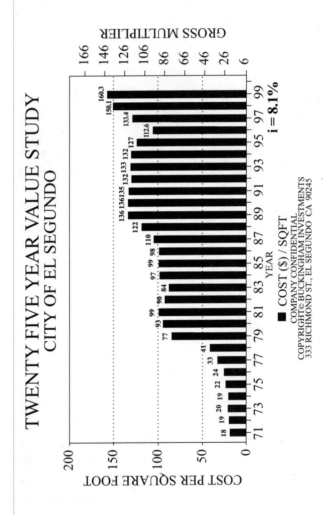

TWENTY FIVE YEAR VALUE STUDY
CITY OF EL SEGUNDO

GROSS MULTIPLIER

COST PER SQUARE FOOT

■ COST ($) / SQFT

COMPANY CONFIDENTIAL
COPYRIGHT© BUCKINGHAM INVESTMENTS
333 RICHMOND ST., EL SEGUNDO CA 90245

i = 8.1%

The more historical data you can get, the better you will be able to make some estimates of the future trends for property in your area. You will want to look for the same information about properties in the past as you got for the properties on the market today. Information about rental rates also will be helpful because you want to see the trends for increase over the years. The further back you can get information the better. You then will also be able to see how trends in real estate values in your area compare to the trends in our economy in general.

The accompanying chart shows the historical trends of real estate values in the city of El Segundo, California. This chart uses a mathematical calculation called linear regression analysis to determine the change in the values from the first year to the last. This is the kind of historical data that would be helpful for your own market. At the very least, the most important facts you want are the trends in values for as many years as you can get. Knowing this percentage increase is important when doing forward projections for an investment plan. Although past history is no guarantee of the future, it is a better way to make an estimate than picking one out of thin air.

Back to the future

Now that you have a handle on the present and the past, it's time to start worrying about the future. This is when you have to go back to school for a review in Economics 101. Many outside factors can impact your real estate business. It is important to be aware of changes in the economy that can affect you both positively and negatively.

You should be reading the business section of the paper with new perspective. Finding out about future business expansion, for example, will mean that there will be more people to rent your units. Likewise, a new shopping mall in your area should bring both more revenue to the city and more employees who need a place to live close to work. Increased inflation means higher prices for goods and services and, best of all, higher rents for you.

In addition to the newspaper, you also should look for other publications that will give you insight into changes in your local economy. Most chambers of commerce have information about what is happening in the local economy. Some banks and savings and loans have research departments that compile this kind of information. Finally, most cities have departments designed for the sole purpose of attracting new businesses. These city departments can be a good source of information about the existing state of your local economy and what they project for the future.

Remember, the goal of all this research is to keep you tuned in to the state of your local economy. This way, you can take advantage of any positive changes in the economy and can make provisions to protect your investments if you see that negative changes are on the way.

Everyone must have a plan

Now that you have accumulated the knowledge to invest and you understand the product, it is time to put a plan together. The foundation of the plan will be your goals. For many years, we have observed investors and—with very few exceptions—the most successful all had very well-defined goals. There is nothing unique about this observation. Hundreds, if not thousands, of authors, scholars, teachers, and so on have, over the centuries, touted the need for goal orientation as a key to success. It's amazing how many of us have a job that requires us to make plans at work for our performance and the performance of the department we head up, but we don't ever do the same for our own lives.

Chapter 9, "Building an Investment Plan," will teach you how to put your investment plan together. Nonetheless, it is important at this point to start thinking about some specific things you want to accomplish through investing in real estate. It's not enough just to say that you want to get rich, that you want to find some good deals, or that you want to make a lot of money. These concepts don't have anything personal to hang on to. Instead, getting specific is the key. A new house overlooking the park in five years or $75,000 set aside for Sydney and Mara's college education are specific goals that have meaning.

Finally, have you ever heard an interview with someone who just won the lottery? The reporter invariably asks "What are you going to do with the money?" The answer usually is a list of things like a new house, a car, trips, and doing something nice for a relative or friend. It's not the money; it's what you can do with the money that keeps people buying the tickets. The right set of personal goals will give you the incentive to work your new business, and in a few years, you'll have the payoffs just like you'd won the lottery yourself.

Make a purchase

The first investment will be a big step for you, but you should have a higher level of confidence than most. You have educated yourself about investing, you are knowledgeable about your target market, you have a plan that lays out what you are trying to

Moneysaver
By properly defining your goals, you will avoid paying extra for a property to satisfy an unfounded emotional need. We always say to buy the ugly property for less; spruce it up with flowers, paint, and awnings; and then manage it into profitability.

❝
It was tough to make the decision to buy that first property. My agent, Eve suggested that we start with just half the capital we planned to start with. This cushion gave us the courage to make the move on that first one.—Shalini P., investor
❞

accomplish, and you know the kind of property you want to get started.

We don't recommend trying to hit a home run on your first purchase. Many beginning investors make the mistake of seeking out bank-owned repossessions or fixer-uppers right out of the gate because they have heard how much money they can make by doing so. Money can be made, but it takes the experience of many years in the business to find success that way. Instead, we recommend that you use your first purchase to apply the sound business skills you are learning here. By starting smart, you will help ensure your success.

Manage your investment

Once you close on your purchase, you have taken on a new job. You are now a property manager. Of course, you can subcontract the management of your property if you so choose. This can be very tempting, especially because the cost of management usually is just a small percentage of the gross income collected. We strongly recommend, however, that you do not hire out management on your first few properties. It is important for you to experience first-hand the duties of running a property yourself. You need to put the knowledge you have learned to the test to see how the real world works. This is like your final exam in school or the thesis you need to write to get an advanced degree.

This hands-on experience will be invaluable to you later when you do turn your properties over to a management company. At that point, your job will be to manage the management company. To do this effectively, you need to have had the actual experience doing the job yourself. It's one thing to read about something in a book; it's another thing to actually have gotten your hands dirty down in the trenches.

Just the facts

- Real estate ownership has three phases of profits—short-term, middle-year payoffs, and retirement rewards.

- One of the greatest advantages of real estate is the fact that it is a business you can start while you keep your regular job.

- As your property equities grow, you can use them to finance luxuries you never thought you could afford.

- Don't swing for the fences on your first purchase; make it a learning experience.

The Secrets of Real Estate Investing

PART II

GET THE SCOOP ON...
The money that will go in your pocket now ▪
Equity growth from loan reduction ▪
The passage of time and how it will make you
wealthy ▪ Tax relief from Uncle Sam

Elements of Return

Chapter 3

With an investment in real estate, four components of return will help you grow rich: cash flow, equity growth from loan reduction, equity growth from appreciation, and tax benefits. In this chapter, you will learn about each element of return individually, and then you will learn how to calculate the combined effect of all four to give you an estimated overall return on your investment.

Learning how to do this will tell you two things. First, it will show you what kind of profit you can achieve on any potential investment. Second, it will give you a benchmark against which to measure all properties you might be considering. Once you are able to do an apples-to-apples comparison of potential purchases, your decision on which one to actually buy should become an easy one.

1800 Mariposa Lane

To help us demonstrate each element of return, we will use an example property that we will come back to time and again. The facts of the example are as follows:

Address: 1800 Mariposa Lane

Asking price: $225,000

Number of units: 4 @ 800 square feet each

Unit mix: 4 units @ 2 bedrooms/1 bathroom each

Income: $550 per unit = $2,200 per month
    = $26,400 per year

Expenses: 30% of gross income = $7,920 per year

Lot size: 50 × 150 foot

Age: 20 years old

Features:

- Newer carpets and drapes
- Built-in stoves
- Natural stone fireplaces
- Four garages

The money in your pocket

The first element of return (and the favorite among many investors) is cash flow. Simply put, cash flow is the money left over after you pay the bills. To calculate cash flow, you need to know three things:

1. The annual gross income of the property
2. The annual expenses on the property
3. The total debt payment on your loans

We will use the example property at 1800 Mariposa Lane to illustrate. Let's say we negotiated the asking price of $225,000 down to a purchase price of $220,000. Our down payment was $30,000, and we financed the remaining $190,000 at a 9 percent interest rate. This gave us a monthly loan payment of $1,450 and an annual debt payment of

Watch Out!
Remember that the four elements of return don't arrive at the same time. As a result, many investors fail to pay close enough attention to all of them and end up missing out on earning the highest possible return on their equity.

$17,400 ($1,450 × 12 = $17,400). We have four units that rent for $550 each. This gives us an annual income of $26,400 ($550 × 4 × 12 = $26,400). Finally, remember that our annual expenses are $7,920 (30% of the gross income).

Knowing this information, we can compute our cash flow return as follows:

Gross Annual Income	$26,400
Less Annual Operating Expenses	-$7,920
Less Annual Loan Payments	-$17,400
Annual Cash Flow	$1,080

After we know the cash flow, we then can find out the percentage return on our investment by dividing the cash flow by the down payment:

$$\frac{\text{Annual Cash Flow} \quad \$1,080}{\text{Down Payment} \quad \$30,000} = 4\% \text{ Return}$$

As you can see, this is a fairly simple calculation. In the real world of buying a property, making sure the components of this calculation are correct is a much greater challenge. The classic conflict starts with determining how much income the property actually brings in.

Factor #1: The annual gross income

There are three ways to look at the income stream of a building. The first way is by examining the scheduled rent. The scheduled rent is the total of all the agreed-upon rents in the building. Scheduled rent makes the assumption that all the tenants are paying and that there are no vacancies.

The second way to look at the income stream is by analyzing potential rent. Potential rent is income you feel you can earn based on the rents other property owners are receiving in your market area. This is where the ongoing research you do can have a

Bright Idea
Don't buy into the belief that a big cash flow is the most important element of return. When you're young, it might be wiser to structure your deals so they will produce a large cash flow only after you retire. That way, you will have money available when you truly need it.

Moneysaver
Make sure you get into the habit of inquiring about available units in your area. By knowing what the competition is charging for rent you can avoid underestimating the market when it comes to your own vacancies.

major impact on your cash flow and, in later years, on the value of your property.

The third way to analyze the income of a building is by examining the collected rent. The collected rent is the actual amount of money the current owner took in over a given period of time. This reflects the market, but more than that, it reflects the current owner's ability to manage in that market. You may do better, or you may do worse. This amount is impacted by the vacancy factor and the credit losses incurred from tenants who did not pay.

When you take over, you will find that the credit loss you suffer from bad debts will depend on three things:

1. Your proficiency as a property manager

2. The economic level of your tenant base

3. The general state of the economy

Factor #2: The annual expenses

Expenses are the second factor in determining the cash flow of a building. It is important for you to become familiar with the kind of expenses you might encounter in your market area and what percentage of the gross income they represent. Your knowledge of what these expenses should be might afford you the opportunity to make a purchase from an owner who is having trouble controlling the expenses of his property. You will encounter the following three types of expenses:

1. Fixed expenses

2. Variable expenses

3. Planned capital expenses

Fixed expenses are the regular recurring costs required in holding a property. These expenses include items such as property taxes, insurance, and city business-license fees. They are called fixed expenses because the amount you pay does not fluctuate, or if it does, it usually is only a nominal change one time per year.

Variable expenses do fluctuate. These are all the other costs you might incur while managing your rental property. These can include utility payments, repairs, and general upkeep.

Finally, planned capital expenses are major items that have a useful life of more than one year. These are items such as a new roof or exterior paint. These expenses must be capitalized for tax purposes. This means you must write the expense off over a period of years. Therefore, to account for these types of expenses in your cash flow, you need to include a reserve of a certain percentage of the income based on the condition of the property. We will cover this in greater detail in Chapter 14, "Managing the Expenses."

The management of all these expenses will play a major role in how much cash flow your property produces. Reviewing the former owner's records can give you insight into how the property might perform, but this information also can be misleading. The seller might be a great manager who has been able to keep expenses under control, or he might be an awful manager who can't control a thing. Therefore, it is important for you to do your homework on the types and cost of normal expenses for your area. The information you learn and your ability to apply this information as the property manager will give you the opportunity to do a better job than your competition.

Unofficially...
You cannot build
an investment
plan for your
area based on
expectations
from other areas
of the country.
Your own market
will dictate the
amount of cash
flow you can
expect based on
a normal down
payment and
financing.

Factor #3: The debt payment on your loans

The final component of the cash flow equation is the payment on your loan or loans. You see, there is a direct correlation between the amount of your down payment and your cash flow. It stands to reason that, if you pay for a property without getting any loans at all, your cash flow will naturally be larger than if you have loan payment obligations. Conversely, if you buy property with leverage (via a loan), your cash flow will be adjusted accordingly. Therefore, you can see that the amount of money you pay on your loans (as is true with any expense you have) directly affects the amount of cash flow you will receive.

Equity growth from loan reduction

The second way your equity will grow is through loan reduction. When you close on a piece of property, your initial equity is your down payment. Know that this equity will change over the years. This is because you will continually make monthly payments on your mortgage, reducing the amount you owe. This small change doesn't mean much in the first few years of ownership, but it accelerates considerably in the later years and is a significant cause of equity growth.

For the purposes of the following calculation, we will assume that the loan payoff is a constant amount. Note that you will be able to get the exact payoff at the end of each year when your lender sends you the 1099 form used by you to file your tax return.

Let's return to the example property at 1800 Mariposa Lane. Recall that we put $30,000 down and financed the balance of the purchase. Our loan on the property was for $190,000, payable at $1,450 per month. That payment included principal reduction and interest at 9 percent per year. The total payments on the loan for the year are $17,400 (12 × $1,450 = $17,400). Roughly speaking, the interest paid to the bank would be 9 percent of $190,000, or $17,100 (.09 × $190,000 = $17,100). The calculation looks like this:

Total Loan Payments	$17,400
Less Interest Paid	−$17,100
Principal Reduction	$300

As you can see, the difference between the $17,400 loan payment and the $17,100 interest is $300. This $300 is the approximate loan reduction the first year. To find out your percentage return on your investment due solely to reduction of the principal balance of your loan, divide that reduction by your down payment as follows:

$$\frac{\text{Principal Reduction} \quad \$300}{\text{Down Payment} \quad \$30,000} = 1\% \text{ Return}$$

Don't let the modest 1% return you see here scare you. As the years go by, principal begins to pay off faster and your percentage return due to loan reduction will dramatically rise. If you have more than one loan on your property, you need to repeat this calculation for each loan. This is part of your overall return on the property because this reduction in principal is paid for with the income you receive from your tenants.

Equity growth from appreciation

The third way you are going to earn money is through value appreciation. Value appreciation results from two factors:

1. Inflation

2. Demand

Watch Out!
A common mistake many investors make is to calculate their return after many years of ownership by using the original down payment in the calculation. You must remember that, with a pay down on your loans, your true equity will surely be much larger than your original down payment.

Bright Idea
As your cash
flow improves,
you might
choose to pay
off some extra
principal each
month on your
mortgage. This
way, you will get
your loan paid
off early, and
you will have
that much more
cash flow
available for
retirement.

Inflationary appreciation

Inflationary appreciation sounds just like what it is—the increase in a property's value due to inflation. This is the same phenomenon you see in supermarket prices. Even when the number of items you purchase at the store stays the same, the prices nonetheless continue to go up every year. This appreciation rate is related to the general inflationary rate of our overall economy. When the country's inflation rate is up, the appreciation rate of property is usually also up.

Two components make up any piece of property: the structure itself and the land. Although land never wears out, structures do. Inflation affects the cost of both of these items, but this component of appreciation can be stagnant because the structure is deteriorating at the same time it may be appreciating. A number of factors combine to give a structure a limited useful life. They include:

1. Wear and tear from usage

2. Wear and tear from the elements

3. Changes in building advances

The factor that makes the biggest difference in this component of appreciation is the value of the land itself. Except in rare cases, usually caused by toxic waste problems, land increases in value. Therefore, the value of the land as compared to the value of the structure itself will have a great impact on the increase in value from inflation. This is called the land-to-improvement ratio.

The land-to-improvement ratio can shift dramatically depending on what area of the country you are in. In many metropolitan areas, for example, the land value can be as much as 90 percent of the value of the entire property. In smaller communities, these numbers can be entirely reversed. The structure might represent 90 percent of the value and the land a mere 10 percent.

To see how this can affect the increase in value, we will look at the example of 1800 Mariposa Lane as if it were in both areas. We will assume that the inflation rate is 3 percent and that there is no inflation increase for the structure because of the offsetting depreciation.

In the smaller community, the value of the land would be $22,000 ($220,000 purchase price × 10% land value = $22,000). This gives us a return from inflation on the land of $660 ($22,000 × 3% inflation rate = $660). In the metropolitan area, the value of the land would be $198,000 ($220,000 purchase price × 90% land value = $198,000). This puts the inflation return at $5,940 ($198,000 × 3% inflation rate = $5,940). Because we put down $30,000 to purchase the property, we can illustrate the appreciation return from inflation as follows:

	Small Areas	Metropolitan Areas
Appreciation	$660	$5,940
Down Payment	$30,000	$30,000
Return	2.2%	19.8%

Demand appreciation

Demand is the second reason your property will make you money because of value appreciation. Demand appreciation is related to four different economic principles. They are:

■ Scarcity

■ Transferability

■ Utility

■ Demand

Unofficially...
Densely populated metropolitan areas usually have the greatest appreciation from demand. This is due to the lack of land available for new construction.

It is the combined effect of all four components that pushes property values up at a greater rate in some areas while pushing values down in others. Let's look at them one at a time.

The scarcity principle can best be seen when comparing a metropolitan area to a rural one. In the metropolitan area, there is very little undeveloped land available. In many cases, to build a new building, an existing older structure must be first demolished. Therefore, developers first have to find someone willing to sell. When they do, they'll be paying for both the land and the structure that sits on it. Naturally, this increases the cost of any property under those circumstances. Rural areas, on the other hand, tend to have large amounts of vacant land. This greater availability of land makes it a lot easier to find willing sellers and lower prices.

Transferability refers to the ease of buying and selling any commodity. As you know, investment vehicles such as stocks and bonds are fairly liquid. That is, you can transfer them from one owner to another pretty quickly. Real estate, on the other hand, can't be transferred as fast. This usually is related to the number of potential buyers and the ability (or lack thereof) to find adequate financing. There might be many buyers and hundreds of lenders for the duplex you are trying to sell, but how many buyers and lenders might there be for the purchase of the Empire State Building? Not too many.

Utility refers to the usability of the property. The value of a property is directly related to its highest and best use. A commercial lot close to a railroad-loading yard, for example, could be a valuable location to build a manufacturing plant. The greater the utility value, the greater the value of the property.

Demand is the last economic principle that drives prices. Demand correlates to the upward desirability of the property. This is the same phenomenon that affects the price of tickets to major sporting events, music concerts, or top Broadway shows. Think about the scalpers that roam the parking lots of these events. The reason they are able to get top dollar for their tickets is because the demand for the product is so great. For example, tickets to see a reunion of the surviving Beatles or the seventh game of the NBA Finals would probably be pretty pricey. If they were scalping tickets to see a revival of your daughter's second grade Christmas pageant, however, the odds are good that prices wouldn't be as expensive.

Demand can increase or decrease due to general trends in the economy. Many investors move from one investment vehicle to another based on the investment's ability to produce a profit. When stocks are hot, their money is there. When bond yields go up, the stocks are sold for bonds. When real estate is moving, they start buying. This sends the message to small investors that it is time to buy. This increased demand for a limited supply causes the appreciation rate to increase.

We can illustrate demand appreciation with our example property. Remember that we bought 1800 Mariposa Lane for $220,000, we put down $30,000, and it brings in an annual income of $26,400. The investor purchasing this property is paying 8.33 times the gross income for the property ($220,000 ÷ $26,400 = 8.33)—see the section on "The Gross Multiplier" in Chapter 4. If the demand for property increases and investors will now pay 9 × the gross income, the value would now be $237,600 ($26,400 × 9 = $237,600). Note that this is a $17,600

Watch Out!
Appreciation is like the frosting on the cake of your investment. Enjoy it when you can but don't build your plans around it.

Timesaver
Most local news-
papers publish
statistics about
increases in
property prices
in the Consumer
Price Index.
Make sure you
check these sta-
tistics often
because they are
a good indicator
of appreciation.

increase in the value of the property with no increase in rental income ($237,600 – $220,000 = $17,600). To determine the percentage return on your investment from demand appreciation alone, you divide the appreciation that took place by your down payment as follows:

$$\frac{\text{Appreciation} \quad \$17,600}{\text{Down Payment} \quad \$30,000} = 59\% \text{ Return}$$

Effect of demand on income

There is another way that demand can affect the value of your property. You see, investment real estate prices are directly related to the net income the property produces. An increased income stream should produce an increased value, even in a market where there is no increase in demand from investors. In this case, the demand would come from the tenants' willingness to pay more rent for your property. This usually happens because of an increased number of tenants in an area with a limited supply of places to rent.

Here's how an increased income affects the Mariposa Lane example. Let's say we raised the rents from $550 a unit to $600 a unit, and therefore increased the gross income from $26,400 to $28,800 a year. If investors were still willing to pay 8.33 times the annual income of the property, Mariposa would now be worth $239,904 ($28,800 × 8.33 = $239,904). This is an increase in value of $19,904 ($239,904 – $220,000 = $19,904). Remember, we put $30,000 down to purchase this property. We now can compute the equity growth from this component of appreciation as follows:

$$\frac{\text{Appreciation} \quad \$13,240}{\text{Down Payment} \quad \$30,000} = 44\% \text{ Return}$$

A value projection example

The following chart is an example of how an appreciation in value projection might look. This is for property values in the South Bay area of Southern California. The chart shows that the area has had some tremendous increases in value as well as some periods with little increase or a loss. Linear regression analysis tells us that the overall increase in value for this area is 7.5 percent.

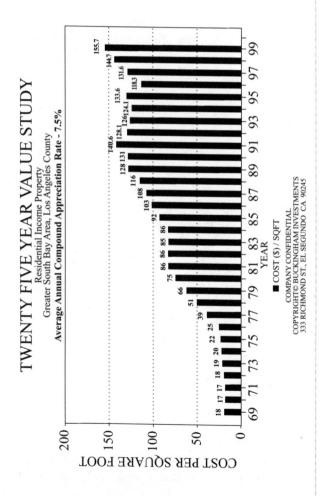

TWENTY FIVE YEAR VALUE STUDY
Residential Income Property
Greater South Bay Area, Los Angeles County
Average Annual Compound Appreciation Rate - 7.5%

COST PER SQUARE FOOT

YEAR

■ COST ($) / SQFT

COMPANY CONFIDENTIAL
COPYRIGHT© BUCKINGHAM INVESTMENTS
333 RICHMOND ST., EL SEGUNDO CA 90245

Watch Out!
Each component of return can vary greatly by geographical area. One location might offer a high cash flow but a lower return from value appreciation. Another might offer good appreciation but minimal tax benefits. Furthermore, these components can vary not only from state to state but from neighborhood to neighborhood.

The idea is for you to make a reasonable estimate of the long-term appreciation rate for your area. In Chapter 6, "Real Estate, the Economy, and Your Target Market," we're going to teach you how to do a value projection chart for your own area. You'll need to enlist some people to help you. Local investment real estate agents who have been in business for a while might have an opinion and might even have historical data that can help you calculate the appreciation rate. Local real estate appraisers also should have some knowledge of the trends in value. In addition, title insurance companies often have research departments that can provide this kind of information.

The important thing to remember is that the more years of data you have, the more accurate your number will be. As you can see from the chart we just reviewed, some years increased at a fast pace while others decreased. For this reason, you do not want to be making projections based on too few years as it would give you a suspect analysis.

To illustrate the impact of appreciation, we will assume that 1800 Mariposa Lane appreciates at a total of 5 percent per year from all the components that affect value. This means an additional $11,000 in profit the first year from appreciation ($220,000 × 5% = $11,000). Remember, we put down $30,000 to purchase the property, so we can compute the appreciation return as follows:

$$\frac{\text{Appreciation} \quad \$11,000}{\text{Down Payment} \quad \$30,000} = 36.6\% \text{ Return}$$

Tax shelter benefits

The final return on your investment from real estate is tax shelter benefits. These are the paper losses you can deduct from the taxable income you receive from the property.

As the owner of an investment property, the IRS gives you an annual depreciation allowance to deduct against your income. The theory is that this deduction will be saved up and will be used to replace the structure at the end of its useful life. This is a necessary deduction in most businesses because equipment wears out quickly. Because most property owners rarely keep their buildings long enough for them to wear out, however, the tax savings from the deduction are a profit you can keep.

Determining depreciation via your tax bill

There are a couple of methods you can use to determine your annual depreciation allowance. The first is to use your property tax bill as your guide. This bill is broken down into two components:

1. The assessed value of the improvements (the structures on the land)

2. The total assessed value of the entire property

Don't be alarmed if the actual dollar amount shown on the tax bill does not agree with what you are paying for the property; it is the ratio we are looking for. You will use these numbers to get the percentage you need to determine the value of the improvements. To do this, use the following calculation:

$$\frac{\text{Assessed Improvement Value}}{\text{Total Assessed Value}} = \text{\% Value of Improvements}$$

The percentage you get from this calculation will be used to determine the amount of improvements as follows:

$$\frac{\text{\% Value of}}{\text{Improvements}} \times \text{Price} = \text{Depreciable Improvements}$$

Watch Out!
Be sure to do your homework on your depreciation. As your income increases, you will need the write-off.

The IRS rarely challenges this ratio because they would be challenging another government entity. Unfortunately, the ratio from your tax bill is not always accurate. Thankfully, the IRS also allows alternate methods of determining your depreciation allowance.

Determining depreciation via your appraisal

A second way to determine the percentage of depreciable improvements is to use the appraisal that was done when you purchased your property. In the section of the appraisal that covers the reproduction cost method, you should find the appraiser's opinion of value for the both the land and the improvements. The appraiser will estimate the cost to build the improvements as of the date of the appraisal. This is called the reproduction cost. An allowance is then made for any depreciation, and the remainder is the appraiser's value of the improvements. Assuming the appraiser is licensed or otherwise qualified in your state, this should be a good estimate to use. Just use the same formula as follows:

$$\frac{\text{Estimated Value of Improvements}}{\text{Appraised Value}} = \% \text{ Value of Improvements}$$

Like before, the percentage you get from this calculation will be used to determine the amount of depreciable improvements. To do this, use the same calculation:

$$\frac{\% \text{ Value of}}{\text{Improvements}} \times \text{Price} = \text{Depreciable Improvements}$$

The IRS does not require you to use this method; it is just recommended for the reason previously mentioned. Because the schedule you pick when you put your investment "in service" stays with you until you have used up the write-off, however, it pays to find an acceptable method that gives you the best deduction.

The good news is that you do not have to establish your depreciation schedule until you file your tax returns. There is usually enough time between the closing and the filing for you to determine which method to use. Regardless, you should discuss the schedule you want to use with your accountant or tax professional.

Modified Accelerated Cost Recovery System

The tax code change in 1986 established the Modified Accelerated Cost Recovery System (MACRS). This code established the recovery period (or useful life) of assets to be depreciated. Like much of the tax code, these periods usually bear no relationship to reality with regard to the useful life of an asset. In the case of improved property (land with structures on it), there are two classes and two recovery periods to know about:

Type of Property	Recovery Period (Useful Life)
Residential	27.5 Years
Non-residential	39 Years

When you calculate the depreciation deduction using this method, remember that it does not matter what the true age of your property is. For residential, you use 27.5 years. For nonresidential, you use 39 years.

When using the MACRS method of depreciation, you will have the same amount of annual depreciation expense over the entire useful life of the building. To arrive at the annual expense, you

Moneysaver
When you get a loan from a lender, make sure you get a written copy of the appraisal. It will be worth its weight in gold when it comes time to calculate your depreciation allowance.

simply divide the value of the depreciable improvements by the recovery period, and this gives you the
deduction as follows:

$$\frac{\text{Value of Depreciable Improvements}}{\text{Recovery Period (Useful Life)}} = \begin{array}{l}\text{Annual}\\\text{Depreciation}\\\text{Allowance}\end{array}$$

Now let's take a look at the calculation using the
Mariposa Lane example. Remember that this is a
two-step process. First find the value of the improvements and then divide by the correct recovery
period. We are paying $220,000 for the Mariposa
Lane property and have decided to use the tax bill
to do the calculation. The tax bill shows the land
assessed at $20,000, the improvements assessed at
$35,000, and the total assessed value of the property
at $55,000. We then would calculate the deprecia-
tion allowance as follows:

$$\frac{\$35,000 \text{ (Improvements)}}{\$55,000 \text{ (Total Assessed Value)}} = 63.6\% \text{ Improvements}$$

$$\$220,000 \text{ Price} \times 63.6\% \text{ improvements} = \begin{array}{l}\$140,000\\\text{Depreciable}\\\text{Improvements}\end{array}$$

$$\frac{\$140,000 \text{ (Depreciable Improvements)}}{27.5 \text{ (Years)}} = \begin{array}{l}\$5,090 \text{ Annual}\\\text{Depreciation}\\\text{Allowance}\end{array}$$

Tax shelter example

Now that we know how much of a depreciation
allowance we can get, let's go back to our example
to determine our overall tax shelter savings. We will
assume that you are an active investor and that you
are in the 28 percent federal tax bracket. To calculate tax savings, we first need to shelter the taxable
profit from our property. As you will recall, we have
a taxable cash flow of $1,080 and a taxable equity

growth from loan reduction of $300 per year. We calculate the carry over loss as follows:

Depreciation Allowance	$5,090
Less Cash Flow	−$1,080
Less Equity Growth	−$300
Tax Benefit	$3,710

The tax savings is calculated by multiplying the tax bracket by the shelter benefit as follows:

28% × $3,710 = $1,039 Tax Savings

Many states have a state income tax. Their rules usually are similar to the federal rules when is comes to deductions and depreciation. If you live in a state with a tax, you will receive additional savings, and you can use this same formula to estimate them.

The combination of all four elements of return

Congratulations, you've made it this far; now let's look at our total first year return on our investment combining all four elements of return. We have a cash flow of $1,080, equity growth from loan reduction of $300, equity growth from appreciation of $11,000, and tax savings benefits of $1,039. Our total tax-deferred return on investment is:

Cash Flow Return	$1,080
Equity Growth (loan Reduction)	$300
Equity Growth (Appreciation)	$11,000
Tax Savings	+ $1,039
Total Return on Investment	$13,419

We can compute the total percentage return on the investment by dividing the first year return by the down payment as follows:

$$\frac{\text{Total Return} \quad \$13,419}{\text{Down Payment} \quad \$30,000} = 44.7\% \text{ Return on Investment}$$

PROPERTY ANALYSIS WORK SHEET

Address: _____

_____

1. Property Value   _____

2. Loans   _____

3. Equity

4. Gross Income _____ Mo. X 12 =   _____

5. Expenses _____ Mo. X 12 =   _____

6. Loan Payments _____ Mo. X 12 =   _____

7. Interest (_____ Loan Amt. X ____%) =   _____

8. Loan Payoff (Line 6 – Line 7) =   _____

9. Cash Flow (Line 4 – Line 5 – Line 6) =   _____

10. Depreciation Deduction   _____

11. Tax Shelter (Line 10 – Line 9 – Line 8) =   _____

12. Tax Savings (Tax Bracket ____% X Line 11) = _____

13. Building Profit (Line 8 + Line 9 + Line 12) = _____

14. Basic Return (Line 13 / Line 3) =   _____ %

PROFIT CALCULATIONS

15. Cash Flow (Line 9)   _____

16. Loan Payoff (Line 8)   _____

17. Tax Savings (Line 12)   _____

18. Appreciation ____% X Line 1   _____

19. Total Investment Return (Lines 15+16+17+18) _____

20. R. O. E. (Line 18 / Line 3)   _____ %

Calculating your return yourself

You can use the accompanying Property Analysis Work Sheet to calculate the components of return. All you need is a calculator.

On the other hand, there are many computer-generated systems for calculating this return. One example is Turbo Tax, which does a great job with depreciation. Some are proprietary systems written by the firms that own them, and many are just modified spreadsheet systems. If you have access to one of these systems it will save time, but having an automated system is not necessary.

Just the facts

- Cash flow is calculated by deducting the mortgage payments and other operating expenses from the rent you collect.

- A key element of return is the reduction in your loan balance paid from rental income.

- Your property might increase in value just because of the effect of inflation.

- An increase in the demand from investors to buy area properties can increase the value of your building.

- It is important to research the history of appreciation in your area so you can make an estimate of this potential return.

- The Modified Accelerated Cost Recovery System allows you to write-off a residential property in 27.5 years and a non-residential property in 39 years.

Valuing Property Correctly

Chapter 4

For people just getting started in investing, picking that first property can be a nerve-racking experience. Of course, the goal is to make your decision based purely on financial parameters, but that becomes pretty hard to do, especially on the first purchase. Usually, your emotions will kick into gear and try to dictate what you should buy. Many first-time investors walk in and indignantly say, "I'm not going to buy anything that I wouldn't live in myself." If you recognize yourself in this statement, know that your emotions have taken over, and you're on the verge of investing with your heart rather than your head.

Don't fret; it's easy to figure out why emotions come into play—you're scared of losing your money. In fact, fear of losing money is as much a motivator (if not radically more so) as is the promise of gain from investing it. To illustrate, let's say you were invited to a meeting at 10 p.m. tonight to learn about an opportunity that could make you $1,000

Moneysaver
If you are in the market for a property with an investment of $10,000 down, don't consider buying that "great deal" you just found that requires $50,000 down. Even if you have the money, stick to your game plan and you will sleep better at night.

on a $10,000 investment. After a bit of thought, you might decide to spend that hour watching television instead. If you got a call, however, and were told you would lose $1,000 if you didn't go to that 10 p.m. meeting, what do you think you'd do? Right.

There is no shame in a bit of trepidation. In fact, a little fear makes for a prudent investor. There are steps you can take, however, to minimize the risk and therefore alleviate your fear. The best way is to educate yourself about the commodity in which you are investing. In this chapter, your education continues with a lesson on appraising value. We will teach you the classic methods of valuing property so you can go into deals without the fear of losing your shirt.

Fair market value

The purchase of an investment property will probably be the largest dollar investment you will make in your lifetime. Unfortunately, there is no Blue Book for establishing value of used property. In addition, each property has unique components that can affect the value. The question then becomes, how do you as an investor determine whether a property is worth the asking price?

From an investment standpoint, the two most important aspects of property are its value as an asset and its return on your invested capital. Your goal is to invest your money and obtain an annual return on that invested capital until you sell or otherwise dispose of the property. Naturally, at the time of sale, you will expect to recover your original investment as well as some equity growth and appreciation. Learning how to buy at "fair market value" will ensure that you will be able to recover your original investment along with the other profit you expect.

Fair market value: The price a willing buyer will pay a willing seller for a property that has been on the market for a reasonable period of time.

As you can see, there are a number of variables to this equation, two of which have to do with the motivation level of the buyer and the seller. Even the "reasonable period of time" component depends on whether you are the buyer or the seller. The truth is, appraising is more of an art than a science. It is nearly impossible for you or even a professional appraiser to look at the information on a closed escrow and know the motivation of the buyer or the seller. At best, you can get a feeling for the market from looking at the trends you see from comparable sales that have recently closed.

Methods of valuing property

Establishing the value of a property can be a complex task. Fortunately, there are a number of acceptable methods for establishing value estimates. We will review each of these appraisal techniques and will show you how to use them yourself. The three commonly accepted appraisal methods are:

1. Comparative analysis
2. Reproduction cost
3. Capitalization of income

To compare or not to compare, that is the question

Comparative analysis is the easiest method to use when estimating value. This is the same technique most of us use when car shopping. Simply put, before you make a deal on a car, you check with several dealers to get an idea of what they each are

Timesaver
Your agent is a great source of information about the seller. Pick her brain to find out the seller's motivation for selling. Once you know what it is, you might just be able to offer exactly what he is looking for.

charging for the same car. The same premise holds true here.

This method of appraisal is not difficult and, with a little practice, can be used by anyone. When doing a comparative market analysis, you will be looking at the major features of the property that affect value. The goal is to find recent sales in which these features are as close to being the same as possible. Because time has an effect on value, the sales should be within the last six months or so, with the greatest weight given to the most current sales. The major features to consider are:

- Square footage of living area

- Number of units

- Mix of bedrooms and bathrooms

- Physical closeness (comparable neighborhood)

- Lot size

- Age of building

- Income-producing capability

- Overall condition of building and lot

- Expense factors (master-metered utilities vs. tenant pays)

- Parking (garages vs. carport)

- Extras (view, fireplaces, multiple baths, patios or decks)

Unofficially...
Comparative analysis can be tricky in areas such as beachfront communities, resorts, or high population areas. In these areas, the properties are not usually "like properties." This will throw off sales prices and make the accuracy of your analysis suspect.

We will show you an illustration of the comparative analysis method using our example property at 1800 Mariposa Lane. Remember that this property is a 20-year-old, four-unit apartment building. It is on a 50 × 150 lot. The units are unfurnished and in good condition with newer carpets and drapes. They all have built-in appliances and even have fireplaces. The neighborhood is good in terms of the condition of all the surrounding properties and their maintenance. The current owner is asking $225,000 for this property. After checking with local brokers and appraisers, you have been able to locate three sales that appear to be comparable to this property.

- **Property A:** This property is identical with respect to the building and looks like it might ever have been built by the same contractor. However, it is on a larger lot, 75 × 150, with nicer landscaping. This property sold two months ago for $270,000.

- **Property B:** This property does not have the same floor plan, but it is the same age, size, and condition as your property. The units lack fireplaces, and they have open parking instead of garages. This building closed escrow three months ago for $200,000.

- **Property C:** This property is another just like yours in every way except it sold a year ago for $215,000. We shouldn't use this sale because it was so long ago, but it is the only other comparable property we can find.

See the chart on the next page for a recap of the facts we have on the properties.

There are enough variations that we will have to make some adjustments to come up with an estimate of value. This is when the comparative analysis method becomes a bit more difficult to use, especially for the first-time investor. The adjustments take the experience of watching enough sales in the market area to be able to estimate the financial impact of the differences. Have heart, though; with a little practice, you will be able to do it, too.

For the purposes of comparing the subject property at 1800 Mariposa Lane to Property A, an

Item	Subject Property: 1800 Mariposa Ln.	Prop A	Prop B	Prop C
Price	$225,000	$270,000	$200,000	$215,000
Footage	Same	Same	Same	Same
Condition	Same	Same	Same	Same
Location	Same	Same	Same	Same
Lot Size	50 × 150	75 × 150	50 × 150	50 × 150
Features	Fireplace	Fireplace	None	Fireplace
Garages	4	4	None	4
Sale Date	Unsold	3 Months	2 Months	1 Year

adjustment will have to be made in the price of Property A because it is on a much larger lot. To do the adjustment, the value of lots in the area needs to be determined. For our example, we will assume that 50 × 150 foot lots zoned for apartment buildings sell for approximately $100,000. The lot on which Property A sits is 1½ times larger than the lot the Mariposa building is on. Therefore, it would have a value of 1½ times the value of the Mariposa lot, or $150,000 ($100,000 × 1½ = $150,000). From this, we can conclude that Property A is worth $50,000 more than the Mariposa property because of the additional land. For the purposes of estimating the value of the subject property on Mariposa Lane, we will decrease the value of Property A by $50,000.

Property B also needs to be adjusted because it doesn't have fireplaces or garages. These items can be estimated by researching the cost of these components with local builders. For our example, we have determined that the cost of installing a fireplace is $1,000. This makes the loss in value of our four missing fireplaces $4,000 ($1,000 × 4 = $4,000). The cost of building a garage in this area is $30 per square foot. The four missing garages would have been 600 square feet, so the total cost to build them would be $18,000 ($30 × 600 = $18,000). To compare the sale price of Property B to the subject property on Mariposa Lane, we would have to add the value of the missing items, or $22,000 ($4,000 for fireplaces + $18,000 for garages = $22,000).

The adjustment to Property C is tougher because a year has gone by since it sold. Appraisers do not like to use comparables that are this old because so many things can happen in that time

Watch Out!
Investors should not trust any appraisal offered by the seller as justification of value. Although such an appraisal might be accurate, investors need to do their own homework as well.

span to affect the value of property. Because we cannot find another sale, however, we will use this one. To be able to use it, we need to know how much property has appreciated in the last year. For our example, we have determined the appreciation rate over the last year to be 5 percent. This means that Property C would have increased $10,750 over the last year ($215,000 × 5% = $10,750). To do our comparison, we would have to add the $10,750 to the sale price of Property C.

Let's do a recap of the adjustments:

Item	Subject	Prop A	Prop B	Prop C
Price	$225,000	$270,000	$200,000	$215,000
Adjust	0	−50,000	+$22,000	+$10,750
Value	?	$220,000	$222,000	$225,750

The last step in doing a comparative market analysis is to make an estimate of value for the subject property. This will be based on the adjusted prices of the comparables. Appraisers usually take an average value of the comps. Therefore, if we avearged the three values of those properties, the indicated value is $222,583 ($220,000 + 222,000 + 225,750 ÷ 3 = $222,583). Rounded off it would be $222,500.

Reproduction cost approach

The reproduction cost method is the "what would it cost to build it today" method. Basically, you establish value by pretending to buy a lot at today's value and then building a "used" building to match the existing building. This method requires a good knowledge of the market for land and an even better knowledge of construction and the current costs of building. Because we can't build a "used" building, we then need to depreciate it based on the fact that it is not new. This requires an even greater knowledge. Nonetheless, let's give it a try.

The first step is to determine the value of the lot. To do this, you need to contact brokers and builders in the area to find out what they are paying for similar lots. If there aren't enough lots of the exact size of the subject property, some adjustments will have to be made. You would then use the same comparative analysis method we just used. It would be easier to do, however, because you would only be making an adjustment based on the price per square foot differences.

Next you will take a survey of the building to determine the square footage of the living areas and the square footage of the garages and other utility areas. These footage costs are based on the type of construction, the size of the building, the quality of construction, and the part of the country in which the property is located. Builders or bankers might be able to give you a general idea of the cost for your local area.

For the purpose of our example, we will assume that the cost to build a standard wood frame and stucco two-story building is $60 per square foot and that the cost to build the garages is $30 per square foot. Now let's return to our example on Mariposa Lane and estimate the value using the reproduction cost method.

The first item to value will be the land. In our example, our lot is 50 × 150, or 7,500 square feet. We previously determined in the comparative analysis method that the land is worth $100,000. This works out to $13.33 per square foot ($100,000 ÷ 7,500 = $13.33).

Timesaver

Building cost tables should be available at your library. These tables provide the current cost per square foot for building the living areas, the garages, and all the other components you might find in a property.

Now we need to determine the value of the structures on the property and all the other amenities such as landscaping, walkways, and driveways. Each of the four units in our example building is 800 square feet and includes two bedrooms, one bathroom, a kitchen, and a living room. There are four garages of approximately 150 square feet each. This gives us a living area of 3,200 square feet (800 × 4 = 3,200) and a garage area of 600 square feet (150 × 4 = 600). In addition, we have determined that the other amenities (driveway, landscaping, etc.) would cost approximately $20,000. The following chart shows the total cost to build our building in today's market:

Item	Square Feet	Cost	Total
Building	3,200	$60 sq. ft.	$192,000
Garages	600	$30 sq. ft.	$18,000
Amenities	N/A	N/A	$20,000
Total			$225,000

We have a problem, though. The building and the garage are not brand new; they were built 20 years ago. Our task is to determine the amount of value that has been used up, or depreciated. For this example, we will use a method based on the estimated useful life of a property. For apartment buildings of average quality with wood frame and stucco construction, a useful life of 40 years is commonly accepted.

The Mariposa property is already 20 years old, so using a 40-year useful life, we see that this building has lost half its useful life and therefore half the value of these improvements. Because the new value of the building is $210,000 ($192,000 building

+ \$18,000 garages = \$210,000), the remaining value of these improvements is \$105,000 (\$210,000 ÷ 2 = \$105,000) given that the property has lost half its useful life. An appraiser would call this the depreciated value of the improvements. Note that we did not take depreciation into account on the amenities because they were only a small part of the value.

We can now finish our estimate of value using the reproduction cost method as follows:

Cost of Lot	\$100,000
Cost of Amenities	\$20,000
Depreciated Value of Buildings	+\$105,000
Total	\$225,000

The banker's way

A third accepted method of appraising value is called the capitalization of income approach. This technique sets value based on the building's profitability. This is the "what would I make on my money if I paid all cash" appraisal method. This is probably the most difficult of the methods to use properly, but it is the preferred method when valuing income property.

The concept of a capitalization rate is well-known to most of us but under a pseudonym. We recognize capitalization rates as interest rates. When you think of putting your money in a bank, the first question you ask is, "What interest rate will I get?" In truth, what you are asking for is the capitalization rate on that bank account.

Before we move on to understanding the capitalization rate in real estate, let's look at the formula for calculating the interest rate from a simple savings account and then expand it to the form we need to use for real estate appraising. Let's assume

Watch Out!
One drawback to the cost approach is that builders' costs can vary greatly depending on the number of units produced and the individual builder's profit margin. You might have to make market comparisons of builders' costs in the same way that sellers' prices are compared.

you have $10,000 in your savings account, and at the end of the year, you earned $500 in interest. The following formula will show your profit percentage:

$$\frac{\text{Interest Earned}}{\text{Amount Invested}} = \text{Percentage Profit}$$

Or:

$$\frac{\$500}{\$10,000} = 5\%$$

Translated to the language of appraising, this becomes:

$$\frac{\text{Net Income}}{\text{Price}} = \text{Capitalization Rate}$$

When dealing with real estate and other investments that have various expenses associated with their operation, therefore, we need to expand the equation to the following:

$$\frac{\text{Gross Income} - \text{Operating Expenses}}{\text{Capitalization Rate}} = \text{Price}$$

When appraising property, remember that we are not trying to find out the profit; we are trying to estimate the value of the property. In the case of investment property, what better way to estimate the value than by using its ability to produce a profit as a guideline? This ability to produce a profit is expressed as the interest rate you earn on your investment. Once we know the interest rate we should be getting on our money when we buy a property, we can use it to project a value. To do this, we need to change our formulas around as follows:

$$\frac{\text{Gross Income} - \text{Operating Expenses}}{\text{Capitalization Rate}} = \text{Price}$$

Simplified, this becomes:

$$\frac{\text{Net Income}}{\text{Capitalization Rate}} = \text{Price}$$

To estimate the value of a property using this method, you need to know a few things, including:

1. The gross income

2. The operating expenses

3. The capitalization rate investors expect in the area where the property is located

We will review each of these items as well as some of the things for which you need to watch out.

The gross scheduled income

The gross income is the total amount of rental income collected in the year plus any other income such as laundry income or garage rentals. Many times, this is referred to as gross scheduled income (GSI). One problem that arises here is how to handle the income from a building in which the current owner has under-rented some or all of the units. This is very common with smaller units because most absentee investors seem to get happy with a certain level of profit and then don't want to rock the boat by changing things.

This problem is a common source of debate between appraisers, bankers, and investors that we won't attempt to solve here. In practice, appraisers will make an allowance for market rents, bankers won't use the market rents when calculating their loan amounts, and investors look for under-rented properties with lower sales prices.

You have to know the expenses

The next component you need to know is the annual expenses on the property including property taxes,

Unofficially...
A couple of generalizations can be made about the relationship between the capitalization rate and the risk of an investment:

High Risk = High Capitalization Rate = Low Value.

Low Risk = Low Capitalization Rate = High Value.

Unofficially...
Appraisals done
for refinance
purposes are
usually more
conservative
than an appraisal
done for a
purchase
transaction.

insurance, utilities, gardening, management fees, repair cost, vacancies, and so on. You do not include interest expense because the capitalization of income approach presupposes that you paid all cash.

We are sure you can appreciate the difficulty in getting a clear picture of what a property's true expenses might be. One owner might do all the management and maintenance himself; another might hire a management company that subcontracts all the work to the most expensive contractors in the area. One owner has low rents and has not had a tenant move in five years; the owner next door is charging market rents and has had some tenants move out. The units have higher rents, but the owner lost some revenue and has had all the fix-up expenses of getting the unit ready to rent.

What this dictates for appraisers is a method of estimating expenses based on the type of property being appraised and the area of the country in which it is located. Take the following examples, for instance:

- A small four-unit building with no amenities will have far less expense as a percentage of the income than a large, full-security building with swimming pools, tennis courts, elevators, and extensive landscaping.

- The cost of heating a building in Southern California will be far less than the cost of heating a building in Minnesota.

You see, factors like these translate into higher operating costs and higher repair costs when the units break down. To attempt to equalize these differences, appraisers use tables of expenses based on a percentage of the gross. The following chart is typical for property in Southern California. Remember, expenses can vary by area so make sure you check with your local experts.

Number of Units	Expenses
2–4	20–25%
5–15	25–35%
15 and Up	30–45%

The range gives appraisers a way to make an allowance for variations in the expenses associated with operating the building and the amenities it has.

The expected "cap" rate

The last item necessary for this appraisal technique is the capitalization rate based on what kind of return investors expect to get in that market area. This rate not only will vary in different parts of the country but it also can vary in different parts of a city, even in buildings within a few blocks of each other.

In addition, different kinds of properties (residential, commercial, industrial) will have a different rate, even in the same location. Remember, the capitalization rate is the measure of the profitability of an investment. Different types of properties have different risks and therefore a different expectation of profit for taking that risk.

Now let's return to the example at 1800 Mariposa Lane and see how this method is used. We determined that the total rental income for the property is $26,400 ($550 per unit × 4 units × 12 months). A rental survey of the area shows that this rent is in line with the market. The expenses are reported at $7,920 for the year. This is 30 percent of the gross income ($7,920 ÷ $26,400 = 30%). We contacted

Timesaver
You probably can obtain the cap rate you need to use from a local investment real estate agent or appraiser. Be sure to ask the person to show you how he or she arrived at the rate provided. It is important to know this figure accurately because most investors give considerable weight to this method of estimating value.

several local appraisers, and they told us the capitalization rate was 8.4 percent. Remember that a capitalization rate can be expressed as a percentage (8.4%) or as a decimal (.084). Be sure to clarify this when someone tells you the rate. If the person gives you the rate as a percentage, you will need to convert it to a decimal before you do your calculation.

Putting this all together, we would calculate the value estimate with the following steps. The first step is to determine the net income:

Gross Annual Income	$26,400
Less Operating Expenses	−$7,920
Net Income	$18,480

The formula to find value is:

$$\frac{\text{Net Income}}{\text{Capitalization Rate}} = \text{Price}$$

To complete our calculation, substitute the following information into the equation:

$$\frac{\$18,480}{.084} = \$220,000$$

The three classic appraisal methods

One way to get a final estimate of value for our subject property is to take the values from the three appraisal methods and average them together:

Comparative Analysis Value	$222,500
Reproduction Cost Value	$225,000
Capitalization Value	+$220,000
Total	$667,500

$$\frac{\$667,500}{3} = \$222,500 \text{ Averaged Value}$$

A word of caution though: In the real world of appraising, it is not always practical or prudent to rely equally on the values by each method. Depending on the type of property being appraised, one of the methods usually gets the most weight in the final value. With single-family homes, for example, the comparative method works best because in most areas there seem to be plenty of similar houses. For that reason, it is easy to find enough current sales to come up with an estimate of value.

On the other hand, the reproduction cost method carries the most weight for specialized properties and for new construction. For a special property such as a church building, this is the only practical way to estimate a value. This also works fine for new construction because the land probably was just purchased, and the cost of the structure is easy to determine because there is no depreciation to estimate.

Finally, for all types of investment property, the capitalization of income method carries the greatest weight. You should use the reproduction cost method and the comparative analysis method to check the value arrived by capitalizing the net income.

The gross multiplier

Real estate isn't any different from any other industry in that people "in the business" have developed a quick and easy way to estimate value. In real estate, we use a number called the gross multiplier. This is similar to the use of the PE, or price earnings ratio, in valuing stocks. It presupposes there is a number, the gross multiplier, that you can multiply times the gross income of a property to estimate its value.

Let's look at our example to see how to arrive at the gross multiplier:

$$\frac{\text{Price of Property}}{\text{Gross Income}} = \text{Gross Multiplier}$$

For our example on Mariposa, the calculation is:

$$\frac{\$220,000}{\$26,400} = 8.33 \times \text{Gross}$$

For estimating value, the equation is changed as follows:

$$\text{Gross Income} \times \text{Gross Multiplier} = \text{Value of the Property}$$

The following chart shows the effect of several gross multipliers on the value of our example:

Gross Income		Gross Multiplier		Value of Property
$26,400	×	8.0	=	$211,200
$26,400	×	8.5	=	$224,400
$26,400	×	9.0	=	$237,600

As you can see, it's easy to see how a small difference in this number can make a big difference in the value of a property. Three financial components of a property can throw the gross multiplier off:

1. The first is the case of a property in which the owner has kept the rents well below market value. In this instance, the multiplier will be way off.

2. The second is when you find a property in which the expenses are too high. The gross multiplier does not take into account the expenses of the property. Some properties have far higher expenses than others, however, which would affect the net income to the owner. The most typical reason is the utilities are paid for by the owner rather than the tenants. If you were to pay the same price for a

building with high expenses as for one with normal expenses, you would end up with a substandard return.

3. Furnished units usually rent for substantially more than unfurnished rentals. If you were to apply the same gross multiplier to this type of property, you would be paying a premium for the right to own used furniture.

It is important to remember that the gross multiplier is only a rule of thumb. It should only be used when you fully understand all the financial details of the area in which you are looking and the property you are considering. It does, however, provide a quick way to rank properties when you are first looking around. You then can review the income and expense figures and determine which property will give you the better net return on your investment.

Finding some hidden value

When an appraisal is ordered on a piece of property, the person making the appraisal will want to know the purpose for the appraisal. The valuation for a loan will be different than the valuation to settle an estate. The valuation of a lot with a home might be less than the valuation of the lot alone if it had the potential to build something more valuable on it such as an apartment building. These variations point to the importance of understanding appraising as a tool for finding hidden value in property.

Knowledge of appraisal methods can be very helpful when it comes time to negotiate the purchase of a property. Most sellers list their property at the price they want, which may or may not be related to its true value when compared to current sales. If you present your offer at a lower price without facts

Moneysaver
By fully under-
standing the
techniques of
appraising, you
can learn to use
the appraisal as
a tool to drive
down the price
you pay. At the
same time, you
can use it as a
tool to dig up
some hidden
profit.

to back it up, the seller might take it personally and
dig in his heels when considering your lower offer. If
you come in with an offer based on recognized
appraisal techniques, however, you have a much better chance of obtaining the property at the lower
price.

Let's make a small change in our example on
Mariposa Lane and see how it affects the value.
Instead of an annual income of $26,400, which is
$550 per month per unit, let's assume the owner has
not kept the rents up to market. In this example, we'll
say the rents are $495, $510, $500, and $525, for a
monthly total of $2,030. $2,030 × 12 months gives us
an income of $24,360. Remember, our annual
expenses are $7920, and the capitalization rate we are
using is 8.4%. In preparing our offer, we include an
attachment with the comparable sales information
and an estimate of value based on the capitalization
of income method. The valuation now looks like this:

Gross Annual Income	$24,360
Less Operating Expenses	−$7,920
Net Income	$16,440

Remember, once you have the net income, the formula to estimate value is:

$$\frac{\text{Net Income}}{\text{Capitalization Rate}} = \text{Price}$$

Or, substituting in our values we get:

$$\frac{\$16,440}{.084} = \$195,714 \text{ Offered Price}$$

Our estimate using the three classic appraisal
methods indicated a value of $222,000, so anything
you can save below that price will be an extra profit
for you. There is no guarantee the seller will take the

lower offer, but if your agent presents a convincing story about your desire to purchase at a fair price, you might prevail.

Now let's use an appraisal to find some additional hidden profit based on potential rent. You have done all your research on the market area and have found that the market rent for these units is $575 per month and that garages add a premium of $15 per month. This gives the building the potential gross of $28,320. The value estimate now is:

Gross Annual Income	$28,320
Less Operating Expenses	−$7,920
Net Income	$20,400

Let's work the valuation formula again:

$$\frac{\text{Net Income}}{\text{Capitalization Rate}} = \text{Price}$$

Or, substituting in our values we get:

$$\frac{\$20,400}{.084} = \$242,857$$

With this information in your possession, you could even pay the full asking price of $225,000 and still have found some hidden profit because of your knowledge of the market. It will take some effort and time to get the rents up to market, but once you do, the profit is there for the picking.

Highest and best use

An important concept to understand in real estate is "highest and best use." Have you ever driven through a commercial area with office buildings and retail stores only to see an old single-family home that looks like someone still lives there? If that home comes up for sale, should it be appraised as a single-family residence or as a commercial lot? The answer is probably as a commercial lot because this is now the "highest and best use" of the property.

Understanding that developed property can have more than one use often will yield a hidden profit. The following are some situations that would warrant valuing a property for it's highest and best use rather than its current use:

- A house or small units on a commercial or industrial lot.

- A house or small units on a large lot zoned for multiunits in an area with many new buildings.

- You get a parcel map on a property and discover that the building sits on two separate lots.

- A four-unit property that consists of two side-by-side duplexes on two separate lots according to the parcel map.

- The apartments in the building currently have one bedroom, but the bedrooms are very large and could be made into two simply by adding one wall and a door for much greater rent.

- A small house on a multiunit zoned parcel where extra units can be added.

- A vacant commercial building that can be converted to loft apartments or live/work lofts.

In all of these cases, the property can be valued in more than one way. The highest and best use for the property might not be its current use. The highest and best use might not always be obvious, as in the case of the building that sits on two lots. In that case, the land value of the two lots might be significantly higher than the value of the building alone.

The lesson here is that real estate is a multi-dimensional asset. If you fail to look at all its facets, you might fail to realize the full potential of your investment. Finding the hidden value in a property does not mean you have to immediately realize it by making a sale. This hidden profit should give you extra confidence in the security of your investment.

In addition, you now have two chances to make more profit in the future. In the example of the building on two lots, the building and its income stream probably will be worth more as the market increases. In addition, the land will be worth more for development purposes, and that value might increase faster than the building value.

Just the facts

- Buying property at fair market value will ensure your success as a real estate investor.

- Comparative analysis is an easy and effective method of appraisal that even the most novice investor can do.

- Capitalization rates tell you how much you will make on your investment if you paid all cash for it.

- The gross multiplier is just a rule of thumb, but it will give you a great head start on your analysis.

Timesaver
When analyzing property, always keep the idea of "highest and best use" in mind. Remember, property not being utilized at its highest and best use will have less value than other, comparable properties based on this standard.

Financing Your Investment

Chapter 5

Locating the right financing is a key component of your ultimate success as a real estate investor. Because not many of us have an extra few hundred thousand dollars to buy a piece of property, you must find a lender willing to loan you a good portion of the money. In this chapter, you will learn how real estate is financed, where to find the right loan, and how to make sure the loan you find is affordable.

Costs of borrowing money

Let's first examine the fees associated with borrowing. As you start shopping for a loan, you will find that costs of borrowing money vary widely. The two greatest factors affecting your costs will be who makes the loan and what type of loan it is. The following list covers most of the most common fees lenders charge.

	Government Loans	Conventional Loans	Private Loans
Good-Faith Deposit	X	X	
Loan Fee–Points	X	X	
Appraisal Fee	X	X	
Credit Report	X	X	X
Tax Service	X	X	
Document Recording	X	X	
Loan Processing		X	X
Drawing Documents	X	X	
Funding Fee	X		
Prepaid Interest	X	X	
Mortgage Insurance	X	X	
Loan Escrow	X	X	X
Alta Title Insurance	X	X	
Set Up	X	X	
Warehouse Fee	X	X	

The Real Estate Settlement Procedures Act (RESPA) requires that all lenders (except private parties) give you an estimate of lending fees. Along with this estimate, it is important to get a statement of the annual percentage rate (APR) of your loan. This estimate will take into account all the fees paid on the loan up-front to give you a true picture of the annual interest rate you will be paying.

The biggest expense of your loan is the loan fee, or "points." Each point is 1 percent of the loan amount. One point on a $150,000 loan would be $1,500 ($150,000 × 1% = $1,500).

In the lending world, interest rates and terms revolve around a current market rate that the lenders call "par." This is the best rate on any given day charging normal closing fees and points. It is important to get a quote at a "par" interest rate when shopping for a loan.

Moneysaver
Do not hesitate to negotiate on points and other lending fees. They are not set in stone.

You will find that many loans are being advertised as having no points or fees. The way they can achieve this is by charging a higher-than-par interest rate. It's an okay tradeoff if you need that kind of help to buy, but know that it can be costly to do business this way. You only pay for points and loan fees once, but you pay the higher interest rate for the full term of the loan.

Unofficially...
Points paid to purchase or refinance an investment property can only be deducted over the term of the mortgage.

Locating a lender

When it comes to financing smaller residential real estate, there are three primary sources to find money:

1. The federal government

2. Local savings and loans and banks and insurance companies

3. Private parties

The Federal Housing Administration (FHA)

The best source for government-supported financing is the Federal Housing Administration (FHA). The FHA's primary objective is to assist in providing housing opportunities for individuals just starting out. The agency generally does not provide the funds for the mortgages; rather, it insures home mortgage loans made by private industry lenders such as mortgage bankers, savings and loans, and banks. This insurance is necessary because FHA loans are made with low down payments and have favorable interest rates and terms compared to the conventional lending market. The following chart gives the maximum loan amounts available for FHA loans at the time of publication:

Number of Units	Standard Loan Amount	High Cost Area Limits
1	$78,660	$155,250
2	$100,600	$198,550
3	$121,600	$240,000
4	$151,150	$298,350

One great advantage of FHA loans is that they offer great leverage to the investor. You can get into a property with as little as 3 percent down. The remaining 97 percent is put up by the FHA-insured lender. Because FHA loans are for individuals just beginning, one requirement is that you live in the property as your primary residence. Don't panic, however; there's no requirement that you have to stay there forever.

Because the goal of FHA loans is to create owner occupancy, you should be fairly certain that you plan to live in your units for a reasonable length of time. Check with your mortgage lender before you commit. This way, you can be clear on the specific rules that ultimately will affect your lending decision.

If you do opt for an owner-occupied FHA loan, the great news is that the one-to-four-unit market usually has the largest selection of properties available. This gives you a great probability of finding a property with a unit that will make a nice home for you and your family and a nice rental for some tenants. We know that the American dream is to own your own home. If you can be patient, make that first buy a set of FHA units. You then can move up to a single-family residence in just a few years and can own a nice piece of income property to boot.

Another great advantage of the FHA program is that it uses FHA-approved appraisers to value the properties. During the appraisal process, one of the

main goals is to make sure there are no major problems with the building and that all the basic safety
measures have been met. If a property does not
meet FHA standard guidelines, the seller must
either comply with the appraiser's request to fix the
problems, or lose the deal. Nine times out of ten,
sellers comply. By the time you move in, all major
repair work will have been fixed.

VA loans

At the end of World War II, Congress approved the
Serviceman's Readjustment Act of 1944. The common term for this program is the GI Bill of Rights.
The purpose of the Act was to give the GI's (general
infantrymen) a new start and to ease their expenses
in civilian life by providing them with medical benefits, bonuses, and low-interest loans. These loans
are not directly made by the Veterans Administration but are guaranteed by it. They work much the
same as FHA loans but with one significant difference. VA loans can be for 100 percent of the purchase price. This means the veteran doesn't have to
come up with any money for a down payment. The
important things to know about VA loans are:

- They are secured by the Department of
  Veterans Affairs.

- VA loans are only for eligible veterans.

- These loans have low- and no-down-payment
  options.

- Eligible properties include one- to four-unit
  primary homes including approved condos.

- Loan amounts can be as high as $203,000.

- They provide the security of fixed payments
  over the life of the loan.

Moneysaver
FHA deals are
great for the
beginning
investor. Because
you will be living
in the property,
you can roll up
your sleeves and
make upgrades
that no doubt
will improve its
value. When it
comes time to
sell or refinance,
you will have
created some
sweat equity for
yourself.

First-time-buyer programs

Many communities offer "first-time-buyer" programs. These loans come in various forms and are designed to help people get their first home at an affordable price. Many first-time-buyer programs require the property to be owner-occupied just like FHA and VA loans. Make sure to check with your local City Hall to see if there are any programs that would work for you.

The conventional route

Conventional loans are offered by banks, savings and loans, and mortgage companies. Most of these loans are packaged using the Federal National Mortgage Association, commonly called Fannie Mae, or the Federal Home Loan Mortgage Corporation, nicknamed Freddie Mac. These are quasi-public organizations with the benefit of government sponsorship. All conventional loans fall into one of two categories:

1. Residential loans for one to four units

2. Commercial loans for five units and up

There are significant differences between these two categories including the number of lenders willing to provide loans for them, qualification criteria, and terms. We will look at residential loans first.

Residential loans for one to four units

Residential loans come in almost unlimited shapes and sizes. Call any major lender in your area and ask for a list of their loan programs; you will be amazed at the options that exist. We will attempt to simplify the list so you can zero-in on the best loan for you.

The standard conventional loan is for 80 percent of the appraised value of the property. This means

Unofficially...
With conventional financing, loans rarely are left on the books of the original lender. Instead, lenders package and sell their loans in the secondary market (that is, they sell the loans to other investors). This way, smaller lenders can avoid using up all their funds available to lend and can continue to make new loans to new buyers.

you will have to put down 20 percent of the purchase price. You can either pay the 20 percent yourself, or you can structure a deal with a seller whereby he finances a portion of it for you in a second loan. The usual scenario has the buyer paying 10 percent, the seller financing 10 percent in a second loan, and the lender lending 80 percent (10% + 10% + 80% = 100%). Some lenders will allow you to get a second loan and some will not, so be sure to check when you do your loan shopping.

In some cases, the appraised value of the property may be less than the price you negotiated. Most standard contracts contain a clause that protects you in the event this happens. In these instances, the clause will allow you to cancel your purchase contract without forfeiting your deposit.

There are two other options available when this happens. First, you can use the appraisal as ammunition to get a lower price. With a lower appraisal in hand, you can go back to the seller and renegotiate the purchase price to make it equal to the appraised value. Second, if you really want the property, you can simply put down additional money needed to complete the purchase. This way, the bank will be satisfied with the final loan to value ratio, so they can justify approval of the loan you are seeking.

Note that it is not unusual in an escalating market for appraisals to come in low. This does not mean the value isn't there for the investor. It just means the appraiser's formula didn't work. In the long run, this has little to do with the profit you will earn from your business.

Sometimes you can find loans advertised that offer financing for 90–95 percent of the value of the property. Unfortunately, most of these loans are

Timesaver
Be sure to let your lender know whether you plan on living in the building you are buying. This information will be critical to the type of loan you qualify for and might even save you some money on the interest rate and fees. Note that loans on properties that are "owner occupied" are generally charged less interest than non-owner-occupied units.

only for owner-occupied properties, and many will not allow them to be anything other than a single-family home. You should know that these kinds of loans usually have an interest rate higher than a loan of 80 percent of value. In addition, they normally require you to pay for private mortgage insurance (PMI). This is insurance that will guarantee the lender not to lose part or all of its loan in the event of a foreclosure. With PMI the lender passes on the cost of the insurance to the borrower by increasing the interest rate. This increase can be ¼% to ½% higher, and the PMI can add another ¼% to ½% on top of that. This can make it more difficult to qualify and will certainly raise the true cost of borrowing.

Qualifying for conventional loans

Qualifying for residential loans depends primarily on your credit worthiness and your ability to pay the loan back. This usually is measured in two ways. One way is by the use of your FICO score. FICO is a rating system based on a standardized ranking by the three major credit agencies as calculated by the Fair Issac Credit Organization. The formula they use is not disclosed by the credit bureaus, per decisions made by the U.S. Congress. Simply put, the higher your FICO score, the better risk you are. Some known FICO parameters are as follows:

- The number of bank card trade lines
- The worst level of delinquency on an installment loan
- The number of months in the file
- The number of months since most recent bank card opening
- The number of months since the most recent derogatory public record

- The delinquency on accounts
- The number of accounts with balances
- The length of revolving credit accounts
- The date of inquiries
- The number of retail accounts

The other method of rating credit is based on a ratio system, consisting of a top and bottom ratio. The top ratio is calculated by dividing the monthly principal, interest, taxes, and insurance payments on your purchase by your total monthly income. The bottom ratio adds all your debt payments to the payment on the property and divides this by your total monthly income. This number takes into account how much debt you have, how much credit you have available on credit cards, late payments, delinquencies, judgments, bankruptcies, and so on.

Most lenders also talk about credit and their loan programs based on a ranking system of A, B, C, or D credit. The following is a summary of the criteria they use to determine your credit grade:

- **A credit:** Very few or no credit problems within the last two years. One or two 30-day late payments. No record of collections.

- **B credit:** A few late payments within the last 18 months. Up to four 30-day late payments or up to two 60-day late payments are allowed on revolving and installment debt. If the late payment is an isolated incident, one 90-day late is allowed.

- **C credit:** Lots of 30- to 60-day late payments in the last two years. Any late mortgage payment in the 60- to 90-day range. A bankruptcy or foreclosure that has been discharged or settled in the last 12 months.

- **D credit:** Open collections, charge-offs, notice of defaults, and so on. Multiple 30- to 90-day or longer missed payments.

The lender also will do an appraisal on the property that will figure into the decision. Make no mistake, however; their appraisal of you is what is most important when lending on one to four units. Your credit ranking and your ratios will be what tips the scales one way or the other, not how the property looks or appraises.

Commercial loans for five units and up

At some point, you probably will start looking at larger properties. Any property with five or more units falls into the commercial lending category. Unlike with residential loans, qualifying for a commercial loan is primarily based on the ability of the property to generate sufficient cash flow to repay the loan. As a matter of fact, many of these loans are nonrecourse loans. A nonrecourse loan is one in which the lender is prohibited from getting any compensation from you for a loss if the lender has to foreclose and take the property back. The exact opposite is true for residential loans.

Most lenders want a debt-coverage of 1.1 to 1.25 of the monthly debt payments. This means that the property needs to have a net cash flow after expenses and vacancy reserves of 1.1 to 1.25 times the loan payment. The property should be able to pay all its expenses, pay the mortgage payments, and have some positive cash flow left over for the investor. Here is what you need to know about commercial loans:

- Commercial loans are harder to find.

- Loan fees and interest rates can be higher than for properties in the one- to four-unit range.

- The appraisal will be more extensive and more expensive than for a one- to four-unit building.

- The lender will want to see specific, up-to-date information about rents and expenses on the building.

- Commercial loans tend to take longer to process because the appraisers are specialized and because it takes longer to get all the environmental reports that are sometimes needed.

Fixed for the life of the loan

Two types of interest rates are available on any kind of loan you get: fixed rates and adjustable rates. At a gut level, most people think they would prefer a fixed-rate loan. You know what the rate is today, and you know what it is going to be tomorrow. This predictability is very attractive and makes a fixed-rate loan desirable. The problem is that in the one- to four-unit market it is hard to get a fixed-rate loan for nonowner-occupied units. If you plan to live in one of the units you buy, that's one thing. If you plan on just having an investment, however, finding a fixed rate on one to four units will be tough.

For argument's sake, let's say you did find a fixed-rate loan on a nonowner-occupied piece of property. Here is what you can expect: The loan usually will be at a much higher interest rate than the typical adjustable loan. In addition, it probably will have higher fees, the loan won't be assumable, and most will have a prepayment penalty for the first three to five years. To add insult to injury, some loans also have a balloon payment due in seven to ten years.

Timesaver
Do your loan shopping before you make any offers on properties that have five units or more. This way, you won't spin your wheels on deals for which the lender won't lend.

Unofficially...
The reason fixed-rate loans usually have higher rates of interest is because the lender has to retain the loan in at the fixed rate for 10–30 years, and take the risk of having the cost of money increase. This is great in a stable economy, but during a period of inflation, the cost of funds for the lenders can erode their profit margin.

Here's how a balloon payment works: Most government and conventional loans on smaller properties are fully amortized. A fully amortized loan is one in which you make 20 or 30 years' worth of payments, and at the end of that time, your loan is paid off in full. In the case of many fixed-rate loans, payments on the loan would be made as though you were paying off the loan with a 30-year amortization schedule, but at the end of seven to ten years, you would have a balloon payment due. This payment would be equal to the balance of the loan at that time.

A quick banking lesson

Savings and loans and banks make most real estate loans for smaller properties. The loans are made for 10–30 years. The money they lend is money they borrow from their customers. Here is how it works: You bring the money in the front door and open a savings account, on which you earn interest. The interest you get is the cost of funds for the bank. The money goes out the back door when your neighbor goes to that very same bank and gets a loan for a new house. The difference between the rate your neighbor pays for his home loan and the rate you get on your savings account goes towards the bank's overhead and profit. The reality, however, is that most people don't put their money in the bank for 10–30 years. Instead, they put it in for a couple of days to a couple of years. What this means is that banks are lending money on real estate for 10–30 years based on their projected cost of funds today. Can you appreciate the risk in long-term lending based on a short-term supply of capital? The banks learned this lesson the hard way in the 1970s, and this is why the adjustable-rate mortgage was invented.

Adjustable-rate mortgages (ARM)

The interest rate of the modern adjustable loan is based on an index plus a margin. It's actually pretty simple. An "index" is a source from which interest rates are determined. It generally is either treasury bills or treasury bond rates or the cost of money in local federal districts. A "margin" is the amount of interest the lender charges the borrower in addition to the interest rate of the index. The margin is to cover the lender's overhead, cost, and profit. It can (and will) vary depending on market conditions and competition. The most common indexes are:

- **COFI:** COFI stands for the Cost of Fund Index. This is the average cost of deposits and borrowing for a savings institution in a given Federal Home Loan Bank District. For example, the 11th District Cost of Funds Index is comprised of California, Arizona, and Nevada.

- **CMT:** CMT is the Constant Maturity Treasury Index. This is the weekly average yield on United States treasury securities adjusted to a constant maturity of one year. For larger fixed rate apartment and commercial loans which may have a maturity date of 7 or 10 years, the index used would be based on 7 and 10 year Treasury Securities.

- **LIBOR:** LIBOR stands for the London Inter-Bank Offered Rate. This is the average of lending rates from a number of major banks based in London, England.

- **CD:** The index based on certificates of deposit (CD) is a weekly average of the secondary market interest rate on certificates of deposit with a six-month maturity date.

You can calculate the interest rate on your ARM loan using the following formula:

Current Rate of Index + Margin of Loan = Interest Rate

As an example, if the index is 4.92 and the margin is 2.25:

4.92% (Rate) + 2.25% (Margin) = 7.17% Interest Rate

Types of adjustables

There are basically two types of adjustable rate mortgages:

1. **"No-neg" loans:** These are loans that do not allow any negative amortization.

2. **"Neg-am" loans:** These are loans that allow for negative amortization.

Amortization refers to the amount your loan balance is reduced after paying for the interest charges. What is negative amortization? Here is how it works: If the agreed upon monthly payment on your ARM for a given year is $850 but $900 a month is required to pay off the loan in 30 years based upon the current interest rate, then the remaining $50 a month will be added to the loan balance. Therefore, instead of decreasing with each monthly payment, your loan balance increases each payment. That is negative amortization.

The "no-neg" adjustable loan

The "no-neg" is an adjustable loan with terms that do not allow for potential negative amortization. In guaranteeing that there will be no negative amortization, the lender builds in protection for potential market interest rate increases. For example, the loan may provide for two interest adjustments each year, one every six months, with a maximum increase or decrease in the interest rate of 1 percent each 6 month period and a corresponding increase or decrease adjustment in the payment. For this maximum increase or decrease, the bank will absorb any costs above the 2 percent (1 percent every six months) increase per year.

To illustrate, let's look at the potential increase on a $190,000 loan at 7 percent interest with a 30-year payment schedule. We'll assume the interest rates increased 1 percent each adjustment period. The change will look like this:

Interest Increase	Monthly Payment	Amount Going to Interest	Amount Going To Principal
1st 6 Months	$1,264.07	$1,108.33	$155.74
2nd 6 Months 1%	$1,394.15	$1,266.67	$127.48
3rd 6 Months 1%	$1,528.78	$1,425.00	$103.78

The difference between your initial monthly payment of $1,264.07 and the jump in a year and a half to $1,528.78 per month is $264.71. As you cn imagine, $264.71 is a pretty large increase to offset by simply raising rents. If you remember, the rents on Mariposa Lane totaled $2,200 per month. If we wanted to preserve the cash flow we had when we began, it would take the following increase in rent every six months:

2ND 6-MONTH ADJUSTMENT

Second Payment	$1,394.15	Increase	$130.08
First Payment	−1,264.07	Rent	$2,200
Increase	$130.08		= 5.9%

$$\frac{\text{Increase} \quad \$130.08}{\text{Rent} \quad \$2,200} = 5.9\%$$

3RD 6-MONTH ADJUSTMENT

Third Payment	$1,528.78	Increase	$134.63
First Payment	−1,394.15	Rent	$2,200
Increase	$130.08		= 6.1%

$$\frac{\text{Increase} \quad \$134.63}{\text{Rent} \quad \$2,200} = 6.1\%$$

The net result is that you'd have to raise your rents 12 percent (5.9% + 6.1% = 12%) if you wanted to maintain the cash flow you started with. Even in a good economy, this is more than most tenants would tolerate. You are left with two choices here: take the no-neg adjustable loan we just discussed and accept a lower cash flow or begin to think like a business-man and consider a neg-am adjustable loan.

The "neg-am" adjustable loan

The "neg-am" loan differs in that the limit is put on how much your required cash payment can increase rather than how much the interest can increase. Additionally, there are payment caps built in to neg-am loans, usually set at a maximum of 7.5 percent increase per year. Using our example loan, this means the required loan payment would only go up $94.81 ($1,264.07 × .075 = $94.81) the first year.

To compensate the lenders for the lower pay-ment, the interest rate may be allowed to adjust every month according to the index to which it is tied. These adjustments usually will start six months after the loan begins. This payment schedule looks like this:

Interest Increase	Monthly Payment	Amount Going to Interest	Amount Going To Principal
1st 6 Months	$1,264.07	$1,108.33	$155.74
2nd 6 Months 1%	$1,264.07	$1,266.67	–$2.60
3rd 6 Months 1%	$1,358.88	$1,425.00	–$66.12

With the neg-am adjustable loan, there would only be one change in the payment in the 18 months of our example. We showed the interest increasing in the second and third periods, however, so it affected the principal reduction part of the loan payment. Because the principal due was not paid (i.e. it actually was negative), the loan amount increased by the amount of the unpaid balance during these periods.

Now let's see how the payment increase compares to the existing rental income. If we want to preserve the cash flow, we'll need the following increase:

Second Payment	$1,358.88
First Payment	−1,264.07
Increase	$94.81

$$\frac{\text{Increase} \quad \$94.81}{\text{Rental Income} \quad \$2,200.00} = 4.3\%$$

This rental increase of less than 5 percent (as opposed to the 12% you would have had to offset with a no-neg ARM) should be much easier for your tenants to swallow, especially because 4.3 percent is very close to the cost of living increase at the time this book was written. A 4.3 percent increase amounts to only $23.65 per month on a unit that rents for $550 per month. With a modest increase like this, the cash flow return will be the same as your original projection.

As you can see, the big advantage of the neg-am loan is that the low payment increase enables you to offset it with an affordable rent increase that maintains the cash flow you desire. If everything goes as planned and the cash flow is not needed, you can always add more money to your payment each month so there's no increase in the principal balance. Remember, however, that the portion of your payment that goes to reducing the principal is taxable because it came from tenant income. There's no real advantage in taking the money out of your bank where it is earning interest and paying down

Moneysaver
If your cash flow is doing well, you don't have to let your loan increase. If you pay the extra interest, it becomes a tax write-off.

your loan. The cash in the bank is your security. If you keep it in the bank, you can pay the loan down anytime.

Finally, people bemoan that neg-am adjustable loans create the possibility that the loan balance can increase rather than decrease. This isn't as much a real problem as it is a psychological one. Take the following examples and apply them to the same thinking you may be using when deciding on a neg-am adjustable loan:

- Everyone knows that the computer system you buy today will be behind the times in less than six months.

- What about that brand new car you just financed? You know very well that the loan will be larger than the car's value when you drive it off the lot.

The fact is, you have been engaging in these kinds of purchases your entire life and you've lived to tell about it. We say, look at the adjustable rate loan as a tool to help you achieve your goals. If you can use an ARM to get rich, go ahead and do it. If, however, you find that it is not in your best interest, make another choice.

Shop the lenders

Regardless of the type of conventional loan you choose, it is important that you shop around for the best possible terms. As you can see, many variables will affect your costs. Use the following uniform checklist to compare programs effectively:

- Interest rate
- Fixed or adjustable
- Loan-to-value ratio

Bright Idea
Feel free to mention other loan quotes to lenders. The best approach often is a straightforward statement: "You know, Steve at Rockland Financial offered me the same loan for ½ point less. Can you beat that?"

- Debt coverage percentage
- Points
- Appraisal fee
- Environmental review fee
- Margin
- Index
- Interest rate cap
- Payment cap
- Required impounds
- Prepayment penalty
- Yield maintenance
- Assumability
- Recourse or nonrecourse
- Processing time
- Good-faith deposit
- Other fees

Watch Out!
It is not just the interest rate you should take into account when shopping for a loan but a combination of all factors on your checklist and how they impact your long-term investment goals.

My loan is your loan

Assumable loans are loans that are already in place and can be taken over by the person purchasing the property. That is, the buyer can "assume" the existing loan rather than finding new financing and paying all the fees to obtain it. There usually are some small fees charged for assuming a loan, but they can be significantly lower than what it would cost to get a new loan from scratch.

When you assume a loan, you still have to qualify just as the original borrower did. There are some loans, however, especially older FHA loans, that allow you to take the loan over and just start making payments. This is sometimes called taking the loan "subject to." Taking a loan subject to leaves the original borrower on the hook in case you default.

One advantage of taking over an older, assumable loan is that it often will have better terms than a similar new loan would have today. The major difference usually is in the margin (remember that the margin is the amount the bank adds on to the index to get the total interest rate on the loan). Once a loan has been in place 10 to 15 years, it starts paying off principal at a faster rate. This means that principal, rather than interest, is now a larger percentage of each monthly payment. Many investors getting ready for retirement look for properties with assumable loans because they do not have to add much additional principal to each payment to get these seasoned loans to pay off at about the same time as they retire. There is nothing as comforting as starting retirement with a nice piece of "free and clear" income property.

Private-party financing

The last source of financing is through private parties. These loans often are made by the sellers themselves, and they have several advantages over conventional loans. The first advantage is that you can save a lot of money in lending fees if you borrow privately. This is because most of the costs associated with conventional financing do not apply to private loans. This is a great help when assembling the initial cash required to close a deal.

Rates to die for

Many times, private loans have interest rates that are lower than the conventional market. If you look at the loan on 1800 Mariposa Lane, which is $190,000, and assume you can save a mere 1 percent on the interest rate through private financing, it adds up to $1,900 per year. The following chart should make your eyes bug out. It demonstrates how a $1,900 per year savings adds up over the span of 30 years:

Year	Savings
1	$1,900
5	$9,500
10	$19,000
30	$57,000

Zero down

The down payment on most transactions is determined by the requirements of the institution making the loan. In the case of private financing, down payments are entirely negotiable. In many instances, sellers don't want any money for a down payment because they are not looking to get cash out of a sale. Instead, they want the monthly income from carrying the paper because any cash they receive is just a tax problem for them. In fact, you will find that many sellers only want enough cash down to pay closing costs.

You pick the terms

In the grand scheme of owning a property, the terms of your financing can be far more important than the price you pay for a building. If you and the seller can agree, anything goes. Not only do many sellers carry the financing at lower interest rates, they also can make the payment plans fit your needs. The golden rule says, "He who has the gold, makes the rules." In private-party lending, this could not be more true.

It is not unusual for sellers to carry financing long term with interest-only payments. This way, they are not using up any of the principal balance of the loan. Remember that any principal the seller

Bright Idea
If money is tight, ask your agent if he would be willing to take his commission in monthly payments. If so, you can close on private-party loans with only as much cash as it takes to pay title and escrow fees.

receives is taxable as a capital gain. Many times, the seller would rather loan the money to you and receive interest-only payments than pay Uncle Sam capital gains tax.

In reality, the seller can make your loan payment any amount he wants. We (the authors) have seen many transactions over the years in which the payment schedules were actually lower than interest-only to accommodate the particular needs of a transaction. In most cases, this is because the seller has not kept the rents up with the market but wants a price calculated on rents closer to what they should be. The seller can carry at a graduated payment schedule to give the buyer time to raise the rents.

The due date

The last major component of a private-party loan is the due date. This also is up for full negotiation. The parties involved can agree for the due date to be in 1 year, 5 years, or 30 years, just like any conventional loan. In addition, it is not unusual for private loans to have partial payoffs at set times. These partial payoffs often coincide with the cash needs of the seller. The seller might have loans he needs to pay off in the future or some special need such as providing a college education for a grandchild. In the case of these partial payoffs, many sellers will allow you to get the funds by refinancing the property and putting their loan in the second position.

A straight note

You might find that some sellers do not need any cash flow at all and are willing to carry a straight note (or notes) with deferred interest. A straight note is a note that has one payment, which is due at

> **"**
> When my agent talked the seller into carrying a straight note for me, it made the difference in being able to buy the property I wanted with a payment I could afford.
> —Jim F., investor
> **"**

the end of the loan. In the period between the start of the note and the due date, the interest accrues and is due at the same time as the principal. Other sellers might only want part of the interest and will allow the unpaid interest to accrue and be paid when the loan is paid off.

All-inclusive loans by sellers

An all-inclusive loan is one in which the loan the seller is carrying includes the seller's equity and any other loans the seller had previously put on the property. Sometimes seller-financed loans take this form because the terms of the existing financing do not allow the loan to be transferred, or in many cases, because of tax reasons associated with the seller's capital gain position. We will discuss the problem of mortgage over basis in Chapter 10, "Planning for the Tax Man," but in short, it is a problem created by taking part of your profit out though refinancing. A taxable event occurs when the seller is relieved of the responsibility for the debt. Rather than allowing you to assume a loan that has a mortgage over basis problem, the seller can carry an all-inclusive loan.

Let's assume the $190,000 loan on the Mariposa Lane example was actually an all-inclusive loan. This might be the actual structure:

Sellers Equity	$90,000
First Loan	+$100,000
All-Inclusive Loan	$190,000

In this case, you make a payment to the seller according to your agreed upon contract, the seller makes the payment on the existing first loan, and he keeps the difference. In this scenario, the seller has not been relieved of his responsibility for the

Watch Out!
When you are using "creative financing" such as a land contract, you always should consult a real estate attorney.

repayment of the $100,000 loan, so in many cases, this will not trigger the taxes due.

Land sales contracts

Another type of private lending is the land sale contract, or the contract for deed. In this case, buyers enter into a contract with a seller to purchase a property, but the buyer does not acquire the title until sometime in the future. These deals often are structured this way because the underlying financing is favorable to the buyer.

Buyers need to be careful here. Many of these loans have acceleration clauses that make the entire loan due and payable if there is a title transfer. Lenders can't accelerate a loan, however, unless they know about the change. Because the title isn't transferred, many times, no one is the wiser.

Land sales contracts and contracts for deed are structured very similar to the way cars are financed. That is, the bank keeps the title to the car even though you are the registered owner. When you eventually pay the car off, the bank gives you the legal title. The same premise holds true here.

Hard money loans

One final source for private financing is known as the hard money loan. This is when third parties make loans on real estate as if they were a conventional lender. Most of these loans are made to borrowers (or on properties) that cannot get financing in the conventional arena for one reason or another. It might be due to poor credit, or it might be that the property is in disrepair, and the buyer is making the purchase as a rehab project. Whatever the reason, know that hard money loans are available for those deals that cannot get financed conventionally.

More often than not, hard money loans are made at a higher interest rate, and they can have even more fees as a percentage of the loan than a typical conventional loan. If you do some looking around, however, you sometimes can find family or friends who would be willing to make loans on property at favorable rates and terms and get a better-than-market return for themselves at the same time. If they are currently getting 5 or 6 percent interest in a savings account, for example, you could offer them 10 or 11 percent to loan the money to you instead—a great win-win situation. You get the money you need, and your friends get an investment that pays a much higher rate than they can get anywhere else. Many self directed IRA/SEP funds can be utilized to make these types of loans.

Watch Out!
Some people with money to loan advertise in the newspaper. You've seen the ads, "Money to loan!" You should use extreme caution here. Read the fine print carefully so you are well aware of what you are agreeing to.

And most important

Remember that financing is just a tool used to acquire the property that best fits your investment plan goals. Don't get caught up in the emotion of the points or the margin being too high and then miss out on an opportunity to acquire a property that is perfect for your plan. Likewise, by carefully investigating the underlying financing of all properties under consideration, you might find one with exceptional assumable financing that makes it a better investment than another property with a lower price.

Just the facts

- FHA loans allow you to get into an investment and a home with a minimal down payment.

- Residential loans for one to four units come in all shapes and sizes.

- Qualifying for a loan on one to four units rests primarily on your personal credit worthiness.

- A lender's primary concern when lending on five units or more is how the property performs as a business.

- If you choose an adjustable loan, the best way to maintain a steady cash flow is with the "neg-am" adjustable.

- The beauty behind private-party financing is that it allows buyers and sellers to negotiate all the terms of the deal.

Mastering the Market

PART III

Real Estate, the Economy, and Your Target Market

Chapter 6

B y the time you finish this guide, you hopefully will have the tools to make an educated decision about what, where, when, and why to buy real estate. Ultimately, you will choose from a limited number of available buildings in a specific target market. Before you do that, however, it is important for you to understand how those few properties fit into the global economy of which we are all a part.

In an effort to accomplish this goal, we need to have a quick lesson in basic economics, specifically how the economy affects real estate. Without this broad overview of the world outside your market area, you can get caught unprepared for troubled times or be lying low because of the troubled times and miss an opportunity to get in on the ground floor of an upswing.

Economics 101

We believe that you must be aware of the big picture of investing; we'll call it the "global view." By understanding the global view and how it can affect you, you can take preventive action to profit from it or ward off any bad times. The second thing you need to be aware of is regional economic trends. This is because these trends directly affect the market in the area in which you are trying to make a profit. Finally, you need to become an expert in the small area we call your "target market."

The global view

Most investment strategies are based on a study of past and present trends and benefits. The idea is to examine what has happened in the past to gauge what might happen in the future. In economics class, we learned about business cycles and the fact that real estate is a cyclical industry. That is, it responds to the overall cycles of our economy. When the economy is moving, so is real estate. When things slow down, real estate does, too. Even in a struggling economy, however, the clever individual can make a profit. This is because our product is a basic necessity of life; everyone needs a place to live.

A closer look at the economy as a whole will show you the dominating influence of real estate. It's easy to see how the buying, selling, and renting of property has a general impact on the economy, but this impact goes much further. Take the savings and loan industry, for instance. This industry is built around lending money to finance every aspect of real estate including its purchase and remodel. Think of the revenue generated from all the goods and services that go into keeping all this real estate functional and looking good. Finally, consider all

Unofficially...
A great many of the richest people in the world owe their wealth to their real estate holdings.

the money spent on property insurance and construction. As you add up all these dollars, the figure becomes staggering.

Real estate is such a powerful storehouse of economic wealth that we literally have built our local city governments around its value. For starters, real estate is the tax basis for most local governments. The money generated provides funding for fire and police protection, education, health and social services, and most of the other services cities provide. This value enables cities to raise the capital they need to function. In fact, some of the greatest advances in local communities come when civic leaders take over a blighted area through the condemnation process or a redevelopment district. They then can use municipal bonds and various incentives to turn these blighted areas into the crowning jewels of the community.

To make a long story short, real estate is the largest single segment of wealth in our nation. It has been estimated that two-thirds of the wealth of our country is composed of land, what's under that land, or what's built on top of that land. We even see the airspace above the land in some highly developed areas being sold as a separate commodity. It is the wealth that attracts investors to real estate.

Regional economic trends

To understand real estate as a vehicle to making a profit, you need to remember that the profit is made when we as consumers get together and utilize that product. Therefore, real estate functions more as a consumer product than as the capital asset it really is. It is a storehouse for wealth on our balance sheet, but we make the maximum profit by recognizing the consumer's needs and desires for it.

> **"**
> A cellular phone company was looking for locations for cell sites. I gave them the use of my roof, and they've decided to supplement my income for the next 30 years.
> —Jeff K., commercial property owner
> **"**

Take an apartment in Bakersfield, California, for example. There, a one-bedroom unit rents for $300 per month. The same size unit in Malibu, California, rents for $1,900 per month. How can this be if the units are exactly alike? The answer is simple enough—because one location is more desirable than the other. As you know, the real value is in the land. If consumers don't want to be there, however, land can be virtually worthless.

The market for real estate is the process in which we as consumers get together to buy, sell, and rent property. It is this market functioning within the economy in general that establishes value and trends. The following list covers some of the major factors that can impact values:

- The supply and value of money
- Occupancy levels (supply and demand)
- Rental rates and controls
- Employment levels
- Population growth and family formations
- Building activity
- Perceptions of the future

The supply and value of money

We buy real estate for one of two reasons. The first reason is to provide a roof over our heads or to house a business. The second reason is as an investment to make a profit. The supply and cost of money isn't as important in the first case because, when purchasing a home, your foremost concern becomes what kind of lifestyle it provides. If it goes up in value that's great, but your life won't depend on how your home appreciates. The same holds true for a business looking for a location.

As an investor, however, appreciation rates do matter. This is because trends in the money market can either make or break your investment. The variables to consider are:

- The supply of money to finance investment property
- The cost of borrowing (rates and fees)
- The percentage that can be borrowed (leverage)
- The length of time that the money can be borrowed (term)

These factors will have the greatest impact on your ability to make a profit. This is because an active money market for financing real estate usually goes hand-in-hand with a market in which you can earn some healthy profits catering to the consumers' desire for that product.

Occupancy rates, rental rates, employment levels, population growth

The next four areas—occupancy rates, rental rates, employment levels, and population growth—all work together to impact the profitability of most real estate investments. When you see these four indicators on the rise in your area, it is a signal that there will be some opportunities to profit from the increased demand.

Obviously, the best environment in which to invest is one with a steady increase in demand and a shrinking supply of land to satisfy that demand. Manhattan and Hong Kong are perfect examples; they demolish fairly new high-rise buildings to build even newer and higher buildings.

We can't all live in or afford to invest in these areas, but we can learn from their example. Growth

Timesaver
You can track most of these statistics through your local chamber of commerce or the business development department of your city.

in an area with a lot of undeveloped land will minimize the increase in value for the existing properties. This is because, as the population increases, developers will build new buildings on the available raw land to satisfy the increased demand. These properties will be brand-new and will have the latest styles and amenities. Human nature being what it is, this attracts the buyers who have the money. These people usually are new residents brought into the market by new jobs.

We are talking about real growth brought on by new jobs that require an increase in population to fill the positions. In areas where unemployment is higher than the national average, jobs can be created that will have little or no impact on real estate values or rental rates. In these areas, real estate can increase in value, but this usually just reflects the impact of inflation rather than true growth.

Building activity

When there is an increase in building activity, it should have a direct impact on the value of existing properties. The amount of the increase usually depends on the amount of vacant land available. In areas with plenty of land available, builders usually can supply the demand for housing easily.

In areas that are more fully developed, however, it becomes tougher to satisfy the demand for new housing. Old homes need to be demolished to build new ones. Therefore, there is some upward movement in the price of the existing product. This is the cost-push increase, and it is similar to the increase from inflation. The biggest increases come from demand pulling the prices up. The consumers bid up the price because they want the product and supply is limited. This is the same thing that drives up

prices at auctions for paintings and other commodities in limited supply.

The one instance in which this growth can be
impacted in a negative sense even in a growth environment is when some kind of price control is put
into effect. This usually is in the form of rent control. Make no bones about it, rent control can have
a disastrous effect on the ability to generate a profit
or to sell a property. It takes a very sophisticated
investor to be able to generate a profit in those
areas.

Perception of the future

The last factor that can influence value is the per-
ception that people have about the future. This
involves emotions and gut feelings based on what
has happened in the past. Perceptions are not
always accurate, but they usually get lots of play in
the press. Once the media gets an idea in its head
and begins to publicize it, people fall in line like
sheep.

Understanding that popular opinion is not
always accurate can be very profitable. It's one thing
to make a good buy when the economy isn't doing
well. It's even better to make that same buy when
the economy is improving but when sellers have yet
to figure that out. The important thing to understand is that you must not be swayed by public opinion. Look for the facts and then make your decisions accordingly; you can wave to the masses in
your rearview mirror.

Defining your target market

Regardless of the size of your community, it probably will have some definite neighborhood divisions.
As is true in most places, there will be upscale areas,

Watch Out!
Unless there is
some allowance
for rental
increases when
existing tenants
move out, you
should be
extremely wary
of investing in
rent-controlled
areas.

working class sections, and areas that are on "the other side of the tracks." You will need to look at all these areas before you make a final decision about which one offers the best opportunities to make a profit. As you zero in on this area, the following checklist will give you some factors to consider:

- Neighborhoods growing or declining
- Criminal activity and trends
- Current supply and demand for housing
- Adverse infrastructure changes
- Positive infrastructure changes
- Economic deterioration of the commercial districts
- Changes in local ordinances that effect real estate

How's the neighborhood?

A class in economic geography would show that an evolution takes place in all cities. We learn how they are founded, how cities expand over the years, how they deteriorate, and then how they're rebuilt through the redevelopment process. Even stagnant communities seem to go through these phases, although they might be harder to detect because the changes lack the momentum of the demand push from new residents. As an investor, what you want to do is make sure you are on the correct side of the growth curve.

Criminal activity and trends

Local crime statistics can be a good indicator of what is happening in neighborhoods. Many communities publish crime statistics, and this kind of historical data can be very helpful. Your goal is to see if you can spot trends rather than to find out

"
I found out a lot about the various neighborhoods I was interested in by just talking to the property owners as I surveyed rental rates.
— Keith C., investor
"

about the specific kinds of crimes. Obviously, you will shy away from an area that consistently has two or three murders per month.

Supply and demand for housing

Local neighborhoods all have their own mix of residential and commercial real estate. There also will be a certain percentage of owner-occupied properties as well as rental properties. Analyzing how much there is of each will dictate what kind of opportunities you will find to profit as an investor. Later in this chapter, we will discuss the actual statistics that help determine which areas offer the best opportunity for you to make money.

Adverse infrastructure changes

The city itself might have a negative impact on some neighborhoods with changes in ordinances or adverse infrastructure changes. We've all heard the story about the small motel that went out of business because the highway was moved. This is the kind of change we're talking about. A trip to city hall will let you know what kind of major capital expenditures are in the works. The most common city projects with adverse effects seem to involve work on streets and highways.

Positive infrastructure changes

You should also be on the lookout for positive infrastructure changes. For example, a new zoo, a federal building, or some other major attraction could improve the neighborhood because of new jobs or other commercial activity that follows. In Denver, for instance, the building of Coors Field in the middle of an empty, drug-ridden war zone resulted in a positive explosion of commercial and residential redevelopment.

Economic deterioration of commercial districts

Most communities have several levels of commercial districts. We'll call them the "A," "B," "C," and "T" districts.

- **The "A" District:** This is the new district with the mall or the freestanding mega-retailers.

- **The "B" district:** This is the area that used to be the "A" area but couldn't keep up because it lacked the space to handle the larger shops.

Watch Out!
Be careful when you see "C" areas deteriorating. This usually is a good sign that the residents who have money to spend are going elsewhere. In addition, it's often the first step before they relocate their residence.

- **The "C" district:** These areas serve as neighborhood business strips. They have the "mom and pop" shops and all the other smaller offices and retailers. You will see accountants, beauty shops, doctor and dental offices, and all the service businesses such as tune-up centers, tire stores, fast-food restaurants, and computer stores. These kinds of small operations thrive on serving the local community.

- **The "T" districts:** "T" districts are commercial or small industrial areas that have deteriorated and are now in transition. Usually they are the old downtown commercial or manufacturing areas. They have deteriorated because the economic growth has moved to the suburbs. The transition and rejuvenation happens as developers and young professionals rediscover them. Old office buildings are turned into retail with offices and residences above, and old warehouses become live/work lofts. Savvy investors can find opportunities in these areas by following the trends where other investors and developers are buying and fixing up formerly deteriorating properties.

Changes in local ordinances that affect real estate

Most cities have master plans for how they see the city developing. Many times, these master plans can include sweeping changes to certain areas to accomplish the projected needs of the community as a whole. That new "A" business district no doubt was in the planning stages for many years. These kinds of changes can offer an opportunity to make a profit if you learn about them early on.

Learning about them in advance also can save you from making a mistake. An apartment building on the edge of a redevelopment area, for example, might suffer through years of waiting for the boarded-up buildings and vacant lots to be replaced by the proposed new shopping mall. This is especially true where public funds are involved. Announced projects are often delayed for years. In Brooklyn, a major development project was announced around the rebuilding of a train station. Ten years have passed and private investors have since opened a mall and new housing has been built, but the promised train station remains a weed-strewn empty lot. The result is that private investors have not been able to realize the profits they had hoped for.

Research local markets

In addition to economic cycles and local trends and changes, it is important to look at historic appreciation in specific areas to help determine your best target market. As noted earlier, real estate is a cyclical commodity. It responds to the ups and downs in the global economy and to things that affect the local economy. There is no guarantee that history will repeat itself, but knowledge of how your local area has responded in the past is a more reliable

Watch Out!
A trip to city hall and the planning department can give you an update as to what kinds of changes are in the works for your city. But be wary. Projects are often announced, commenced, then stalled indefinitely or even abandoned. Public projects are notorious for delays; private ones may go bankrupt.

forecasting tool than pure guesswork. Without something to base future projection on, it is tough to make a long-term plan of where you are going with your investments.

It is worthwhile to take another look at the chart you first saw in Chapter 3, "Elements of Return," on the next page. It shows value appreciation as seen in the greater South Bay area of Los Angeles. Notice that value is expressed as a price per square foot of living area. We showed the price-per-square-foot chart because the trend in price from this information enables us to calculate the yearly increase in value over the entire period. That is, the 7.5 percent average appreciation rate shown at the top of the chart. This is the interest rate used in the compound interest formula (i) to estimate your rate of return over an extended period of time. (See the section "Determining your general plan" in Chapter 9, "Building an Investment Plan.")

Look once again at the chart. You can see that the increase in value was not constant over the last 30 years. For this reason, you should not do any projecting based on data from just a couple of years. Looking at the chart, if you had done your projecting based on the data from just 1977–1981, you would have gotten pretty excited about investing because the market kept getting better and better. If you only had data for 1991–1996, you might have decided never to invest at all because we were in a downswing. As you can see, the market has started moving upward again. The lesson is to make sure you get plenty of years of data because that is the only way to determine a true appreciation rate for any given area.

You might find that it can be pretty difficult to gather this type of information, especially if you're

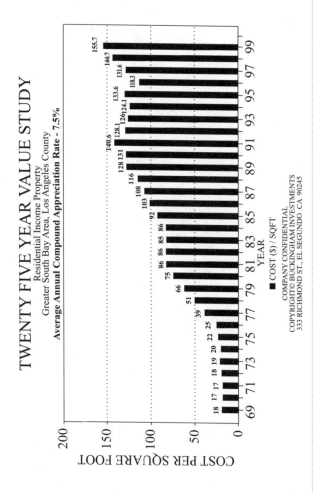

TWENTY FIVE YEAR VALUE STUDY

Residential Income Property
Greater South Bay Area, Los Angeles County
Average Annual Compound Appreciation Rate - 7.5%

COST (\$) / SQFT

YEAR

COST PER SQUARE FOOT

looking for income property alone. If you are fortunate enough to find a real estate agent who specializes in income property in your area, he might have saved the kind of data you need. If not, you will need to do some research on your own to get some sense of the trend in property values. This is vital in projecting the long-term growth of your investments. The following list covers the data you should look for:

▪ **Price per square foot:**

$$\$/sq.\ ft. = \frac{\text{Sale price of the property}}{\text{Square feet of living space}}$$

▪ **Gross multiplier:**

$$G.M. = \frac{\text{Sale price of the property}}{\text{Gross income of the property}}$$

▪ **Price per unit:**

$$\$/unit = \frac{\text{Sale price of the property}}{\text{Number of units in building}}$$

▪ **Rental rate**

$$\text{Rent}/sq.\ ft. = \frac{\text{Total rent per month}}{\text{Square feet of living space}}$$

Bright Idea
Recruit a local librarian to help you research values in your area. Most libraries have great databases, and the librarians probably would be happy to help.

In the event that you are not able to find data for income property sales, you can use sales information for homes to give you some indication of the trends. Many realty offices save sales data to assist in estimating the sales prices for listings and sales they make. If not, it's time to do some detective work. The information is out there; you just have to find it. The following are three good sources that can help you find this information:

1. Tax assessor's records
2. Appraisal services and title companies
3. Newspaper ads

Ask the tax man

Your local assessor's office should have records of the property values for many years in the past. The problem with the assessor's data is that the assessed valuation does not always reflect the actual fair market value of the property in the area. Some of these valuations are so old, or are based on original valuations done sometimes 50 or more years ago, that they occupy the realm of fantasy. The truth is, it is impossible for these departments to appraise all properties every year, so the valuations are based on current data combined with any historical data they might already have.

When using the tax assessor's records, it is important to choose a section of property that hasn't changed much for many years. A large tract of homes, for example, would be a good place to start. Then you need to check valuation changes in that area back as many years as you want your study to cover. Once you do this, it should show you a trend in the valuation of property in that area.

Appraisal services and title companies

Most appraisal services and title companies keep large databases for comparable sales of property. By contacting their customer service departments, you might be able to find one that would let you look through files of buildings that have changed hands. Some companies, however, use outside services to gather this kind of information. If they do, ask them who they use and then contact the service yourself. It might cost you something, but in the long run, having

Bright Idea
As the use of the Internet increases, more sources are available to track comparable sales (as well as any other data you may require). If you're computer savvy, go online and give it a try.

Timesaver
It isn't necessary
to look at every
paper for every
month of the
year. Ask your
agent which
months of the
year seem to be
the most active
in your area.
This usually is
just after school
is out because
most people
don't like to
move their kids
in the middle of
the year.

this understanding about the history of value for your target area will be well worth a small expense.

Newspaper ads

A third method of acquiring appreciation data requires spending some time in the archives of your local newspaper or library. As with the research at the assessor's office, you will want to pick a section of your community that hasn't had much physical change for the time period you are researching. The best choice would be a housing tract in which the houses are advertised using the name of the tract. As an example, in Hawthorne, California, the most popular housing tract in the city is called Holly Glen. In Holly Glen, there are only a couple of floor plans in the entire tract, and they each have 3 bedrooms and 1¾ bathrooms.

When you find the ideal tract of homes, it's time to do your research. Look at the "For Sale" ads in the Saturday and Sunday papers as far back as the year the tract was built. You should be able to get enough sales prices to get a good feeling about the average price in the tract. Because you know the average number of square feet in the homes in this tract, it will be easy to get the average price per square foot for that year. When your research is complete, you will have enough data to do an estimate of the appreciation rate.

We'll assume you have reviewed past newspaper ads and have identified a tract of homes as previously discussed. The following shows how you could lay out your chart.

The percentage change can be calculated by dividing the change in dollars by the price the year before. For example, the dollar increase from 1989

Year	Price	Change in Dollars	Percentage Change	Average Change
1989	$89,500			
1990	$93,500	$4,000	4.4%	4.40%
1991	$98,500	$5,000	5.3%	4.85%
1992	$97,500	−$1,000	−1.0%	2.90%
1993	$95,000	−$2,500	−2.5%	1.55%
1994	$95,000	0	0	1.24%
1995	$97,500	$2,500	2.6%	1.46%
1996	$101,500	$4,000	4.1%	1.84%
1997	$106,500	$5,000	5.0%	2.24%
1998	$113,000	$6,500	6.1%	2.67%
1999	$119,950	$6,950	6.2%	3.02%

to 1990 was $4,000. The percentage change is $4,000 ÷ 89,500 = 4.4%.

The average change is calculated by dividing the percentage changes by the number of years of changes. For example, the average change from 1989 to 1991 is 4.4% + 5.3% ÷ 2 = 4.85%. We divide by two because we have owned the property for only two full years, 1989 and 1990. The percentage change shown on the line for 1991 is the value at the start of the year.

You have now entered "The Comfort Zone"

At a minimum, you now have a reasonable idea of what is happening in your area. It's time to start narrowing down the geographic area and deciding on one or two areas in which you'd feel comfortable investing. Establishing this zone where you feel comfortable will be a combination of the economic cycles of your specific community and your personal feelings about the areas.

Timesaver
Most new calculators and computers have programs that can do linear regression analysis. If you can learn to use those programs you will be able to chart appreciation rates quickly and easily.

The best way to pick areas is by doing a comparison of the financial returns of all the areas in which you could buy. Pick a property size, let's say a four-unit, and find one for sale in each of the areas in which you could invest. Next, calculate the return on investment for each property. Use the same down payment and loan terms so you get an apples-to-apples comparison.

Invariably, you will be drawn to some areas emotionally but will not be able to afford them. Other areas will have an exceptional return, but you wouldn't feel comfortable in them. In the end, you should find several areas that could work for you, and we'll call these your comfort zones. As you learn about financial planning in Chapter 9, you will use this comfort zone information and the other statistical facts you've accumulated to complete your investment plan.

Just the facts

- A clever investor always can make a profit because housing is a basic necessity of life.

- Understanding the economic principles of supply and demand will help you succeed as a real estate investor.

- Be wary of letting public opinion influence your investment choices.

- To make long-term projections for your investments, you need to chart value appreciation in your target market.

- Finding your "comfort zone" is the first step in long-term real estate planning.

GET THE SCOOP ON...
Raw land and why it's a risky investment ▪ The
truth about condos and single-family homes ▪
Small apartment buildings and why they are
golden opportunities ▪ The allure of larger
rental properties ▪ How to make money by owning and renting out commercial space

Broad Categories of Real Estate

Chapter 7

Much of this guide is built around our sample four-unit apartment building. This allows us to demonstrate the concepts of real estate investing with an easy-to-understand example. There is more to this game, however, than just four-unit buildings. There's land for development, larger apartment buildings, condominiums, single-family homes, commercial strip malls, and industrial properties to name just a few.

Many investors develop tunnel vision when they are making money in real estate. If someone is doing well buying small apartment buildings, the odds are good that they won't even consider investing in homes or commercial centers. Maybe an owner of an office building hasn't had a vacancy in five years. Why should he sink his money into vacant lots when he's doing great as it is? The reason is that there are opportunities to make money by investing in all kinds of property. In this chapter, we will give you a guided tour of the entire market so you can choose the venue that will produce the best return.

Let's begin with the foundation of all real estate, land itself.

Land ho!

When you own real estate, it's the dirt that holds the real key to the ultimate value of your property. A beautiful house on the beach that goes up in value every year isn't appreciating because the 2 × 4s that went into building it are worth more annually. It is appreciating because the demand for the location is increasing—the demand for the land. You will learn that the secret to making money on land is being able to recognize an increase in demand and then being able to capitalize on your insight.

We will focus on three different types of land investments. The classic purchase is raw land that sits in the path of progress. The other two involve buying land in areas that already are developed. Once you know the principles behind these three, you will gain a basic understanding of the opportunities and pitfalls that exist in this market.

Raw as raw can be

Investing in raw land has inherent problems associated with it. First, it is a capital-intensive investment. You have to start with a lot of money and be willing to wait a long time for any financial return. Unfortunately, this is just the nature of the beast. Many smart investors try to get ahead of the game by researching growth trends in certain areas and then rolling the dice and hoping their predictions come true. Sometimes they pan out; sometimes they don't. Here's a real-life example:

> In California, the communities surrounding the Los Angeles airport had become so crowded that there was talk of building a new

Timesaver
The county planning office is a good place to start when considering a raw land investment. Ask them to help you plot out the business, industrial, and residential growth of the community over the past 30 years. Your map of the past should give you insight into plans for the future.

airport 100 miles away in the city of Palmdale. The thought was that this would take the pressure off Los Angeles and would provide millions of affordable acres for jobs and new homes. In the movie *Field of Dreams* it was said, "If you build it, they will come." In *Field of Dreams* it worked. Kevin Costner had a vision to build a baseball diamond in a cornfield. He built it, and the people came. In Palmdale, however, they never built it, but the people came anyway. They sunk their savings into raw land thinking they were going to get rich, but the project fizzled. Will Palmdale ever be the thriving center envisioned? Probably, but not in the lifetime of those who had the dream.

As you can see, investing in raw land is inherently risky. This is because a land investment:

- Often has enormous up-front costs including the cost of the land, sewers, utilities, roads, plans, permits, engineering, and so on

- Pays you no income at the beginning

- Might be highly taxed

- Usually is very slow to rise in value

- Might come with legal barriers to hurdle

- Is highly speculative

This is not to say, however, that you can't make money here, because you can. If you are in an area of rapid growth and see raw land as a potential winner, you should:

- Do an in-depth analysis of growth trends, the speed of growth, and the direction of growth

- Determine which uses grow fastest in your area: commercial, residential, or industrial properties
- Attend planning meetings
- Obtain utility expansion plans
- Review historic examples of similar growth

In-fill opportunities

An "in-fill" project is another type of land investment. It involves buying a vacant lot surrounded by existing buildings of one type or another. The idea is to buy the lot, build something useful on it, and then sell it off for a profit. Compared to a raw land investment, these projects have considerably less risk for the investor because these opportunities are found in areas that already are developed.

In many cases, an owner has held a vacant lot next to his home or business for as long as he can remember. His original idea was to keep it just in case he needed it. Now he is getting ready to retire, and he realizes that he really doesn't need the property. Therefore, he decides to sell. This is where you come in.

Remember that, when buying this kind of lot, you need to do the same kind of research you would do if you were buying raw land. Check with the city and utility companies to see what can be built on the site. It would be disastrous to buy a lot with the intent and resources to build an apartment building only to find out it is zoned for a parking lot only.

One important issue that comes up when doing an in-fill deal is determining whether there are any pollutants in the soil. As the developer of vacant land, this concern is now your problem. Think back to all the old gas stations and "mom-and-pop" manufacturing sites that closed near your property's location. If one of those types of businesses was located on your lot, and if it left any pollutants behind (which is very common), you are the one who is legally required to clean it up. Most cities require developers to do extensive environmental testing. These tests always are expensive, and if any problems are found, the cost of removal can be staggering.

We (the authors) developed many apartment and commercial projects in the late 1980s. One time, while doing the foundation excavation for an apartment building, we found concrete and asphalt mixed in with the soil that filled the rear of the lot. The city did not care that the problem was not toxic. They still forced us to excavate the entire rear portion of the lot, remove the concrete and asphalt, and then re-compact the soil. This was because the dirt was not natural. Instead, it was fill-dirt and was not compacted properly. The concern was that it would cause settling problems after the foundation was built. Because the integrity of the entire structure rests on the foundation, the process had to be observed and regulated by an expensive licensed soils-engineer. This unexpected problem cost us all the money we had in reserve and then some.

Redevelopment projects

The last type of land investment we will touch on is called a "redevelopment opportunity." This is when a piece of property is worth more for the value of the land itself than for the value of the land plus the existing structure that sits on it. In this situation, you are not looking for vacant land to build on as you did with the in-fill project. Instead, you are looking for a bargain property that should (and will) be

Unofficially...
The purpose of zoning laws is to establish a well-distributed community for the development of working areas, industry, parks and recreation, homes, apartments, and so on.

torn down eventually. Like an in-fill, however, once you have an empty dirt lot, the goal is to build on it and then sell it off for a profit.

When doing a project like this, the rewards for the developer can be hefty. As an example, let's say you found an older two-bedroom house on a 50 × 150 R-3 (multiunit) lot. The house can be had for $60,000, and after checking, you determine that R-3 land in that area is going for $10 per square foot. Here is how a redevelopment deal could yield a profit even before you build on it:

Value of Land (50 × 150 × $10 Per Square Foot)	$75,000
Cost of The House	−$60,000
Potential Profit Before Building	$15,000

One great thing about redevelopment deals is that the structure sitting on the lot might already be producing income when you purchase it. This is especially helpful if the market for land isn't real hot when you find the property. You still can take advantage of the opportunity by buying the lot and then renting out the structure until the market improves. This way, you avoid the high cost of holding undeveloped land while you wait for the appreciation. In addition, you could begin the development process with the city and be able to have a turn-key project to sell to a builder when the time is right.

Can you do it with condos?

Condominiums are not the best way to get rich in real estate. The trouble is that you are quite limited in terms of what can be done to the property to increase its value. As an investor, you must always ask yourself, "How can I add value to any property I purchase to make it worth more when I sell?" The idea is to buy a property for X, find ways to add value to

Moneysaver
Find an architect who is willing work for a percentage of the profit when your project is completed. He will get paid on the back end, and you will save cash on the front end.

it, and then eventually sell it for Y. With condominium ownership, however, most associations will not allow you to make any improvements at all to the outside of your unit. They want your unit to look like your neighbor's unit, which looks like his neighbor's unit, and so on. For that reason, any profit to be made buying condos is limited to:

- Finding a bargain in the market (preforeclosure, foreclosure, desperate seller)

- Appreciation in value over time

- Adding value by doing interior upgrades only

Most people do not buy condominiums to make a profit; they do it to buy their first home. This is pretty smart because, as you can see, there is very little profit here, especially when held up against other real estate opportunities. If you are looking for a home *and* an investment, a single-family residence is a better way to go.

Single-family home sweet home

A single-family home offers a better opportunity to create some extra profit from your efforts. A primary reason has to do with the desire of most of us to own our own "plot of land." In addition, the diversity of the properties in the typical single-family area offers many chances for you to add value. Unlike condo tracts, there is hardly ever (except in planned communities) a requirement for a single-family home to look just like the neighbor's. Check with the local buildings department to see whether there are any restrictions due to zoning regulations. Wealthier communities often impose severe zoning restrictions. Historic districts undoubtedly will have restrictions as well.

Become a detective

Begin, as always, by researching your market. Start by identifying areas that have some diversity in the homes and that sell well. A good rule of thumb is that the more conforming the area, the fewer opportunities to find a bargain. The typical conforming area is a housing tract that has hundreds of homes in it but only three or four different floor plans. You can make money here, but because there is so little variation, it limits the possibilities.

If you are looking to add some value to increase your profit, you first should take a trip to City Hall. The first thing you need to know is how difficult the permit requirements are. Obtaining permits can be easy and inexpensive or costly and time consuming. Answers to these questions will tell you if it's worth pursuing or not.

Talk to your real estate agent and get his opinion about what is out there. When searching for a bargain in the single-family residence market, knowing the following information will help you spot homes that are under-priced:

Bright Idea
Have a lender prequalify you for a loan before you start looking at properties. This way, once you start looking, you will be able to see what you can get for your money and will be able to adjust your needs to what you can afford.

- The amount of time on the market
- The price per square foot
- The price per bedroom
- The value of extra bathrooms
- The value of a family room or den
- The value of amenities (pool, deck, garage, hot tub)
- The premium for condition

Adding value to your single-family residence

You can find even more profit by using other facts from your research. Let's say you've found an older two-bedroom house that has about 1,300 square feet. Your research shows that most of the three-bedroom houses also are about 1,300 square feet, and they sell for about $125 per square foot (1,300 square feet × $125 per square foot = a sales price of $162,500). The house you found could be bought for $110,000 because it only has two bedrooms, it is older, and it needs carpet, paint, and window coverings.

Watch Out!
Beware of homes or units that have termites or termite damage. If either is found, it should be up to the seller to have treatments done and make the necessary repairs or to adjust the sales price accordingly.

The plan would be to upgrade the house in general and to redesign the interior to turn it into a three-bedroom. You have determined that this can be done with a minimum of expensive structural work because you would only have to move some walls and build a new closet. The budget would look like this:

Construction of Bedroom	$15,000
Floor Covering	$1,300
Interior Paint	$750
Window Coverings	$500
Exterior Paint	$2,000
Landscaping	+$750
Total Cost to Improve	$20,300

Now you would have a sharp, three-bedroom home that should sell for $125 per square foot just like the other three bedrooms in the neighborhood. Your gross profit would look like this:

Value Added Price	$162,500
Less Original Cost	–$110,000
Less Cost to Improve	–$20,300
Gross Profit	$32,200

One of the extra bonuses of this type of investment is that you combine this purchase for profit with your desire to live in and own your own home. Many investors have started out exactly this way. They pick a house for the investment and profit value and also live in it as their personal residence.

Moneysaver
Before buying a
house with the
idea of rearrang-
ing the interior,
have your con-
tractor make sure
he can do the
work without any
major structural
alterations.

The main goal isn't the personal desires you might have for a home but the profit you can generate by purchasing a particular piece of property. The property just happens to also provide a temporary place for you to live. Living in this kind of investment provides several advantages:

- You gain an investment and a residence in one shot.
- You become your own boss.
- When you sell it, the profit might become tax free if you meet certain criteria.

The first two advantages are obvious, but the last is a new twist because of current tax laws in effect. As of 1999, you can exclude the entire gain on the sale of your main residence under the following conditions:

1. Up to $250,000, or
2. Up to $500,000 if all of the following are true:
   a. You are married and file a joint return for the year.
   b. Either you or your spouse meets the ownership test.
   c. Both you and your spouse meet the use test.
   d. Neither you nor your spouse excluded gain from the sale of another home after May 6, 1997.

The IRS says you can claim the exclusion if:

1. During the five-year period ending on the date of the sale, you have owned the home for at least two years (ownership test).
2. Have lived there as your main residence for at least two years (use test).

This is probably the greatest method of delivering tax-free wealth that the government has ever enacted. Think about it. This isn't a way of deferring your taxes; instead, you have absolutely no tax due whatsoever. What's more, Uncle Sam says that you can take advantage of this technique every two years. This can work for both beginning and experienced investors.

For people just starting out, the message is: When you buy a home, don't buy with the idea that you are going to live there forever. Instead, buy a property that will generate the greatest profit within the two years following your purchase. You might want to consider a house in an up-and-coming location, a place with an extra lot that you can sell off separately, or even a classic fixer-upper—anything that will help create some sweat equity.

After you have lived there for two years, the idea is to sell it, take all that free profit, and start over again. This time, however, you might have made enough money from the sale to buy both a home and a piece of income property. Now think about your portfolio. It would include two great pieces of real estate—a home and an apartment building. If you're game, you could even do it again in two years.

The plan will work just as easy for people who already have substantial equity in their current residence. It can be particularly helpful to people nearing retirement. A person can make money using the same methods previously mentioned, but a significant portion of the capital gain could be put into cash reserves for his latter years.

A final word on this benefit: Our government uses these kinds of tax benefits to stimulate the economy. Other methods are used to slow the economy. Conventional wisdom says that, because this benefit is so huge, it probably won't be around very long. If you wait, you might be left mumbling, "If only I had..."

Single-family homes as rental properties

Single-family homes also can be purchased as rentals and, as such, can generate the same returns previously discussed in this book. There are pros and cons to owning single-family homes as investments. The primary advantage is that the management and expenses of renting a house should be minimal. Management will be easy because you only have one primary tenant to be concerned with. As for expenses, you should make the tenant be responsible for all of his own utilities and general maintenance. Of course, you have to pay for major items such as new roofs and broken water heaters, but the tenant should basically live in the house as though he owned it.

There also are some disadvantages to buying and then renting single-family homes. The biggest disadvantage is that the financial return on single-family residences in a given area is far less than the return on an apartment investment. Go back to our discussion earlier in this chapter about the value of the dirt under any property. Because the land holds a great percentage of the value of any property, the rent you earn is being paid not only for the structure but also for the land. This is the only reason why there's a difference in rental rates for homes in differing economic areas in the same city. People don't pay more for the house; they pay more for the location, which is the land. Location, location, location!

> **"**
> I own several single-family homes. On two different occasions, I had tenants skip out on the rent and leave me to pay my mortgage without any income coming in from the properties.
> —Jillian L., property owner
> **"**

Let's say you have a four-unit building on a 7,500 square foot lot. You have four tenants paying rent on that lot. If you had one house on that same size lot, you would only be getting income from one person. It is true that one house will always rent for more than one apartment, but it is doubtful that it would rent for more than four apartments. It is a rare case that the premium for a single-family residence will give you the same return as an investment in apartments in the same area.

The second disadvantage is that, when you have a vacancy in a single-family home, your vacancy rate is 100 percent. If you own a positive cash flow four-unit, however, the cash flow from the other three units might be enough to still make the mortgage payment and pay for your other expenses.

Two- to four-unit properties

One step up from buying a condo or a house is purchasing a small apartment building. We will define "small" as a duplex, triplex, or fourplex. As you learned in Chapter 5, "Financing Your Investment," these properties fall into the residential loan category. For that reason, they are easier to finance and will always be priced differently than units of five or more.

The privacy factor

Your tenants should feel a sense of privacy. If given a choice, most people would like to live in a house. Because houses rent at a premium, however, most renters can't afford them. The next best thing for them is to pay a premium for a nice apartment that has the feeling of a single-family home.

The best way to create that single-family feel is to find properties that have separate units on the lot.

Even if fences do not separate the units, these kinds of apartments give the tenants more privacy than, say, three or four units in one building would.

As a general rule, the more private you can make the rentals, the less the tenants will call and ask for things to get done. This is because privacy makes the tenants look at the unit as their home as opposed to a temporary residence. In addition, if you can add fences to separate the units, you can save on gardening costs as you make each tenant responsible for his own yard. You will see both of these benefits on the bottom line because your overall expenses will be kept at a minimum.

One lone building

The next best thing to completely separate units is to buy a building that sits on just one level. These properties do not have the inherent noise problems that come with tenants living over one another. Many of these situations offer the opportunity to fence off a private area for each tenant behind or in front of each unit. Again, this gives some private open space, and it should save on gardening costs.

Two on the bottom, two on the top

If you are not able to find these single-family-style properties, you will have to settle for standard apartment-style buildings. These usually are two-story buildings with a couple of units downstairs and a couple more upstairs. A parking area usually is either attached or separated, depending on the size of the lot. Although these buildings do not have the appeal of the other style properties, don't worry. There will always be a tenant available for a nice unit.

In many older urban areas you have two-family ("Philadelphia" style) houses and three-deckers. You also often find formerly single-family residences split into two to four units. The "feel" of these residences is somewhere between a single-family house and an apartment building. With growing gentrification, as in New York or Boston, some older neighborhoods with this type of housing could be a wise investment.

Finding the right one

One of the keys to finding the right property is to survey the market and get a feeling for the kind of style and amenities that seem to command the highest rent per square foot. Your goal then will be to acquire that type of property or one that can be converted at a minimum cost.

In finding the right property, it is important to pay particular attention to your potential expenses. Look for properties that have all the utilities metered separately. This way, the tenants will pay the utility bills instead of you. Also look for units that have individual laundry hookups versus common laundry rooms. Again, this means that they pay for their gas and electric, not you. Tenants also should supply their own appliances. Not having to purchase and maintain refrigerators and stoves will save you a lot of money over the years. From a practical standpoint, the bigger the items your tenant has to move in, the less likely he is to move out.

You will be restricted based on what tenants in the area expect when they rent. If you find that you will have to provide most of the appliances, make sure you become an expert on the second-hand market and local repair services. This will help you keep costs under control.

> " I bought a 4-unit row house in Boston in the '80s, converted to condos and sold them for triple my investment (purchase plus improvements). Twelve years later, the units were selling for 100% more than I sold them for.
> —Matthew K., Investor "

Watch Out!
It is not uncommon to find owner financing with properties of five units and up. Although owner financing helps with the purchase today, it passes the problem on to you when you go to sell.

Five units and up

When you graduate to the five-unit and larger category, you have moved into the arena of commercial loans and the economy of scale that comes from more units per square foot. The first time you start looking at these properties, this discount usually is very apparent. Again, this is primarily because there is a limited availability of financing for these size properties versus one- to four-unit buildings.

With five-unit buildings, specifically, there is a good method of creating some added value. Surprisingly enough, it is not by adding bedrooms like we did with the single-family example earlier. Instead, you can add value by turning a five-unit building into a four-unit building. In doing so, you turn a property that required a commercial loan into one that only requires a buyer to obtain a residential loan.

Let's say you find a five-unit building in the same neighborhood as our four-unit example. The four-unit is worth $220,000, and we can buy this five-unit for $175,000. (This is not uncommon. Once you start to research the market, you will see it to be true.) The four-unit is made up of all two-bedrooms. The five-unit has three two-bedrooms and two one-bedrooms. If the layout of the one-bedroom units is such that they are located right next to each other, you probably can take out a couple of walls and combine them into one really nice two- or three-bedroom unit. All of a sudden, you have turned your hard-to-finance (and hard-to-sell) five-unit building into an easy-to-finance (and easy-to-sell) four-unit.

It is easier to get a conversion like this through city bureaucracy because you are down-zoning the property, which is a preferred situation to creating more units. You are decreasing the density and increasing the parking on your property, which most cities like.

You will have to do diligent research before you attempt this kind of project. You need to know in advance what kind of permits and costs will be involved. If you find that the city is going to require extensive drawings or engineering work before they issue permits, make sure your contractor and architect are in the loop. Their expert opinion will help you to determine whether the project will be worth the expense.

Big apartment buildings

When you buy big apartment buildings, your decision-making becomes entirely dependent on the analysis of the financial operations of the property. The good news is that when you get into this range of properties, there are usually plenty of loans available. Know, however, that when it comes to commercial loans like these, you are going to have to come up with a great deal of money for a down payment. With these purchases, lenders usually require you to come up with 25–30 percent of the purchase price. On a $2,000,000 piece of property, 25 percent comes to $500,000 down.

Tenants who rent in larger properties tend to be looking for a different environment than tenants who like the privacy of smaller properties. These tenants have similar thinking to people who want to buy and live in large condo developments. They want the luxury of pools, workout rooms, and clubhouses, but they don't want the hassle of paying for or taking care of these amenities themselves. Items that attract tenants to larger apartment complexes include:

Moneysaver
When buying big apartment buildings, always be on the lookout for any available owner financing. If you can find some, it will increase your leverage considerably.

- An attractive appearance from the street

- Well-maintained common areas

- A security entrance system

- A secure parking area

- Recreational amenities (pool, sauna, barbecues, tennis courts, clubhouse, and so on)

- Laundry rooms

- Large square footage apartments

- Appliances provided

- Multiple bathrooms for two-bedroom units

- Walk-in closets

- A private balcony or patio area

- Air-conditioning

- Upscale amenities (wet bar, fireplace, and so on)

- Cable or satellite television services

Timesaver
Unless you have confidence that you can manage a large apartment building yourself, you should pick a property management company before you buy. Make sure you take a company representative with you to look at each and every property you are considering. The representative will provide valuable insight.

Providing these amenities, combined with a strict maintenance program, enables owners to charge the highest rent per square foot and helps keep turnovers to a minimum. It is not unusual for tenants in larger properties to move more frequently than those who rent in smaller properties. By maintaining a high degree of pride-of-ownership, you will make it harder for tenants to justify moving for a purely emotional reason.

As you move into progressively larger properties, you will be leaving the "mom-and-pop" phase of real estate investing and entering the "just business" phase. The properties produce good cash-on-cash income, but they need the kind of organized management that any larger business would need. The principles we will be discussing in Chapters 13–15 will be most applicable to these size properties.

Commercial and industrial properties

Commercial and industrial properties can be one of the best investment vehicles you can find because, like residential tenants, businesses also need a roof over their heads. In fact, you should think of these properties as "a home for a business." These properties fall into many categories including:

- Free-standing stores
- Small strip-malls
- Office buildings
- Mobile home parks
- Mixed-use commercial and residential
- Parking lots
- Garages
- Multistory office buildings
- Specialty commercial (restaurants, gas stations, and so on)
- Small factories
- Larger industrial buildings

Let's be partners

When you rent commercial or industrial space to a tenant, you really are becoming a partner in their business. If they do well in your location, the odds are good that they will continue to be a tenant and will continue to line your pockets with money. The fact of the matter is, however, most new businesses fail in the first year or two of operation. If one of your long-term tenants fails, your real estate investment could be in serious trouble. For this reason, you should personally interview all the tenants in any commercial property you consider purchasing. You need to find out the following information:

- The length of time the owners have been in business
- The credit rating of the owners and the business
- Why they left their last location
- Why they chose this location
- The goals of their business
- The type and term of lease they desire

Be especially wary of a property in which most of the leases are coming up for renewal. Many clever sellers have unloaded a prize building with a great long-term tenant because they got wind that the tenant was going to move. You don't want to get stuck owning a great strip-mall without any tenants.

Types of leases

The foundation of most commercial properties is the lease as opposed to the month-to-month agreement used in residential property. Having long-term leases with successful tenants/businesses is one of the greatest advantages of owning a commercial property—provided your lease is structured properly. Before you invest in this type of property or negotiate any leases, hire a real estate lawyer to help you. Generally speaking, leases fall into two categories:

1. Gross leases

2. Triple net leases

The difference in the two depends on whether the property owner or the tenant is going to pay the bills. In a gross lease, the tenant pays the rent, and the property owner pays all the expenses of operation except the tenant's utilities. In a triple net lease, the tenant pays for everything including the rent, the taxes, the insurance, the utilities, and most of the maintenance of the property. In some retail leases, the tenant even pays a percentage of their sales as part of their rent.

There are many variations in leases. Custom usually dictates what most tenants and landlords expect. It is best to consult a leasing expert before you buy a commercial property so you can find out what is usual and customary for the area.

Bright Idea
When negotiating rents with big commercial tenants, try to get a percentage of their gross as well as monthly rental payments.

Commercial and industrial vs. residential

Commercial and industrial properties have some distinct advantages and disadvantages when compared to residential purchases:

Advantages

- Long-term tenants
- Limited management
- Consistent return on investment
- Consistent value appreciation

Disadvantages

- Limited availability of tenants
- Limited availability of financing
- Significant holding costs between tenants

A couple of niche markets

There are a couple of interesting trends in this type of real estate. The first is the niche market of providing small office and commercial space for new enterprises. One of the effects of the leaning of our new entrepreneurial economy in the late 1990s is the emergence of the displaced or energetic person who has an idea for how to make a better mousetrap. This started with more and more people working from home. These workers usually end up looking for a small space to rent where they can have a desk, a copy machine, and maybe a secretary instead of a house full of kids. They are willing to pay a premium rent per square foot, and in some areas, there seems to be an unlimited supply of people always looking for office space.

The other phenomenon is the conversion of older commercial and industrial buildings into loft apartments or live/work spaces. This mirrors the trends in cities such as New York and San Francisco for a "hip," open environment for young adults and trend-setting businesses. These older buildings sometimes can be purchased at a very low price per square foot. Then, with a minimum of improvements, they can be rented or sold at a fantastic profit. If the structures are of any historical significance, there are some very attractive tax benefits. In these cases as well as the other commercial/industrial properties, the secret to your success will be staying on top of the market so you are not caught owning a "white elephant."

Just the facts

- A real estate investment in land requires two things from you: money and patience.

- Adding value to a condo or a single-family home is the best way to get more out of that kind of investment.

- An investment in a single-family home will never bring you the same return as a unit investment on that same lot.

- Because of the great financing available, two- to four-unit buildings can be huge money-makers.

- Big apartment buildings require huge down payments and intensive management.

▪ There are a lot of opportunities to make money by buying commercial and industrial properties.

GET THE SCOOP ON...
Whether fixer-uppers are really for you
▪ Mismanaged properties and why they're an
investor's dream ▪ The truth behind the fore-
closure market ▪ Getting in on "short sales"
▪ Buying property with little or no money down

Special Types of Properties

Chapter 8

S everal types of properties offer an extra opportunity to make a profit. These are the ones
that get most of the "get rich quick" publicity
on late-night infomercials. You've probably seen the
nouveaux riches testifying to the glory of foreclosures and no-money-down deals.

The truth is, these kinds of properties do present
an opportunity to make an extra profit, but based
on 30 plus years in real estate, we believe that they
are best left for later in your career—after you've
had considerably more hands-on experience.
Nonetheless, many people have made loads of
money (and others have lost a bundle) investing in
these "sure things." Here are the facts so you can
make an educated decision for yourself.

Have tools will travel

The classic property that offers a chance for the
investor to make an extra buck is the fixer-upper.
These properties are run-down and need considerable work and TLC to bring them back to life.

Countless books have been written about these types of investments. They offer an opportunity to add value to a property, thereby increasing the investor's equity over and above the down payment. We will use a variation of our example property to illustrate how fixer-uppers pencil out.

How the numbers stack up

Let's assume that 1800 Mariposa Lane is in a state of disrepair. During our inspection, we find that the following items need attention. Here are some estimates for what the repairs will cost:

Exterior Paint	$2,500
Landscaping	$500
Garage Doors	$800
Fence	$750
Roof	$3,000
Rehab Unit	
Carpet	$750
Interior Paint	$350
Misc.	$75
Lost Rent	$550
Total	$1,725
Grand Total	$9,275

In our example, 1800 Mariposa Lane was listed on the market for $225,000, but we estimated the value to be $222,000 using the three classic appraisal methods. In this instance, because the property needs some fixing up, we were able to negotiate the purchase for $205,000.

Now let's take a look at what this means in terms of our potential profit. The first assumption is that the building will be worth the full $222,000 as soon as we finish the work. Therefore, our gross profit from the project will be:

Finished Value	$222,000
Purchase Price	−$205,000
Gross Profit	$17,000

Now we deduct the estimated cost of the repairs from the estimated gross profit to find the net profit:

Gross Profit	$17,000
Less Upgrade Costs	–$9,275
Net Profit	$7,725

There are two ways to look at the return from this kind of effort. The first way (and the one most people look at) is the percentage return on the effort itself. In other words, "What is my estimated profit compared to how much it will cost to do the work?" This calculation looks like this:

$$\frac{\text{Estimated Profit} \quad \$7,725}{\text{Cost of Project} \quad \$17,000} = 83.2\%$$

This 83.2 percent return looks pretty impressive. Most first-time investors would look at this potential profit and jump at the opportunity, but let's look at this profit in terms of the overall investment.

To recap, remember that, in the first year of ownership, 1800 Mariposa Lane had an estimated profit of $13,419. We had $1,080 from cash flow, $300 in equity growth from loan reduction, $11,000 in equity growth from appreciation, and $1,039 in tax benefits. If we combine these returns with the returns from the work we did to fix up the property, our overall return now looks like this:

$$\frac{\text{Returns} \quad \$13,419 + \$7,725}{\text{Investment} \quad \$30,000 + \$9,275} = 53.8\%$$

As you can see, when you add both of the profits together, add both of the investments together, and then divide the two, there isn't that big a difference in the overall profit you would make between this kind of project and the original example which had a 44.7% yield (see Chapter 3).

Watch Out!
You can find any number of book and tape courses that claim you can make a fortune with little or no money invested. If they sound too good to be true, they probably are.

The return starts to drop, however, when you look at the future return. This is because the extra profit you gain in fixer-uppers is a one-shot increase in value, while the cash investment is a permanent investment of capital. If we make the assumption that the profit in the second year would be about the same as the first year, look at what happens to our overall return because we now have the extra cash invested:

Timesaver
Compile a note-book with the cost of basic property mainte-nance items as well as a list of work you have had done on your property. This will come in handy when a crisis arises and you need to know how much it will cost to fix it.

$$\frac{\text{Returns} \quad \$13,419}{\text{Investment} \quad \$30,000 + \$9,275} = 34.1\%$$

From a practical standpoint, it would make bet-ter sense to take the extra capital it would take to fix up 1800 Mariposa Lane and, instead, put it toward the down payment on a second building.

In one year—out the next

Many people who make money buying fixer-uppers don't look at property as a long-term investment. To them, buying real estate is like buying raw materials to produce a product to resell. If that's the case, let's examine the profitability on the Mariposa fixer-upper the same way. This time, we will assume that you will hold the property for just one year and then sell. Of course, you will get the normal returns as well as the fixer-upper profit, but we have to add in the costs of selling. We'll estimate that to be $15,000. Our profit now looks like this:

Profit from Operation	$13,419
Fix Up Profit	$7,725
Less Sale Costs	−$15,000
Net Profit	$6,144

Now let's look at the return on our investment over the year it took us to do the work:

$$\frac{\text{Profit} \quad \$6,144}{\text{Investment} \quad \$30,000 + \$9,275} = 15.6\%$$

As you can see, 15.6 percent isn't a very impressive profit, especially when you consider the added risk of having to do all the necessary repairs.

The truth is, when you see an opportunity to make an extra profit, you need to evaluate whether it will be truly worth the extra risk and investment. Remember, the added capital investment decreases your leverage. As you are learning, leverage is one of the most significant elements that drives the return on your invested capital. For that reason, the return from any fixer-upper project needs to be pretty darn good to warrant the loss of leverage and the increased risk.

The other side of the coin: management fixer-uppers

A different type of fixer-upper property offers a fine opportunity to add value to your bottom-line profit. This is a property that has been mismanaged for one reason or another. Management fixer-uppers are buildings that often can be described as ones in which "the inmates are running the asylum." Rents usually are below market, and they always arrive late or, sometimes, not at all. Often, mismanaged buildings cause their owners so much grief that they discount the price dramatically just to be rid of the headache.

As you know by now, real estate is not a "get rich quick" investment. You can't get in and get out quickly like you can when buying stocks or bonds. Unfortunately, many people jump into real estate not knowing this reality. This can work to the advantage of people who truly understand investing and

Watch Out!
You are taking on an extra risk when you buy a property that needs work. Many times, a job that looks like it will only take a month to complete and only cost a few dollars ends up taking 6 months and costing four times the original estimate.

who are looking for a way to create some extra profit on their investment. This is especially true when it comes to the management fixer-upper.

How they came to be

Mismanagement is a common problem for both part-time and out-of-state owners of small properties. It also is common with properties owned by partners or groups of investors. Owners of these buildings either get tired of owning property, get tired of the losses their properties produce, or both. The truth is, they have given up and are ready to do whatever it takes to get the property off their books.

When individual investors find themselves in this situation, it usually is because they have something more pressing than landlording to attend to in their lives. Many people find out after the fact that they don't have the time, energy, money, or desire to make the building perform. For groups, the problems come from the fact that they usually lack a leader willing to do the job necessary to save the investment. That person would have to put in a larger amount of effort only to receive his proportionate share of the profit.

Enter Sherlock Holmes

Your real estate agent will have to do much of the detective work to find a mismanaged building. This is because many of these opportunities are not reflected in the asking price. Instead, your agent will have to network with other agents who have the listings. They might not come right out and say "You can steal this property," but they will give your agent hints along the way. Common clues that might lead you to a mismanaged fixer-upper opportunity are:

Unofficially...
Mismanaged buildings are a much wiser choice for the real estate investor than standard fixer-upper opportunities. They generally require less money and very little physical effort to straighten them out.

- The sellers are retiring and just want out.
- The partners are having problems.
- The seller can't handle the problems anymore.
- The partnership is breaking up.
- The owners moved out of state.
- The seller needs the money for (fill in the blank).
- This is the last property the seller is getting rid of.
- The sellers are getting a divorce.
- The sellers have found their up-leg property in their IRS 1031 exchange.
- There is high vacancy or credit losses.
- Deferred maintenance is obvious.
- Expenses are out of control.
- Nobody is watching the property.
- Theft by the staff is happening.
- The rents are under market.

A management fixer-upper illustration

When you find a property with a motivated seller and some management problems, it's time to sharpen your pencil, because this is where you can make some good money. The first thing to do is analyze the value that might be there. As with the standard fixer-upper, you want to be sure there is adequate profit available for the risk you will take by buying someone else's problem.

Let's go back to our example property. Assume that, because 1800 Mariposa Lane has been mismanaged, we can buy it for $205,000. In fact, not only has the listing agent indicated that the owners are anxious to sell, we can tell they have lost interest altogether. Here is why:

1. **The exterior looks shabby.** Paint is peeling, and the landscaping is terribly overgrown.

2. **There has been a unit vacant for more than two months.** There are two reasons for this. First, the unit isn't rent-ready. The carpets need cleaning, it needs new blinds on the windows, and the kitchen and bathroom need painting. The second reason for the vacancies is probably due to the "For Rent" sign stuck in the window of the vacant unit. It can barely be seen from the street, it doesn't say anything specific about the building, and it only lists a phone number that is hard to make out. What's more, the agent tells us he hasn't been advertising the vacancy in any way.

3. **The rents are all too low.** The market rent for the neighborhood is $550, but the current rents in the three occupied units are just $475, $490, and $505. The reason it's under-rented is that the current owners didn't want to rock the boat by raising them. In addition, because the owners have been reluctant to maintain the property, they didn't want to have to worry about cleaning units up if tenants decided to move out because of a rental increase.

Before we raise the rents on the existing units, we first decide to offer some upgrades to ease the pain of the increase. The budget for all of the repairs and upgrades is as follows:

Exterior Paint	$500
Landscaping	$250
Rehab Unit	
Clean Carpet	$75
Paint	$350
Misc.	$100
Lost Rent	$250
Total	$775
Unit #1: Garbage Disposal	$75
Unit #2: New Blinds	$125
Unit #4: New Screens	$110
Total	$310
Total Cost of Upgrades	$9,275

Bright Idea
Offer your existing tenants a referral fee if they recommend a new tenant for one of your vacancies. The whole idea of successful landlording is to keep your units full. A small cash outlay to achieve that result will always be well worth it.

Let's review the profit from the purchase and see how this compares on a percentage basis. The gross profit is:

Finished Value	$222,000
Purchase Price	-$205,000
Gross Profit	$17,000

Now we deduct the estimated cost of the repairs from the estimated gross profit to find the net profit:

Gross Profit	$17,000
Upgrade Costs	-$1,835
Net Profit	$15,165

Now let's see what kind of return this is on our investment:

$$\frac{\text{Estimated Profit} \quad \$15,165}{\text{Cost of Project} \quad \$1,835} = 826\%$$

As you can see, 826 percent is definitely a healthy return on the extra capital we had to put into this project. We could do the same calculations that we did on the standard fixer-upper, but this should still show an exceptional profit margin because it only requires an extra $1,835 of capital to capture the extra profit. If we look at the profit the second year will bring, assuming no change as we did in the standard fixer-upper, it looks like this:

$$\frac{\text{Returns} \quad \$13,419}{\text{Investment} \quad \$30,000 + \$1,835} = 42.1\%$$

This return is very close to the original return because we haven't diluted the equity.

If we looked at the management fixer-upper as though we were purchasing for only a one-year hold and then selling, the return would look like this (using the same assumptions we used for the standard fixer-upper):

Profit From Operation	$13,419
Fix Up Profit	$15,165
Less Sale Costs	−$15,000
Net Profit	$13,584

This is what the return looks like as a percentage of the total investment after one year:

$$\frac{\text{Net Profit} \quad \$13,584}{\text{Investment} \quad \$30,000 + \$1,835} = 42.6\%$$

You can see that the effort needed to correct the management problems would make the management fixer-upper well worth your while. The important thing to learn is how to assess the potential profit before you invest. If you don't do this kind of research, you might stumble across a diamond in the rough and not realize it, or, you might end up with a property that needs a lot of extra work but has little or no financial payoff.

Bank-owned properties

Throughout the late 1990s, there have been a rash of bank-repossessed properties on the market. In the business, these are known as REOs, which stands for Real Estate Owned. REOs can offer the investor an opportunity to purchase at a substantial discount, but as is true with most things in life, with a discounted REO, you often get what you pay for.

No warranties

Keep in mind how the bank came into possession of the REO. Someone probably bought it with one of two ideas in mind: to get a nice home or to get a set of units that was hopefully going to make a decent profit. Along the way things started to go wrong. It might have had to do with the economy in general, a problem with the building itself, or perhaps some issues in the person's own personal life. Whatever the reason, the lender was forced to take the property back. The problem for you is that you will never know the reason why. With a foreclosure property, the bank is not required to give any disclosures or warranties at all. In fact, with foreclosures, you will be going into the deal with your eyes wide shut.

When REOs are put on the market, they usually have a large discount in price compared to the average property listed. This discount can give buyers a false sense of profitability. Remember, bankers are not interested in losing money. They are out to make a profit just like the rest of us. The truth is, when they set the price of foreclosure properties, they do diligent market research just like any other seller would. In fact, they have their own appraisers on staff who can give them an opinion of value based on market research, the property's current condition, and the needed repairs. Although banks might leave a bit of extra profit on the table, don't assume that every REO will make you a windfall profit.

Watch Out!
One drawback to buying REOs is that you will not receive any type of disclosures regarding the condition of the property. Therefore, you bear all the risk of any hidden problems the property might have. This is the classic example of "Let the buyer beware."

Difficult financing

One of the major problems associated with purchasing a bank-owned property is obtaining financing. Some banks will carry the financing on their repossessions, but these usually are repossessions that are still in decent condition (which is harder to find), and there often is a stipulation that the building must be owner-occupied. In addition, if the property has a lot of deferred maintenance and is partially (or completely) vacant, it might not be possible to get financing from a conventional source at all. At a minimum, you probably will have to put cash to a new loan, and you might have to go to a "hard money" lender (See Chapter 5, "Financing Your Investment") to get the money needed for the purchase.

An REO illustration

Moneysaver
When buying any REO property, it is advisable to have a thorough inspection done by a professional contractor or a licensed property inspector before you sign on the dotted line.

The first thing to do when purchasing an REO is to do an accurate assessment of the current condition of the property and any management problems it might have. In most cases, you have to purchase the property "as is" and will not get any reports or clearances from the lender. Once you gather all your data, you then will do the same kind of review you learned earlier.

To illustrate, let's revisit 1800 Mariposa Lane. We will assume it has the same kinds of repair problems as a standard fixer-upper, but it has more severe management problems (which is not uncommon with REOs). In this case, three of the four units are vacant and need a complete overhaul. The last unit has a tenant, but the tenant isn't paying rent and will need to be evicted after you close. We will use the same market value of the finished building

($222,000), but because it's owned by the bank and has some serious problems, we can get it for $170,000. Some additional facts are as follows:

1. The rent loss and eviction expense will be higher than in our first example. This is because we won't be able to start the work or the eviction until we take possession. We will assume that it will cost $300 in legal fees and will take one month to get the tenant out.

2. It will take one month to do the repair work on the units.

3. We will rent one unit in July for an August 1st move in. We will rent two units in August for a September 1st move in. The last unit will be rented in September for an October 1st move in.

Here is what the profitability looks like:

General Fix Up

Exterior Paint	$2,500
Landscaping	$500
Garage Doors	$800
Fence	$750
Roof	$3,000
Total	**$7,550**

Interior Repair (Four Units)

Carpet @ $750 Each	$3,000
Paint @ $350 Each	$1,400
Misc @ $100 Each	$400
Total	**$4,800**

The time line of the vacancies, assuming we close June 1st, looks like this:

	Close	End Month 1	End Month 2	End Month 3	End Month 4
Month	June	July	August	September	October
Vacancies	4	4	3	1	0

As you can see, we have lost a total of 12 months of rent (4 months in June, 4 in July, 3 in August, and 1 in September). We also have lost the cost of the eviction plus the cost of the repairs. With an assumed rent on the units of $550 each, our total expenses are as follows:

Rental Loss	$6,600
Eviction Expense	+$300
Total	$6,900

Let's look at what kind of return we made on our investment. The total cost of the project is as follows:

General Repairs	$7,550
Interior Repairs	$4,800
Rental Loss	+$6,900
Total	$19,250

Now we will review the profit and see how it compares on a percentage basis. The gross profit is:

Finished Value	$222,000
Purchase Price	−$170,000
Gross Profit	$52,000

We deduct the estimated cost of the repairs from the estimated gross profit to find the net profit:

Gross Profit	$52,000
Upgrade Costs	−$19,250
Net Profit	$32,750

Now let's see what kind of percentage return this is on our investment.

$$\frac{\text{Estimated Profit}}{\text{Cost of Project}} \quad \frac{\$32,750}{\$19,250} = 170\%$$

170% is a pretty sizeable return on the capital we had to invest. Let's see, however, how the overall profit margin is affected. We will look at the return for the second year, assuming no change in the

> 66
> It all looked good from the start, but completing the work took longer than projected. The negative cash flow because of the lost rents tapped me out and made me rethink this approach to investing.
> —Blake M., Investor
> 99

ordinary profit from the property. Because this is an REO that required a considerable amount of work, we would have had to get a loan that required 20 percent down. Twenty percent of $170,000 is $34,000. Therefore, the return is:

$$\frac{\text{Return} \quad \$13,419}{\text{Investment} \quad \$34,000 + 19,250} = 25.2\%$$

As you can see, the large amount of capital required for a project like this dilutes the overall return in future years. 25.2% is a significant drop off. For that reason, these kinds of projects don't always fit with investors that have long-term growth in mind.

The hold-for-one-year strategy

Let's look at this project as if we were going to sell after one year. If so, the profit would look like this:

Profit from Operations	$13,419
Fix Up Profit	$32,750
Less Sale Costs	–$15,000
Net Profit	$31,169

Once you know the net profit, you can determine the percentage profit on the project as follows:

$$\frac{\text{Net Profit} \quad \$31,169}{\text{Investment} \quad \$34,000 + \$19,250} = 58.5\%$$

58.5% is a pretty decent return on your invested capital. We believe that because most bank REOs take so much capital, the "fix it up and get out in a year" strategy might be the best approach for maintaining a strong return on your invested capital. As you will learn later, keeping the return on equity at your target level is the key to achieving your goals.

One of the attractions of repossessed properties is the fact that they offer the possibility of a deep discount in price over fair market value. We have

Watch Out!
When banks are forced to take a property back in foreclosure, they usually do the least amount of work necessary to get the property off their books. As far as they are concerned, peeling paint, rotting stairways, and overgrown landscaping are all just fine.

learned, however, this comes with a price measured in additional capital requirements and usually a lot of work. Another similar class of properties offers some of the same benefits without the larger capital requirements—preforeclosure properties.

Buying a property through a "short sale"

Preforeclosure properties are advertised as "short sales." A short sale is one in which the lenders have agreed to take less than is owed on the loans to get a payoff on the balance owed. At this stage, the owners have been doing the best they can to keep the building running. All the units are probably rented, but the owners are still drowning for one reason or another. In situations like this, lenders have found that they can minimize their loss on bad loans by getting the property sold before they have to go through the complete foreclosure process.

In these instances, you will be negotiating with the actual owner, subject to approval by the lender. Most owners in this situation aren't too concerned with what kind of price they accept because they will be walking away with nothing for themselves; the bank is going to get it all. This is a chance to sharpen your pencil, do your homework, and show off your knowledge of appraisal methods.

To get the best pricing, you need to present a well-organized story to the lender. A good way to present your offer is as follows. The first section of your proposal should include:

■ A brief biography of you and your knowledge of real estate

■ A complete financial package on you and two years of tax returns

- A prequalification letter from a reputable lender
- A copy of the purchase contract
- A deposit check

The second section of your proposal should include a detailed discussion of the physical condition of the property. It should include the following:

- A professional property inspection report
- Photos of all items that need repair
- A termite report if necessary
- Disclosures on other systems as needed
- Bids to repair any deferred maintenance items

Next you need to give them your estimate of value, which will justify the price you offered. At this point, you could consider hiring a professional appraiser because he could present the valuation in a format to which the lender is accustomed. If this is not practical or cost effective, you can present the information yourself. Make sure you get your agent's help to find the best comparable sales to justify your offer. Your opinion as to the value of the property should include:

- Copies of comparable sales with pictures
- Details of how you determined your price (appraisal)

You should end the proposal with a strong statement as to why the lender should accept your offer. The format of the letter on the following page should give you an idea of what you might say.

Will a strong proposal guarantee acceptance? Unfortunately, the answer is no. We admit that, after 30 plus years in real estate, we are still baffled by some of the decisions made by banks and savings and loans.

Moneysaver
Lenders who have said they would consider a "short sale" are already tipping their hand in admitting that they will take a lower amount than is owed on their loan.

January 1, 2000

Bodian Savings and Loan
333 Richmond Street
Anytown, CA 90245

Re: Short Sale Proposal Loan # 14283

Gentlemen,

Enclosed you will find our proposal to purchase the property secured by your loan number 14283. As you know, this loan is in default, and we are asking you to consider a short sale to avoid the long and costly process of doing a foreclosure.

We have included our financial information so you can verify that we have the background and capability of closing this transaction quickly if you grant your approval. We have chosen a lender to handle the financing and have included their letter to show their willingness to make the loan.

The price we are offering is based on careful consideration of current sales in the area and a detailed inspection of the property in its current condition. We felt it was important for you to have this information about the current condition because it does impact the value, based on a comparison with current sales. If you were forced to take this property to foreclosure, your expenses would increase significantly, and the condition of the property would no doubt worsen.

We are prepared to close the purchase within ___days of opening escrow. We urge you to accept our proposal, and we will get this nonproducing loan off your books as soon as possible.

Sincerely,

[signature]

John Flanagan
2220 Jose Way
El Segundo, CA 90245

Although these properties offer an opportunity to get a great discount in price, that doesn't mean this is the right type of property for you. You will need to do the same analysis that was done for the previous examples to see if the overall returns are worth the extra effort and capital investment.

Minimum down payment deals

Our last class of special properties is those you can purchase with a low down payment. In these situations, the owners are fed up and just want out. There are several common motivations of sellers in this situation. Some have purchased rental property and then realized that landlording just isn't the business for them. Many are moving out of the area or have had a career change that makes it difficult to continue running the property. Many are just retiring and want to quit being a landlord.

No matter what the reason, what they want is someone to take the property off their hands and give them enough cash to pay selling expenses. Some of these owners might even be willing to take money out of their pockets to move the property. Their primary goal is to protect their credit by removing the liability of the loan. Properties in this category offer two advantages:

1. Lower down payments

2. Seasoned financing

The first advantage is obvious. If you only need to put closing costs or less down, you are getting into a property with great leverage. This leverage will work to your benefit and will greatly increase the percentage return on your investment in the first few years of ownership.

Bright Idea
Many lenders have lists of approved appraisers. You might be able to hire one from this list, which should help you sell your bid.

Bright Idea
It's not unusual to be able to pay a loan off in 10 years that actually had a 20-year payment schedule by just a small increase in the payment from the cash flow of the building. Collecting the cash flow from a property with no mortgage is a great position to be in during retirement.

Second, seasoned financing offers a distinct advantage to you as an investor. It is the nature of conventional financing that there will be very little payoff on a loan balance in the initial years of the life of a loan. In the middle years, this increases; in the final years, principal pays off quickly. What this means is that, if the loan you are taking over was written for 30 years and has 20 years or fewer to go until paid off, it is beginning to make some significant reductions in principle. This is a great benefit to you.

A word to the wise

The examples in this chapter have given only a broad overview of these kinds of special circumstance properties. Our goal was to expose you to the opportunities and how they give you the possibility to make some extra profit. The most important lesson is that you must look at these special properties closely to be sure the extra profit is worth the increased risk and the increased capital required. Make sure you do a complete analysis of each special opportunity before you make a purchase.

Just the facts

- Fixer-uppers are better left for the later years of your investment career.
- Management fixer-uppers are relatively easy to cure and are the vehicle of choice for the savvy investor.
- REOs usually require too much money out of pocket to make them profitable.
- A short sale gives the investor an opportunity to buy a troubled property from a lender at a considerable discount.

Setting Your Investment Goals

PART IV

GET THE SCOOP ON...
The five keys to a profitable investment plan ▪
Learning how to set attainable real estate goals
▪ Projecting your future net worth ▪ The compound interest formula and how it will make
you rich ▪ Creating a detailed year-by-year
investment plan

Building an Investment Plan

Chapter 9

When was the last time you heard someone say, "I'm happy just scraping by," or
"I don't care if I get ahead in life." Never,
right? This is because people strive to be successful.
In fact, we're obsessed with it. We dress for success,
read about success, and above all, we spend money
(borrowed at 18 percent) as if each of us was the
most successful person on earth. Truth be told, however, most of us aren't any closer to our dreams than
we were last year at this time. How come?

We believe that planning is the road map to success. In Chapter 1, "Basic Investment Concepts," we
talked philosophically about taking control of your
own destiny. Unfortunately, if you take control but
don't have a clearly defined set of goals with a plan,
you'll probably spend most of your time simply spin-
ning your wheels.

The purpose of this chapter is to teach you how
to turn your good intentions into achievable results
through planning. The end result could be a great
future you designed yourself.

Good intentions vs. planning

Most people's lives are so complicated that they put things off until they absolutely have to do them. This is true whether it's something as simple as taking out the trash or something as vital as planning for retirement. We all might have the best of intentions, but in reality, no matter what the chore is, we put it off until we decide to get around to it.

We learned of a sales tool many years ago that might help you overcome this problem. Get a piece of card stock about three inches square and cut it into a circle. With a red marker, write the following words across the middle of your circle: "to it." After you have done that, put the card-stock circle in your pocket and keep it with you at all times. Problem solved. You no longer have the excuse of being able to wait until you get around to it because you now have one—a round "to it."

In all seriousness, having a plan with stated goals is one of the most important foundations of successful investing. The following are some characteristics that differentiate a good intention from a plan:

- A good intention is the desire to have the better things in life. For example, "I want to be worth a million dollars one day." The problem, however, is that just saying it doesn't bring you any closer to achieving it.

- Good intentions always are very general and are never written down.

- A person who plans expresses a specific goal or goals and how to get there. For example, "I plan to have a net worth of $500,000 within 10 years by purchasing small rental properties."

■ A plan is put in writing, and it is made public to friends and family.

The five key components of a winning investment plan

Although good investment plans do not start out in minute detail, they should be in writing from day one. Your plan gradually will grow in detail as you proceed though your investment career. To get things started, buy yourself a three-ring binder in which to put your plan. This way, you can change the contents easily as you make progress. Your planning binder should contain the following four sections:

1. **Goals:** Here you will lay out your long-term investment goals and the time frame you have scheduled for their achievement.

2. **General plan:** This spells out how you will achieve your goals over the time limits set forth in the plan.

3. **Detailed plan:** The detailed plan is similar to the "profit plan" of a business. It establishes the year-by-year goals of the plan. This is the measuring stick to determine how you are doing along the way.

4. **Follow-up and goal review:** Here you will enter predetermined dates to periodically monitor your progress. This is a perfect opportunity for equity and property budget reviews.

Your long-term investment goals

The goals section of your investment plan should be divided into the following subsections:

■ Cash flow requirements

■ Net worth projections

Bright Idea
Give copies of your investmer plan to people whose opinions and knowledge you respect. By knowing your intentions, you respected conf dants will help keep you on track.

- Tax shelter benefits required
- Cash withdrawal from plan
- Other goals

Planning for cash flow

Cash flow requirements refer to your cash flow projections during and after completion of the plan. The point at which you will begin to achieve a significant cash flow depends on two things:

1. The amount of cash you invest in the plan initially
2. How well you manage your plan

Let's look at some ways of setting cash flow requirements with a few typical examples.

- **Case #1:** You are well-employed, expect to remain so for the immediate future, and would like to retire in 10 years. You have available to you between $30,000 and $40,000 for investment purposes. Your current salary is $40,000 per year, and you expect to be making about $50,000 per year in 10 years. To supplement your company-sponsored and social security retirement income, you would like to have about $20,000 per year of income from your real estate equities at retirement. Because you feel that you can support yourself and your family adequately until you retire, you will require no cash withdrawal from the plan; however, you would prefer no significant negative cash flows during the life of the plan.

  Your cash flow requirements from the plan would be:

  "Cash flow of $20,000 each year after the 10th year. No significant negative cash flow during the plan."

Unofficially...
Properties that yield large cash flows in the beginning generally produce low tax benefits. This is because the higher the cash flow, the less depreciation left over to shelter your normal income.

- **Case #2:** You are young, ambitious, and single. You have a good job that pays $35,000 per year. You borrow $10,000 from your parents and are willing to invest that money in real estate. Your plan is to parlay that nest egg into $500,000 in real estate equities in 15 years.

  Your cash flow requirements from the plan would be:

  "Generate $500,000 in net equities at the end of 15 years. Pay off loan from parents from cash flow over first five years. The $500,000 invested at the end of the plan at 10 percent in trust deeds should yield $50,000 per year income."

- **Case #3:** You have been employed in the aerospace industry for 15 years, and your salary is $40,000 per year. Over 50 percent of the employees in your department have been laid off recently due to budget reductions. You suspect that you, too, might someday lose your job, and your prospects for a new job in this field are slim. You have saved $50,000, but you know that amount won't last long without other income to supplement it. With the right real estate purchase, you believe your net equity could grow to $350,000 in 8 to 10 years. If you are laid off after that date, you could sell the property and carry the financing. At a 10 percent interest rate, you would have $35,000 in interest per year. With your company retirement and this interest, you could live comfortably in case you couldn't find other work.

  Your cash flow requirements from the plan would be:

  "Invest $50,000 into a four-unit building that will appreciate to yield $350,000 equity in 8 to

Bright Idea
Make it a habit to read and reread your investment plan When you look your goals daily you keep yourself tuned in to the future you want.

10 years. No cash flow is required during the plan. All cash flow proceeds are to be put back into the property to promote payoff of the financing."

How to generate cash flow

Cash flow is generated from a property in two ways:

1. **The net income from the property after paying all the expenses and loans.** This cash flow should increase yearly as you increase rents. By retirement, this cash flow can be significant, depending on the amount of financing you have left on the properties.

Timesaver
When it's time to sell, make sure to let your listing agent know that you are interested in carrying an installment note. This way, she will make sure to bring you buyers who desire this type of financing.

2. **The sale of the building and the carrying of your equity as a note against the property.** As a general rule, the cash flow at that time will be equal to the going rate of interest multiplied by the net equity of your property. The great thing about this is that you generally can get a larger percentage yield by carrying the financing than you could get in a typical savings account or certificate of deposit. Another advantage is that you postpone the capital gains taxes due when you carry the financing because the government considers this to be an installment sale.

Let's say you need $20,000 per year cash flow to supplement your retirement income. It normally is safe to plan on a 9 percent interest yield. To find out how much net equity you would need at retirement, you would use the following formula:

$$\frac{\text{Cash Flow Required}}{\text{Interest Yield}} = \text{Net Equity Needed}$$

Or:

$$\frac{\$20,000}{.09} = \$222,200$$

What this tells you is that you will need at least $222,200 net equity in order to generate the cash flow you need. By knowing this number, you will be able to create a target for your own investment plan.

Your future net worth

Your net worth projection is the amount of money you want to be worth at the end of a given period of time. As we have previously shown, net worth and cash flow are related. In cases where your investment plan is set up as a retirement vehicle, your net worth projections probably will be about 10 to 12 times your net annual cash flow requirements. This assumes that, at the time of retirement, you will be able to locate savings investments that offer yields of 8–10 percent per annum. This is a very reasonable assumption based on the available returns for the last 10 to 20 years.

One of the advantages previously discussed is the installment method of selling property. By acting as a banker and carrying a note when you eventually sell or trade up, you usually can earn a higher interest rate than the market is offering. What's more, you can postpone the payment of your capital gains taxes and can even earn interest on the tax money you are keeping. This is a great advantage, and you need to remember to factor this possibility into your calculation when setting your net worth goals.

If you decide against carrying paper and instead decide to take the profit and run, you will need to make an estimate of the capital gains taxes due when you sell. This is because settling up with Uncle Sam will dilute the net amount you have to invest when you retire. The calculation to determine your net equity for reinvestment looks like this:

Unofficially...
Under current IRS rules, you cannot sell a depreciable property to a relative and have an installment write-off.

Gross Equity at Sale
−Sale Costs
−Capital Gains Taxes
_____
Net Equity for Reinvestment

If you decide to use the installment method, you can eliminate the tax from the calculation. Capital gains tax rates have been known to change with the wind depending on who holds political office. You need to factor in a reasonable tax rate in the event you decide to sell at the end of the plan because it will have a significant impact on your net equity.

You might want to establish your net worth projections for reasons other than just cash flow requirements. For example, you might want to provide a college education for your children, you might want to purchase a business to run in your retirement, or you might just have the old American desire to be a millionaire. Regardless, if that is what you want, your goal might look like this:

"Attain a net worth of $1,000,000 at the end of 15 years."

Tax shelter benefits along the way

Tax shelter benefits in real estate investments are complicated and can vary widely. Therefore, we are going to devote the entire next chapter to this subject. For now, however, we will provide a few necessary guidelines and warnings for you to keep in mind. Here are some general tips:

- We do not recommend buying real estate for tax benefits only. The tax benefits have been diluted by the tax law changes in the late 1980s.

- It is important to consider the amount of depreciable improvements when making your final decision on a purchase. All things being equal, the property with the highest improvement ratio will give you the best return because of the higher write-off.

■ We recommend the use of the tax-deferred exchange and the installment sale.

A reasonable tax benefit goal would look like this:

"Maximize tax benefits on purchases and use tax-deferred exchange and installment sale when available."

Cash withdrawal from the plan

Cash withdrawal refers to any lump sum amounts of cash you take out of the plan. You have the opportunity to make provisions for these expenditures when you first make up your plan. As a matter of fact, building in perks for you is a great way to stay connected to your plan's ultimate success. You could make provisions for your children's education, a trip to Europe, a second home, or building a dream home on the lot you own.

Major withdrawals can occur either by selling or by refinancing. In some cases, money in your property accounts can adequately cover the withdrawals. Examples of these types of goals are:

■ "Withdraw $2,500 in year 2 to go on a fly-fishing vacation with my buddies."

■ "Generate $75,000 in year 5 to pay for an addition to the house."

■ "Withdraw $15,000 in years 7–10 for Adam's college fees."

Other goals

The last subsection is for any other goals you would like to accomplish with some of the earnings from your real estate investments. This section could involve family and friends in your investments or

Moneysaver
Tax-deferred exchanges are best made after you have had a few years of experience in real estate investing. Why? Because the experience with your own properties will improve your ability to judge potential winning trade opportunities.

Watch Out!
Exercise considerable care and thought in setting your goals; they form the cornerstones of your investment plan.

perhaps benefit a charity. Examples of these goals are:

- "Buy a four-unit apartment building that has a nice owner's unit for the folks to live in."

- "Donate the expected second trust deed from the sale in the 5th year to the college scholarship fund."

- "Buy new carpet for the pulpit at the synagogue."

Determining your general plan

As we already have seen, setting future net worth at a given interest rate also sets future cash flow. Therefore, we will concentrate most of our discussion of the general plan to achieving a given future net worth.

The first step in developing a general plan is knowing what you can logically expect to achieve. This depends on a few key criteria:

1. The capital you have available to invest

2. The length of time for which you will be invested

3. The amount of your own effort you can afford to contribute to the plan

In making these projections in real estate, we commonly use the compound interest algorithm. Relax, it's not so intimidating. The mathematical formula for this is:

$$FV = PV(1 + I)^N$$

We told you to relax! In language the math-challenged student can understand, this translates as follows:

- FV = Future value of the investment

- PV = Present value of the money invested (down payment)
- I = Average interest rate you earned on your investment
- N = Number of years the money is invested

This formula states in simple language that, if you invest an initial amount of money (PV) at a compounding rate of return (I) for a given number of years (N), your total investment will have a future value (FV) at the end of the period. If you invested $50,000 (PV) for 10 years (N) at 30 percent (I) compounded interest, for example, the value of your investment at the end of the period would be $689,292 (FV). The equation would look like this:

$$FV = \$50{,}000(1 + .30)^{10}$$

The following is a table of various combinations of the compound interest formula. It will quickly give you an idea of the kind of future equities you might expect at various times with differing investment amounts. The compound interest percentage on the following page might seem high and unattainable to you, especially if you are used to the 4–6 percent interest you receive from your bank, but this is where real estate rises head and shoulders over any other investment vehicle. Study the chart, do the math, and see for yourself how the money adds up.

It's important to remember that this is the average expected return on your investment, combining all four components of return: cash flow, equity growth from loan reduction, equity growth from appreciation, and tax benefits.

The underlined portion of the chart is an example of how to use the chart to make a projection for yourself. Down the left column (PV), locate the amount of the original investment of $50,000. Move over one column to the right to locate the number of years of the plan, (N), which in this case is 10. The next columns are the future values, (FV), based on the range of returns, (I), located at the top of the chart. For our example, we are projecting an average return of 30 percent, so the final value is $689,292. If you are starting with an amount that isn't on the chart, you can combine totals to estimate the return.

PRESENT VALUE/FUTURE VALUE TABLE

PRESENT VALUE	YEARS	I = 10%	I = 20%	I = 30%	I = 40%
$10,000.00	5	$16,105.00	$24,883.00	$37,129.00	$53,782.00
	10	$25,937.00	$61,917.00	$137,858.00	$289,255.00
	15	$41,772.00	$154,070.00	$511,858.00	$1,555,681.00
	20	$67,275.00	$383,376.00	$1,900,494.00	$8,366,822.00
$20,000.00	5	$32,210.00	$49.766.00	$74,259.00	$107,565.00
	10	$51,875.00	$123,835.00	$275,717.00	$578,509.00
	15	$83,545.00	$308,140.00	$1,023,717.00	$3,111,361.00
	20	$135,550.00	$766,752.00	$1,800,989.00	
$30,000.00	5	$48,315.00	$74,650.00	$111,388.00	$161,347.00
	10	$77,812.00	$185,752.00	$413,575.00	$867,764.00
	15	$125,317.00	$452,211.00	$1,535,576.00	$4,667.042.00
	20	$201,825.00	$1,150,128.00	$5,701,483.00	
$40,000.00	5	$64,420.00	$99,533.00	$148,517.00	$215,130.00
	10	$103,750.00	$247,669.00	$551,434.00	$1,157,018.00
	15	$167,090.00	$616,281.00	$1,047,434..00	$6,222,722.00
	20	$269,100.00	$1,533,504.00	$7,601,977.00	
$50,000.00	5	$80,526.00	$124,416.00	$185,646.00	$268,912.00
	10	$129,687.00	$309,587.00	$689,292.00	$1,446,273.00
	15	$208,862.00	$770,351.00	$2,559,293.00	$7,778,403.00
	20	$336,375.00	$1,916,880.00	$9,502,471.00	

Now let's look at how we use the table to determine what financial goals you can logically expect to meet. If you have $30,000 to invest and require a net worth of $1,500,000, there are two variables to work with to meet this goal:

1. The rate of return on the investment (I)

2. The number of years invested (N)

If you look at the chart, you will notice that you can meet this goal in 15 years at a 30 percent rate of return. You can do it in about 11 years at a 40 percent return. These percentage returns seem high, but surprisingly, they are not unrealistic.

Let's refresh your memory of the return from the example property at 1800 Mariposa Lane. The return components were:

Timesaver
Most business calculators have the compound interest algorithm, which you can use just in case you aren't carrying this book around with you for the rest of your life.

Cash Flow	$1,080
Equity Growth (Loan Reduction)	$300
Equity Growth (Appreciation)	$11,000
Tax Savings	$1,039
Total	$13,419

Therefore, our percentage return the first year was:

$$\frac{\$13,419}{\$30,000} = 44.7\%$$

Each year, your percentage rate of return will reduce from the previous year because your equity in the property will increase significantly faster than your total annual return. For this reason, you should use a percentage return of the compound interest column that is lower than the initial return you expect so as to offset this decrease. This compound interest number should be the rate you can expect as an average over several years of ownership.

Now that you have a handle on how to use the compound interest chart, let's return to determining a general plan and setting your future net worth goals. Most of us start with the primary constraint of a limited amount of capital to work with. Knowing the amount you plan to invest initially, we will combine the percentage return we can expect with the

number of years we are going to invest to estimate
our net worth. We are, of course, constrained by the
maximum rate of levered return (compound interest) we can achieve, but 20–30 percent should be a
comfortable rate for the average investor.

Using the formula, let's review a couple of the
cases we used earlier in this chapter when we were
discussing setting goals.

- **Case #1:** You have $30,000 to $40,000 to invest
  and have the goal of having $20,000 per year
  income in 10 years. This requires approximately
  $200,000 in equity invested at a 10 percent
  interest rate. Because this is your first investment, it would be wise to only invest $30,000
  and keep the other $10,000 for contingencies.
  You will see from the table that this goal
  requires a sustained rate of return of 20–25 percent, which is in our comfortable rate range.

- **Case #2:** You can borrow $10,000 to invest and
  want to have a total equity of $500,000 in 15
  years. Again, using the table, we can see that
  this requires a rate of return of 30 percent for
  the 15 years. This is at the top of our range, so
  our young and ambitious investor will need to
  devote the energy and sacrifice to attain this
  goal.

Now we are ready to pull all this work together
and set your general plan. There are three steps in
this process:

1. **First determine how much cash you have available to invest comfortably.** Always keep some
   cash in reserve. You can always invest some of
   your reserves later as your experience and confidence increases.

2. **Next set the feasibility of your future net worth.** You can convert this to a cash flow at retirement by assuming it can be invested at an 8–10 percent interest rate return.

3. **Set the number of years you want for the overall plan.** Using the table, move down the column on the far left (PV) to the amount nearest your available capital. Move across this row until you come to a value at least as large as your future net worth goal. The rate at the top of this column is the rate you will have to maintain to meet your general plan goal. Remember, you can combine two lines and add the totals to get a combination that equals your capital investment if it isn't on the chart.

Your general plan should look something like this:

"I am going to invest $_____ for _____years in real estate investments at a sustained rate of return of _____ percent and be worth $_____ at the end of the plan term."

Establishing a detailed plan

In establishing a detailed investment plan, we will use the $30,000 it took to buy 1800 Mariposa Lane as our capital, and that property will be the beginning investment of the plan. We will have the following general investment plan:

"We are going to invest $30,000 for 10 years in real estate investments at a sustained rate of return of 30 percent and be worth $350,000 at the end of the plan term."

It's now time to crunch the numbers and make our detailed plan. We (the authors) are fortunate to have a proprietary computerized system for building investment plans that makes this process much easier. For the benefit of those without access to a

Bright Idea
If time is not a particularly important factor in your plan, you would be well-advised to pick a conservative rate of return and extend the years of the plan accordingly.

computerized system, we will demonstrate how to do this manually. It necessitates eliminating some of the fine-tuning a computer is capable of doing, but it will give an adequate plan to measure your progress against. We have included a copy of a computerized investment plan of the four-unit at 1800 Mariposa Lane in Appendix D.

Bright Idea
Consider seeking out an investment real estate agent who has access to a computerized planning system. With a simple click of the mouse, any variable in the equation can be changed to suit your needs.

The next step in building your detailed plan is to establish the variables to be used in making the estimates for the future calculations of the plan. You will need the following:

- The appreciation rate

- Interest rates for first and second loans

- Loan-to-value ratios

- Income and expense increase rates

- Buy and sell costs

- Gross multipliers for various size properties

You will establish these variables after you have done your research and with the help of your investment real estate agent. Your agent's input will be helpful because the prior history of the market helps establish the future trends, and this will help you set the rates for the future years of the plan. Using these variables, you will be estimating the financial performance of the properties you will be acquiring in your detailed plan.

We will start the detailed plan with the specifics of 1800 Mariposa Lane and then use our estimated rates for the preceding factors for the balance of the plan. The heart of the detailed plan is the accompanying projection worksheet on the next page. The horizontal lines are the year-by-year estimates of the performance of the property we acquire. The vertical columns are the financial parameters of the plan. The most important columns are the last two columns—the return on equity (ROE) and average return on equity (AVG. ROE).

The return on equity is essentially the same concept as the return on investment. In the first year of ownership, the return on investment and the return on equity are the same because your equity is your investment. In the second and succeeding years, the equity is the initial investment plus the profit you made during the year. This is why we call your investment in subsequent years your "equity." Recall that in our example, our return on investment for the first year is:

Cash Flow	$1,080
Equity Growth (Loan Reduction)	$300
Equity Growth (Appreciation)	$11,000
Tax Benefits	+ $1,039
Total	$13,419

The percentage return on investment (ROI) is:

$$\frac{\$13,419}{\$30,000} = 44.7\%$$

To make the estimates for the second year of the plan, we will assume there are no changes in the cash flow, loan reduction, and tax savings. The appreciation will be adjusted because the property appreciated $11,000 during the first year of ownership, as we used an appreciation rate of 5 percent. Our investment, now called our "equity," is:

Original Investment	$30,000
First Year Profit	+ $13,419
Equity Second Year	$43,419

This calculation is repeated in successive years to find the equity.

The appreciation for the second year is calculated as follows:

TRANSACTIONAL POSITION

_____ YEAR

YEAR	MARKET VALUE $	TOTAL EQUITY $	INCOME __%INC	OPER'G EXP'S __%INC	TOTAL INTEREST $	AMORTI- ZATION __%DWN	CASH FLOW __%DWN	APPRE- CIATION __% M/V	TAX REBATE __%DWN	ROE %	AVG ROE %

Starting Value	$220,000
Appreciation	+ $11,000
Value Second Year	$231,000

Value Second Year	$231,000
Multiplied by Appreciation Rate	× .05
Second Year Appreciation	$11,550

The profit the second year is now:

Cash Flow	$1,080
Equity Growth (Loan Reduction)	$300
Equity Growth (Appreciation)	$11,550
Tax Benefits	+ $1,039
Total	$13,969

The percentage return on equity the second year is:

$$\frac{\$13,969}{\$43,419} = 32.1\%$$

The average return on equity (AROE) is:

44.7% + 32.1% ÷ 2 = 38.4%

The following worksheet shows the calculations through the third year. You'll see that in the third year the average return on equity (AROE) dropped below the target of 35 percent. No need to panic. It just means it's time to do something to increase the average return. You have two options. You can either refinance or do a tax-deferred exchange. We will do a tax-deferred exchange because it is the most common way for investors to reposition their equity.

Now is when the experience of your investment real estate agent will really help with your plan. This is because you will have to make an estimate of what property will sell for and how it will perform years into the future. If you are not fortunate enough to have an agent who tracks value appreciation trends,

Watch Out!
When doing a 1031 tax-deferred exchange, make sure the money from the sale of your property is placed in trust and not co-mingled with the funds of others. Also, if an individual holds your money, make certain that person is bonded and that you are protected with a letter of credit from a bank.

we suggest using "the world doesn't change that much" method of estimating probable future value.

Let's assume you can make almost the same purchase in the future as you can make today. We will eliminate the cash flow, equity growth, and tax benefits from our calculation as a way of evening up any errors and simplifying our estimate. In some locations, the cash flow and equity growth might be the most significant aspect of the return. In these areas, you will need to keep these elements of return as part of the planning process.

The next step is to estimate the costs of the transaction (selling and then trading via a 1031 exchange) and then build the model of our new property for the plan. Here's how: At the start of year four, 1800 Mariposa Lane is valued at $254,600, and you have $71,907 in equity. Remember that this assumes you have put aside all the cash flow and tax benefits from this investment. The costs of doing this trade will be the sale expenses on the existing property and the purchase costs on the new building.

To simplify this step, we will assume the selling expenses of the existing property to be 5 percent of the sales price, and we will round this off at $12,000 ($254,600 × 5% = $12,730). In addition, we will assume that we get the seller of our new property to pay our purchase costs. This technique usually can be accomplished in the negotiation process by adding the costs to your final offer. The benefit to you is that you get to finance these expenses in the price you pay for the building. The equity left for reinvestment now is:

Equity Start of Fourth Year	$71,907
Costs of Transaction	– $12,000
Equity for Reinvestment (Rounded)	$59,900

_____ YEAR

TRANSACTIONAL POSITION

YEAR	MARKET VALUE $	TOTAL EQUITY $	INCOME _%INC	OPER'G EXP'S _%INC	TOTAL INTEREST $	AMORTI-ZATION _%DWN	CASH FLOW _%DWN	APPRE-CIATION S_% MV	TAX REBATE _%DWN	ROE %	AVG ROE %
1	220,000	30,000	26,400	7,920	17,100	300	1,080	11,000	1,039	44.7	
2	231,000	43,419	26,400	7,920	17,100	300	1,080	11,500	1,039	32.1	38.4
3	242,500	57,388	26,400	7,920	17,100	300	1,080	12,100	1,039	25.3	34
4	254,600	71,900	TRADE UP EQUITY LESS $12,000 COSTS								

Bright Idea
When using a
manual system
for planning,
don't hesitate
to round off the
numbers to
make your cal-
culating easier.
This plan is just
an estimate of
where you are
going, and the
rounded-off dol-
lars will not
make a signifi-
cant difference
in the final
numbers.

For the next step in our plan, we will invest these proceeds in one or two new properties using a 1031 tax-deferred exchange. To calculate the correct size of the next property that will fit in with our plan, we need to use the following formula:

$$\frac{\text{Equity to Invest}}{\text{\% of Down Payment}} = \text{\% Value of New Property}$$

Using our available funds, the value of the next property value can be calculated by plugging in these numbers:

$$\frac{\$59,900}{.10} = \$599,000$$

So, as you can see, the next property you buy, to keep your plan alive, will cost $599,000.

The accompanying chart has the values added for the trade in year four (the trade we just worked together) and the trade that was needed in year seven. The trade was needed in year seven because the average return on equity (AROE) again fell into the low 30 percent range. Through trial and error, we determined that one more year of ownership would make the average less than the target 30 percent. Note that the further into the future your plan gets, the tougher it will become to estimate the smaller components of return. For that reason, when planning for future trades, you can eliminate any estimates for income, operating expenses, total interest, amortization, cash flow, and tax benefits.

Follow-up and goal review

Just as important (if not more important) as preparing your investment plan is managing the plan to its successful completion. This involves, among other

_____ YEAR

TRANSACTIONAL POSITION

YEAR	MARKET VALUE $	TOTAL EQUITY $	INCOME _%INC	OPER'G EXP'S _%INC	TOTAL INTEREST $	AMORTI-ZATION _%DWN	CASH FLOW _% DWN	APPRE-CIATION S_% MV	TAX REBATE _%DWN	ROE %	AVG ROE %
1	220,000	30,000	26,400	7,920	17,100	300	1,080	11,000	1,039	44.7	—
2	231,000	43,419	26,400	7,920	17,100	300	1,080	11,500	1,039	32.1	38.4
3	242,500	57,388	26,400	7,920	17,100	300	1,080	12,100	1,039	25.3	34
4	254,600	71,900	TRADE UP EQUITY LESS $12,000 COSTS								
4	590,000	59,900						29,500		49.2	—
5	619,500	81,400						30,975		34.6	41.9
6	650,475	117,400						32,500		27.6	37.1
7	682,975	149,100	TRADE UP EQUITY LESS $34,000 COSTS								
7	1,160,000	116,000						58,000		50.0	—
8	1,218,000	174,000						60,900		35.0	42.5
9	1,278,000	254,900						63,900		27.2	37.4
10	1,342,800	298,800						67,000		22.4	33.6
11	1,409,800	365,800								—	—

things, monitoring the progress of the plan to make sure you stay on plan at both the general and detailed levels.

Reviewing your general plan

The general review of your plan starts with your goals for your family and how they affect your investments. As things change in your personal life, you sometimes need to make alterations in your financial commitments. A job change might take away some of the time you had to dedicate to the properties. A bonus at work might now allow you to buy another property, which will get you to your goal sooner or will raise the amount of your final net worth. The market might change, which will affect what you buy or sell.

Reviewing your detailed plan

This book started out by recommending that you gain knowledge about the market and property. The secret of a successful plan is to never stop that education process. Monitoring your plan at a detailed level requires that you stay in touch with the market. It is easy to get involved in the day-to-day operation of your property and forget to look at what is happening around you. In the review section of your planning binder, you should keep a blank copy of the projection worksheet previously shown in this chapter. At the end of each year, make it a point to meet with your investment real estate agent and do an estimate of value based on the current market conditions. Discuss how the market is doing and where it looks like it is going in the next 12 months. Use the new value and the actual performance figures from the year's operation of your property to complete the next line of your worksheet.

Now compare what really happened in that year with the plan you laid out 12 months earlier. How did you do? If there are any significant changes—good or bad—go back, revise your plan, and get ready for next year. This will force you to stay involved in reaching your final goals. There is no doubt that many changes will occur over the life of a 10–15 year plan. Some changes will be positive; some will be negative. The secret is to take full advantage of the positives and take the necessary steps to minimize the negatives. This requires staying informed by monitoring what is really happening.

Just the facts

- A written plan with stated goals is critical to successful investing.

- An installment sale is a great method to help you achieve a desired net worth.

- The compound interest formula demonstrates how your equity will rapidly multiply in real estate.

- Your detailed plan will give you a year-by-year projection of where you are headed.

- It's advisable to revise your plan as necessary along the way.

GET THE SCOOP ON...
The tax laws and how they affect you as an
investor ▪ The two types of expenses and the
tax deductions you can take on them ▪ How the
depreciation allowance works ▪ Capital gains
tax and how to calculate it accurately ▪ The
three types of IRS 1031 tax-deferred exchanges
▪ Installment sales and refinancing options

Planning for the Tax Man

A s the cost of government increases, the burden of individual taxation increases proportionately. Built into the framework of federal, state, and some local tax laws, however, are certain techniques whereby investors can legally defer their taxes due for an indefinite period of time. To take advantage of these techniques, you need to have an understanding of certain taxation rules.

There is no beating around the bush; these rules can be complicated. To that end, we suggest you seek the advice of your accountant, tax attorney, or other tax expert from the outset. You do need to have a basic understanding yourself, however, because it is not practical to have professionals review every transaction under consideration.

There are two broad areas in which knowledge of taxation is important. The first is during the ownership and management of the property.

Chapter 10

The second is upon the sale of the property. This chapter will examine both of these areas in great detail, making them easy to understand and almost enjoyable.

Deductions, deductions, and more deductions

As a real estate investor, a number of tax benefits are now yours for the asking. They are:

1. The deductibility of your purchase costs
2. The deductibility of your operating expenses
3. The corresponding annual depreciation allowance that Uncle Sam provides

Purchase costs

As a general rule, most of the costs incurred at the time of your purchase are tax deductible in the year of the purchase. The following list covers some of the most common:

- Prepaid interest on the loan
- Fire and liability insurance
- Property tax prorations
- Escrow fees
- Title insurance costs
- Miscellaneous fees from the lender and escrow company

You'll notice that loan fees and points are not in the preceding list. The rule is that any money paid to secure a new loan for income property must be written off over the period of the loan. As an example, if the loan for our example property at 1800 Mariposa Lane required a loan fee of 1.5 percent and the loan was a 30-year loan, the yearly deduction would be calculated as follows:

Loan Amount	$190,000
Loan Fee Rate	×.015
Fee (Points)	$2,850

To calculate how much of a deduction you could take, you then would divide the loan fee by the term:

$$\frac{Loan\ Fee\quad \$2,850}{30\ year\ term} = \$95\ per\ year$$

In the past, points could be written off in the year of purchase, but after years of abuse, this loophole was closed.

Operating expenses

In addition to the purchase costs, all the expenses you incur in the operation of the property also are deductible. The biggest problem in determining deductibility is distinguishing between expense items and capital items. As a general rule, if you incurred the expense by fixing a problem in your building or merely by maintaining the value of the property, it should be considered an expense item. These normal operating expenses are deductible in the year you spend the money. Examples of these include:

- Utilities

- Interest on loans

- Insurance

- Taxes

- Gardening and cleaning expenses

- License and city fees

- Roofing, plumbing, electrical and miscellaneous repairs

- Management fees

Watch Out!
Be sure to check with your tax expert each year to see if there have been any changes in the tax laws. It would be a shame to miss out on opportunities for write-offs because you were uninformed.

- Advertising and rental commissions
- Mileage, postage, and phone expenses associated with the operation of the property
- Any other noncapital expenses

On the other hand, if the improvement increases the value or completely replaces a component of the property, it should be considered a capital expenditure. With capital expenses, the cost needs to be depreciated rather than expensed in the year the money is spent. The tax code says that capital items must be written off over the period of time they contribute to the usefulness of the property. Capital expenses include:

- Carpeting
- Drapes or window coverings
- New roof, plumbing, or electrical systems
- Building additions
- Major appliances or furnishings
- Major repairs—a new driveway, replacing stucco or siding, replacing landscaping, and so on

Timesaver
You don't need to worry about calculating this amount. Your lender will send you a statement at the end of each year showing you how much of your payments went towards principal and how much went toward interest.

It is important to note that the principal paid each month on your loan payment is not a deductible expense. It actually is one of those returns on your investment that you must pay tax on, but you never see the money because you have to give it to the bank to pay down your loan. If you have a positive-cash-flow property, you are paying off your loan with the income you are receiving from the tenants. The rule says that you cannot deduct the portion of your payment that goes towards paying off the loan.

The depreciation allowance

As the owner of your own real estate business, you now are able to deduct a certain amount of expenses for the loss of value on the improvements (improvements = the structures on the land) of your property—things such as wear and tear from aging. Remember that, because land does not depreciate (it appreciates), this depreciation expense is only for the physical structure of the building and other improvements, not the land.

The most important point to remember is that the depreciation schedule you originally calculate will be with you as long as you own that property. If you sell the property and pay your taxes, you can start fresh with the next property. If you trade via a 1031 exchange, however, that basis and its schedule stays with you.

As you learned in Chapter 3, "Elements of Return," the most important component of the depreciation schedule is the land-to-improvement ratio. (See the section "Inflationary appreciation" in Chapter 3.) For any improved property, part of the value is for the land and part is for the improvements. Because you can't depreciate the land, a property that has a high ratio of improvements has a high depreciation deduction. To set your ratio, you must make sure to use an accepted method. If you don't, the IRS might disallow your schedule, force you to set a new one, and probably end up sending you a bill for additional taxes and penalties.

Limitations on deductions

To calculate the tax benefits from a property, you need to understand the rule changes adopted from the Tax Reform Act of 1986 (TRA '86). These new rules affected the amount of depreciation property owners can take per year, and they also defined investors into different classes depending on the amount of their involvement in their properties.

Moneysaver
Keep detailed records of each expense related to your property. This way, you will be able to take advantage of every single deduction to which you are legally entitled. We would rather see you keep your money than give it to Uncle Sam.

The new tax code recognizes two classes of investors: passive investors and active investors.

Passive investors

Generally, you are a passive investor if you buy property as a limited partner or with a group of more than 10 partners. As a passive investor, you can use the depreciation deduction to shelter any profit from the property. Any excess write-offs must be carried forward to be used as the profit from the building increases. It's like having a savings account of tax benefits that can be drawn upon to cover future profits.

Active investors

You probably are an active investor if you purchased your property alone or with a couple of partners and are active in the management of the building. The IRS calls this "materially participating" in the management. This means that you have a say in how it runs, how the bills are paid, and how much you are charging for rent. You might not actually run the property if you have hired a company to do this, but the key is that you have the ultimate responsibility for it. There are two classes of active investors:

1. Those who consider real estate investing and management as their primary career
2. Those who invest in real estate as a secondary career

Rules for active and passive investors

If you are "in the business" of real estate and it is your primary career, you have no restrictions whatsoever on the dollar amount of losses you can claim against earnings.

Most people, however, fall into the category in which real estate is a secondary career. If this

Bright Idea
If your spouse does not work outside the home, he or she can help you qualify for unlimited deductions by obtaining a real estate license and handling the management of your properties. This may qualify your spouse as a full-time property investor.

describes you, your real estate losses are limited to $25,000. If your adjusted gross income before real estate deductions is $50,000, for example, and your losses from property are $30,000, you can only deduct $25,000 of the $30,000. You don't lose the remaining $5,000. Instead, it goes into that tax shelter bank account previously mentioned. What this deduction means is that, instead of paying tax on $50,000 of income, you only pay tax on $25,000. The tax you save is profit and therefore is included in the overall return from your investment.

The earnings limitation

A second code change from the Tax Reform Act of 1986 limits your ability to use the losses from your real estate against the earnings from your regular career. This limit occurs when your earnings exceed $100,000. For every $2 you earn over $100,000, you lose $1 of deduction. This means that, at $150,000, you have no deduction against your income. Remember that these are not lost; they're just saved up for future use.

Calculating capital gain

Capital gains taxes are taxes on the profits you make when you sell your property. To understand capital gains and how to calculate them, you first need to be familiar with some new terms:

- **Sale Price**: The price for which you sell the property
- **Adjusted Sale Price**: The net price after deducting sale costs
- **Cost Basis**: The original purchase price plus capital expenses

■ **Adjusted Cost Basis**: The cost base minus depreciation

To estimate your capital gain, you would complete the following calculation:

$$
\begin{array}{r}
\text{Sale Price} \\
-\text{ Sale Costs} \\
\hline
\text{Adjusted Sale Price}
\end{array}
$$

$$
\begin{array}{r}
\text{Cost Base} \\
+\text{ Capital Expenses} \\
-\text{ Depreciation} \\
\hline
\text{Adjusted Cost Base}
\end{array}
$$

$$
\begin{array}{r}
\text{Adjusted Sale Price} \\
-\text{ Adjusted Cost Base} \\
\hline
\text{Capital Gain}
\end{array}
$$

To illustrate this formula, let's use the Mariposa property that we bought for \$220,000. We've depreciated the property for five years at \$5,090 per year for a total depreciation of \$25,450 (\$5,090 × 5 = \$25,450). We also just put on a new roof for \$5,000 (a capital expense). We can sell it for \$320,000, and our total expense to sell will be \$20,000.

Knowing this information, we can calculate the capital gain as follows:

Sale Price	\$320,000
Sale Costs	−\$20,000
Adjusted Sale Price	\$300,000
Cost Base	\$220,000
Capital Expenses	+ \$5,000
Depreciation	−\$25,450
Adjusted Cost Base	\$199,550
Adjusted Sale Price	\$300,000
Adjusted Cost Base	−\$199,550
Capital Gain	\$100,450

As you can see, the capital gain of $100,450 is a sizable chunk of money to have to pay tax on. Instead of giving it to Uncle Sam, let's learn about some methods of deferring or reducing these taxes.

The beauty of the 1031 Exchange

As far as saving on taxes is concerned, the IRS 1031 tax-deferred exchange is probably the single most important technique available to the real estate investor. An exchange enables you to pyramid your equity while deferring the payment of taxes. In effect, Uncle Sam becomes your partner by letting you use the taxes you owe on your capital gains as a down payment on the buildings you trade into. When you trade into larger properties, the government figures that, in turn, you will make more profit. By making more profit, you eventually will owe more tax. It's a win-win situation.

You must be aware of the three rules to qualify for a tax-deferred exchange:

1. You need to trade for like-kind property. Like-kind property in this instance would be a property you are purchasing for investment purposes. You can't trade a duplex you've been renting out for a new dream house. This is because the duplex is income producing property and the dream house would be a primary residence. You can, however, trade the duplex for an office building or a strip mall. The idea is to trade income producing property for other income producing property.

2. The property should be of equal or greater value than the existing property, hence the phrase "trading up."

Unofficially...
The capital gains tax rate is a political and economic "football." Politicians advocate raising or lowering it to get votes. The government in general uses the raising and lowering of the rate as a way to speed up or slow down the economy.

Unofficially...
In an exchange, "boot" is the term used to describe something of value given in addition to the like-kind property, as in "this acre and cash to boot."

3. You should not receive cash, mortgage relief, or "boot" of any kind in the transaction.

Three categories of exchanges

Most 1031 tax-deferred exchanges fall into one of three categories:

1. The straight exchange
2. The three-party exchange
3. The delayed exchange

The straight exchange

The straight exchange occurs when two parties get together and simply trade properties. At the end of the transaction, each party goes his separate way. This scenario doesn't happen very often because most investment property owners either trade up or just get out altogether. By trading straight across the board, one party probably ends up with a lesser property, which fails to meet the requirement of trading into a property of equal or greater value.

The three-party exchange

The most common type of tax-deferred exchange is the three-party exchange. As its name suggests, three different parties are involved in the process. One of the key elements of doing a tax-deferred exchange is that the party trading up never receives the equity in the property being traded. For that reason, the party cannot just sell the property, collect the proceeds, and go out and buy a larger property. Because most people with bigger properties don't want to trade into anything smaller, these three-party exchanges have evolved so that each party can get what it wants and stay within the framework of the law. Here's an example of how one might work:

Facts:

- Party A owns a four-unit building and wants to trade into an eight-unit building.

- Party B owns an eight-unit building and wants to sell, pay the taxes due, and retire to Florida.

- Party C is just getting started investing and wants to buy the four-unit building of Party A.

    Solution: Parties A and B enter into an exchange escrow in which Party A gets the eight-unit and Party B gets title to the four-unit. In a separate escrow, Party B agrees to accommodate the exchange and deed the four-unit building to Party C immediately

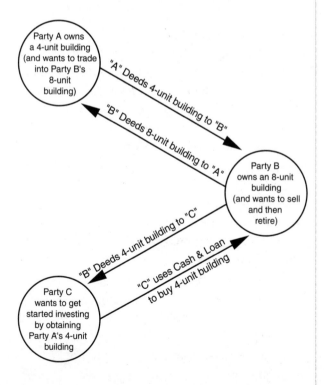

after he acquires title from Party A. Both of these escrows contain contingencies stating that they must close concurrently. This means that, if Party C can't buy the four-unit for some reason, Party B will not have to take Party A's four-unit in trade for his eight-unit.

Result: At the close, Party C owns the four-unit he wanted, Party A owns the eight-unit he wanted, and Party B is sipping margaritas at his beach house in Florida.

Recap: In case you're wondering, Party B doesn't pay any tax by taking the title to the four-unit because it is sold for the same price at which it was taken in trade. This is what is called a non-taxable event.

The delayed exchange

The final category of exchange is the delayed or Starker exchange. Starker refers to one of the principles in *T. J. Starker v. U.S.*, a case in the Ninth Circuit Court of Appeals. In this case, Starker exchanged some timber acreage for 11 different parcels of property owned by Crown Zellerbach. As was agreed between the parties, Starker selected the properties and they were transferred to him by way of the exchange. This was called a delayed exchange because the transfer spanned more than two years.

Because of the two-year delay, the IRS questioned whether this was an exchange at all and took Starker to court. Fortunately, for all investors, the Ninth Circuit Court approved of the process, and this has since been codified nationally for use by all U.S. investors. The Starker court held that:

1. A simultaneous transfer of title was not required.

2. IRS Section 1031 should be broadly interpreted and applied. Treasury regulations under IRC 1001 to the contrary were deemed invalid.

In an effort to update the rules concerning exchanges in light of the new rulings, a number of additional changes were made to IRC 1031. These changes included:

1. Partnership interests are no longer of "like kind" for exchange purposes.

2. The exchange property the taxpayer desires to receive must be identified within 45 days after the date upon which the taxpayer transfers his property in the exchange.

3. The taxpayer must receive the identified property within the earlier of 180 days after the date he transfers his property in the exchange or the due date of his tax return for the year of the exchange including extensions.

To accomplish a delayed exchange, an accommodator is used. An accommodator is an unrelated party (or entity) that holds the exchange proceeds. The accommodator can even take the title to the property you trade into in order to complete the exchange.

In choosing an accommodator, make sure you check their credentials, business history, and insurance coverage. Remember that the accommodator will be getting all your funds from the sale of your property. He or she holds it for you until it's time to purchase the replacement property. Be sure to choose your accommodator wisely. Over the years, some have been known to close up shop, pack their bags, and get the heck out of Dodge—taking the trust funds with them.

Watch Out!
Before you do a 1031 delayed exchange, you should be very sure of your next purchase. If you miss the 45-day or 180-day deadlines imposed by the IRS, you will have to pay the capital gains tax on the sale.

Watch Out!
None of these
tax-deferral
methods get you
out of paying
your taxes.
Instead, these
techniques
simply help you
put the taxes off
until sometime
in the future.

There are some additional complicated rules associated with a delayed exchange. Therefore you should make it a point to consult with your tax advisor before making any decisions in this regard.

Exchanging vs. paying your taxes and buying another

An additional problem created when you do a tax-deferred exchange is that you limit the depreciation deduction on your new property. Part of the exchange process is that you carry forward your profit and your basis from the traded property. Whatever the depreciation schedule was on the old property now becomes the schedule for that part of the new property.

We'll illustrate this using our example property. Assume that 1800 Mariposa Lane can be sold for an adjusted sale price of $300,000. We will net $80,000 from our sale, and we'll use that $80,000 as a 15-percent down payment (with a seller carrying another 10 percent) on a new property worth $550,000. This new property has a land-to-improvement ratio of 80 percent. The depreciation deduction we will be carrying forward is $5,090 per year. This means that, if we started fresh, the depreciation deduction on the new property would be:

Price of The Property	$550,000
Percentage of Improvements	× .80
Depreciable Improvements	$440,000

In order to find the depreciation deduction, you do the following calculation:

$$\frac{\text{Depreciable Improvements} \quad \$440,000}{\text{Useful Life} \quad 27.5 \text{ Years}} = \begin{array}{l} \$16,000 \\ \text{Depreciation} \\ \text{Deduction} \end{array}$$

Now let's see what the deduction will be if we trade up via an exchange. Because we carry the depreciation schedule with us from the old property, we are only allowed to calculate a new schedule on a portion of the new price. Therefore, the portion of the new value we can depreciate on a new schedule is:

Purchase Price	$550,000
Value Transferred In	−$300,000
New Cost Base	$250,000

New Cost Base	$250,000
Percentage Of Improvements	× .80
Depreciable Improvements	$200,000

$$\frac{\text{Depreciable Improvements} \quad \$200,000}{\text{Useful Life 27.5 Years}} = \begin{array}{l}\$7,272 \\ \text{Depreciation} \\ \text{Deduction}\end{array}$$

To find the total deduction, you add the old and the new schedules as follows:

Prior Deduction	$5,090
New Deduction	+ $7,272
Total Deduction	$12,362

As you can see, trading up represents a $3,638 decrease in the annual depreciation ($16,000 − $12,362 = $3,638). Remember, it is important to review the impact of a proposed trade on your annual depreciation because this new schedule will be with you for the life of your holding period for the new property.

One last problem that should not be overlooked is related to your goals from your investment plan. Although the use of the exchange allows you to pyramid equities, it also pyramids the tax liability on a future sale. If you have plans of cashing out at the end of your plan, paying your taxes, and then retiring, this could leave you with a very large tax bill. If this is your goal, you might consider paying your taxes as you go along or consider the next alternative, the installment sale.

The installment sale

The installment sale is another significant technique for deferring payment of capital gains taxes. In an installment sale, sellers elect not only to sell property but to put up some or all of the financing needed to make the deal work. Because the property is being sold now but is being paid for later, such deals are called installment sales. As far as taxes are concerned, it differs from the 1031 exchange in that you actually sell the property without getting a new one in return, but you still delay paying some or most of your capital gains taxes due. Here's how:

With an installment sale, instead of taking all the cash and walking, you become one of the lenders on the property. You find a qualified buyer, he takes over your existing loan, and you carry a note (and your profit from the sale long-term), all the while receiving interest-only payments. The idea is to keep earning a high interest on the taxes due for many years and put off paying the capital gains until the contract is complete. The wonderful thing about an installment sale is that you don't owe Uncle Sam a penny until you actually receive the profit from the sale. If you structure it correctly, that could be years down the road.

The rules for qualifying for an installment sale were significantly modified by the Installment Sales Revision Act of 1980. In the past, there were rules regarding the amount of the down payment and the number of years needed to qualify. These rules no longer exist. The advantage of an installment sale now is that you are only required to pay capital gains tax on the amount of the profit you receive in one year. You pay the balance of the tax due as you collect the profit in subsequent years.

Because an installment sale can be relatively complex, we need to simplify our example. Let's assume you are selling 1800 Mariposa Lane and need to decide how to handle the tax on the $100,450 capital gain we calculated earlier. We'll estimate the tax rate at 28 percent. To find your after-tax net equity, use the following formula:

Capital Gain	$100,450
Tax Rate	× .28
Tax Due	$28,126

Capital Gain	$100,450
Less Tax	−$28,126
Remaining Profit	$72,324

As you can see, your profit is $72,324. If you have no plans to spend the money and you want to invest it in a passive, cash-flow-generating vehicle, the installment sale is for you. The only tax due will be on the amount of cash you take as a down payment.

Let's assume you take a 10 percent down payment on the $320,000 sale of 1800 Mariposa lane; this would be $32,000. You then carry the rest of the profit as a note due on an installment contract. See how this affects the net cash profit:

Down Payment	$32,000
Tax Rate	× .28
Tax Due	$8,960

Down Payment	$32,000
Less Tax	−$8,960
Net Cash Profit	$23,040

Capital Gain	$100,450
Less Down	−$32,000
Installment Note	$68,450

In this example, we have a net cash profit of $23,040 and an installment note on the property of $68,450.

The real advantage of the installment sale comes from what you can earn from the installment note versus what you can earn by putting your net cash in another investment vehicle. Let's say that, by putting your cash into a certificate of deposit or a savings account, you could earn 6 percent on your money. Conversely, by carrying the financing on Mariposa, you could earn 9 percent on your money. The contrast would look like this:

Outright Sale:

Cash Out Profit	$72,324
Interest Rate	× .06
Profit	$4,339
Per Month	$362

Installment Sale:

Installment Note	$68,450
Interest Rate	× .09
Profit	$6,160
Per Month	$513
Net Down Payment	$23,040
Interest Rate	× .06
Profit	$1,382
Per Month	$115
Installment Total	$7,542
Per Month	$628

As you can see, the difference of $628 per month by carrying an installment note versus $362 per month at 6% interest is quite dramatic. There are two main reasons for the difference:

1. You usually can get a significantly higher interest return on your money by carrying financing

versus putting it in a bank or a comparable investment.

2. You are earning interest on the capital gains you have yet to pay the IRS.

You can increase this profit even more by varying the amount of down payment you accept. In theory, because you are the banker on your loan, you could agree to no down payment at all. By doing this, you would not have to pay any tax, and all the down payment money could earn the same 9 percent interest you were earning on the rest of the note.

Refinancing your loan

There is one more technique to avoid paying the taxes due on some of the profit from your real estate. This technique is to secure new financing to pay off the existing loan, netting additional cash at the closing because of the increased value of the property. Let's use our example to illustrate.

Time has passed and the Mariposa property is now worth $320,000 with an existing loan balance of $185,000. Our current lender tells us that it will make a new loan of 80 percent of the appraised value, and the fees will be about $3,000. This new loan will generate the following cash for us:

Appraised Value	$320,000
Loan Amount	× .80
New Loan	$256,000
Loan Amount	$256,000
Loan Fees	−$3,000
Payoff On Existing	−$185,000
Cash Generated	$68,000

As you an see, you now have extracted $68,000 of equity to spend any way you want without selling

Bright Idea
An alternative to down payment money is to require additional security on your loan by securing it with not only your property but another property of the buyer that has significant equity. In this instance, the buyer gets a property with no down payment, and your note is secured by two properties, not just one.

your property. If we are still in the equity-building years of our plan, we probably will use that money to acquire an additional property.

One of the great advantages of getting at some of the profit by using this method is that there is no tax due on the money. Because we borrowed the money from the bank, we are obligated to pay it back; therefore, no tax is owed. What's more, we also can write off the interest as a deduction on the property you refinanced.

If you've done your job managing the property, the increased rents should more than cover the increased mortgage payments on the refinance. As you can see by comparing the net cash from an outright sale ($72,324) versus the cash you can generate by refinancing ($68,000), the bottom-line numbers are pretty comparable. The advantage of refinancing is that you will still be receiving rents, will still be building equity, and can still be taking advantage of tax benefits.

Refinancing, however, can create a future tax problem you should know about. The IRS doesn't make you pay tax on borrowed money because you have to pay the loan back. What if you were to take most of your profit out on a loan, however, and then sell the property and let someone else take over the loan? This is a situation in which you are taxed on the "boot" you receive. Remember that boot is something you receive in addition—something extra in a real estate transaction.

To illustrate the problem, let's assume we held 1800 Mariposa Lane for five years and took the depreciation deduction of $5,090 each year. Our adjusted cost base would be:

Purchase Price	$220,000
Less Depreciation	−$25,450
Adjusted Cost Base	$194,550

When the buyer assumes the new loan, we are relieved of the obligation to pay the $256,000 loan back; however, it creates the following mortgage relief obligation:

Loan Amount	$256,000
Less Adjusted Cost Base	−$194,550
Mortgage Relief	$61,450

Remember, as long as you keep this property, there is no tax to pay. Once you sell, however, you have to pay tax on the boot.

A tax lesson summary

The information in this chapter is designed to give a basic understanding of real estate taxation and some deferral methods. The goal is to make you aware of the complexity of this area so you will seek the advice of professionals before you make (what could be) a costly mistake. To cover all your bases, we recommend a three-stage process when contemplating a move with one of your properties:

1. Schedule a general review meeting with your tax consultant before you list your property for sale. Review your goals, discuss all the alternatives, and get a general idea of your position.

2. When listing the property, make clear to your real estate agent and in the listing contract that any transaction must be reviewed and approved by your tax consultant.

3. When negotiating a potential sale or exchange, include a contingency that gives you

Moneysaver
Before you select a tax-deference method, you should consult an expert so you can pick the method that best suits your long-term financial goals. Because of the current liberal tax treatment of capital gains, it is not always advisable to postpone paying the tax as the rates might someday increase.

the right to have the final purchase agreement
reviewed and approved by your tax consultant.

Just the facts

- As an owner of improved real estate, you can
  deduct most of the purchase costs and operating expenses from your taxes.

- The depreciation deduction allows you to take
  a deduction for the wear and tear from aging
  on your property.

- Several great techniques are available from the
  IRS that allow you to delay paying your capital
  gains tax.

- The 1031 tax-deferred exchange lets investors
  trade into new properties and postpone paying
  any capital gains tax.

- An installment sale can defer taxes due and
  also can bring in significant cash flow for years
  after the sale of a property.

- A smart way to extract cash from your property
  is to refinance your loan.

Putting Your Money
on the Line

PART V

GET THE SCOOP ON...
The difference between a buyer's agent and a
seller's agent ▪ Where to find the perfect agent
for you ▪ The keys to narrowing down your
search for property ▪ How to determine the
seller's motivation and why it is critical to your
success ▪ Three good methods of writing offers

Purchasing Your Investment

Chapter 11

Y ou have come a long way in your education.
Among other things, you have learned why
real estate is the best choice for your investment dollar. You also know how to appraise property, finance your deal, create an investment plan,
and make Uncle Sam a partner in your business. It
is now time to put all the pieces of this puzzle
together and buy yourself a piece of property.

For many investors, this is when emotions take
over. They find (what they perceive to be) an incredible piece of property, and they just have to own it.
Their investment plan and goals are now the fur-
thest things from their minds. But be careful, this
kind of thinking is a dangerous trap to fall into. If
your emotions dictate your investment choices, they
might keep you from acquiring the very property
you need to get the best start.

One of the best ways to stay focused during this
process is to think of this as a mere shopping trip

rather than the important financial commitment it really is. Remember the times you set out to buy that new car or living room set? You made the decision to buy long before you left the house. In fact, the trip to the store was only a formality to find the best value for the item you already had decided to purchase. The same holds true here. You already have decided to invest in real estate. You have read books, taken notes, and analyzed properties until you are blue in the face. Now you only need to find the right fit for your plan.

Real estate agent: friend or foe?

Throughout this process, one of the key players in the hunt will be your real estate agent. In the beginning, his job will be to sift through all the properties on the market to find the ones that best suit your goals. Once you have found a property, he then will become the primary negotiator in communicating the terms of your offer to the seller. Finally, your agent will be there to guide you every step of the rest of the way, from the moment you first sign an offer to the day you close on the deal.

There is no rule in real estate that says you have to use an agent to buy property. Many excellent investments have been bought without ever having a real estate agent enter the picture. Many times, buyers and sellers do a great job of finding each other and negotiating deals themselves. The problem is that the vast majority of properties available are under contract to be sold through real estate companies. The fact is, unless you have access to properties that no one else knows about, you are going to have to work through an agent whether you want to or not.

Buyer's agent vs. seller's agent

When an owner decides to sell his property, he usually hires an agent to give him an opinion as to value. This agent is called the listing agent or seller's agent. Once they agree to work together, the seller and the agent sign a listing agreement. This agreement outlines the price and terms at which a seller is willing to sell. It confirms all the vital statistics about the property including the mix of the units, the size of the property, the income it generates, the year it was built, and so on. It also serves as an employment contract between the seller and the agent. Most listings are then put on a multiple listing service (MLS), to which all the other agents looking for property have access.

In more than 50 percent of the cases, a second agent will get the information from the MLS and will tap into his resources of willing buyers. This second agent is called the buyer's agent. He then gets an offer and presents it to the seller through the listing agent. Counter-offers usually are exchanged until the parties come to a meeting of the minds. At that time, a deal is consummated.

For many years, it was not uncommon for the same agent to handle both sides of a transaction (and this is still legal and common in most states). That is, the agent who obtained the listing also brought in a buyer to buy it. This created a "dual-agency" relationship. In theory, a dual agency might work just fine, but in most business situations, it is tough work to look out for the interests of both parties in a transaction. When was the last time you saw an attorney effectively represent both sides in a legal dispute? It's a conflict of interest.

Unofficially...
The MLS is a real estate agent's most powerful tool. It is an online computerized service that provides up-to-the-minute information about available properties. Only a few years ago, the MLS was an antiquated service. It was published in hard copy and, in some places, was updated only once a month. As you can see, the Internet has changed real estate, too.

Unofficially...
To clarify who
represents or
doesn't represent
whom, real
estate profes-
sionals in more
than 40 states
are required to
disclose their
roles to
the buyers
and sellers.

Finding the right agent for you

The following are the best ways to locate potential agents to represent you:

- Signs and advertisements for property
- Property management companies
- Escrow and title companies
- Referrals from other income property owners

Signs and advertisements for property

Once you start looking for property, you'll find that ads and "For Sale" signs on small apartment buildings will begin to jump out at you. Most will give you an idea about pricing, and they all will tell you which agents are dealing in income property. Keep notes about which agent's ads and signs you see most often.

Property management companies

Get to know the property management companies in your area because you might need to hire one someday. In the interview process, ask for references of agents who handle income property.

Escrow and title companies

Escrow and title companies have the most contact with agents in your area. Most should be willing to give you some recommendations for good agents who are easy to work with.

Other income property owners

Other owners are a great resource. When you are getting to know your market, you will be visiting a lot of properties. In many cases, you will be talking to the property owner rather than the manager. Ask them if they can recommend an agent or company that could help you.

Once you've compiled your list of names and numbers, start making phone calls. These calls will be like phoning someone before a blind date. You don't know him and he doesn't know you, but you might have something to offer each other. Your goal should be to see whether you can develop rapport over the phone.

You might not find the right agent for you on the first interview, so keep looking. At this point, you are searching for a licensed agent with whom you have some rapport and who is willing to give you his time. The following is a list of characteristics you should look for in an agent:

- You feel you have a rapport with the agent.

- The agent has time to work with you.

- The agent has access to the MLS.

- He has knowledge of the market area in which you are interested.

- The agent is willing to teach you about the market.

- The agent deals in investment property and not home sales.

- The agent understands your goals in investing.

- The agent owns or manages rental property.

- The agent has made investment property sales or has listing experience.

If you start looking for an agent when you first begin researching your market, you will have the best chance of finding someone with whom you feel comfortable. The bottom line is that you want an agent to be able to get you the property you decide to buy. That is the agent's job. If you can find (or train) an investment expert along the way, all the more power to you.

Bright Idea
Once you have compiled your list of potential agents, be sure to check them out with the Better Business Bureau, the local real estate board, and even your state licensing bureau.

Don't steal their commission

Most professionals (doctors, lawyers, and so on) get paid a lot of money per job or per hour. Real estate is different. Real .estate agents earn a commission based on a percentage of the price of the property they are selling, regardless of the amount of work they put into the deal. Easy deals combine with tough ones, and transactions that never work combine with some that do. These all even out and result in a commission for the agent now and then.

Many times, near the end of negotiations, the principal parties find themselves only a few dollars apart on price. Invariably, they start looking to the agent(s) and what they see as their "big commission" as the perfect source to make up the difference. This might be tempting for the seller, but if you're smart, it won't work for you. Remember that your agent is the person who is going to help make you your fortune. If you have been lucky enough to have found a good agent, you will need him to help you buy and sell many properties over the years. Don't alienate him by dipping into his paycheck to make one deal work. In the end, your agent will save you—and make you—a lot of money, especially if you respect his way of earning a living.

Make a list and check it twice

At this point, you have learned enough about the market, have developed a workable investment plan, and have found an agent with whom you feel comfortable working and who understands what you are trying to accomplish. It is now time to narrow down the field of available properties and buy the one that best suits your needs.

You probably will have a list of several properties you are considering. You need to rank your list and

Moneysaver
If you are buying a lot of property and don't like paying commissions, consider obtaining a real estate salesman's license. You then can find and negotiate your own deals and can keep the commission for yourself.

determine which property will be the one you make a run at. You should have made some estimates of return by now based on the financial picture of each property and how the market looks to you and your agent.

Again, make sure you do an apples-to-apples comparison when comparing properties. In other words, don't make the property you personally like most look the best by using a lower expense ratio compared to the other properties. Yes, maybe one is more pleasing to the eye than another, but that does not mean it will run at lower expenses or make you more money. Only an analysis of the books will yield that information.

Your list of potential buildings should only have properties on it that have the capability to satisfy the goals of your investment plan. Many times, you will run into great opportunities that are outside the goals of your plan. Even if they are affordable, stick to your plan, especially in the beginning; it's your best guarantee of success.

You should rank your list based on two pieces of information:

1. Bottom-line return and value based on estimates

2. Your personal opinion of the property

The first criteria is how the numbers look. The second is how you would feel about owning the property. Yes, your feelings do matter, and this is the time to take that into account. When you have boiled the list down to a few final choices, the bottom-line numbers probably are fairly close. Don't hesitate at this point to make the final decision based on your personal feelings about the property. You probably will do a better job of running the building if it starts out

Bright Idea
When deciding between property A and property B, ask your agent to bring in a colleague for his or her opinion. An unbiased third party might shed some light on something you have yet to consider.

as one you really want to own. Just don't base your whole decision on how you feel about a property.

Determining the seller's motivation

As you have learned, many variables go into determining the right property for your investment plan. It took careful thought about your own dreams and goals to put it together. Now that it's time to buy a property, you need to consider the seller's goals as well. This is where your agent turns into a modern day Sherlock Holmes. His job will be to find out why the seller is selling and what he wants out of the deal. This knowledge will be key to structuring a winning offer. The following is a list of some of the kinds of information you and your agent need to know before you start writing offers:

- How long has the seller owned the property?

- Does the seller own other income property?

- What are the seller's plans for the proceeds from the sale?

- Have there been any other offers yet?

- If so, what were the terms and what happened?

- How flexible is the price?

- Will the seller consider carrying any financing?

- Is the seller easily offended?

- Is the seller willing to negotiate on price and terms?

Answers to these questions and any others your agent might ask will help you achieve your ultimate goal—being able to buy the property you want. Here are a few examples to help illustrate how helpful this kind of insider information can be.

Case #1: Seller needs a quick close

Facts: You find a four-unit building that is in good condition and that appears to be priced at market value. It has a large assumable loan on it with a better-than-market interest rate.

Seller's motivation: In talking to the listing agent, your agent finds out that the seller has been transferred out of the area and needs to sell now. He would like to get cashed out but might consider carrying some paper if the transaction will close quickly.

Result: Knowing that he is desperate, you can make a low offer guaranteeing a quick closing and the seller carrying a portion of the financing.

Case #2: Seller's previous deal fell through

Facts: The price on the four-unit seems a little high, but the property is in excellent condition.

Seller's motivation: Your agent talks to the listing agent and finds out that the sellers have owned this property for almost 20 years. They are selling so they can buy their daughter and her husband their own home as a wedding present. The last offer was 15 percent below the asking price, and they accepted it. The buyer did not qualify for the financing, however, and the deal fell apart.

Result: You can make an offer well below the asking price, include a glowing pre-qualification letter from a lender, and promise a 30-day or less closing time. This closing date, coincidentally, is a week before their daughter's wedding.

Case #3: Seller wants to carry an installment note

Facts: This four-unit is in a good location and is in decent condition. The rents are really low, but the price is close to market value.

Seller's motivation: Your agent learns that the seller is retiring and doesn't need any cash from the

Timesaver
Knowledge of previous negotiations or deals that fell through are great indications of what the seller might do with your offer. Make sure your agent asks what has happened before you entered the picture.

sale. He would rather have the monthly income that comes from carrying a note than pay any capital gains tax.

Result: You can offer just enough cash down to pay selling costs and can ask the seller to carry the balance. You could even ask for reduced payments for the first two years to give you a chance to increase the rents.

Motivation summary

These examples have been structured to show you how information about the seller can be used to your advantage. Most of the owners you will be dealing with are not sophisticated real estate investors, and they often have a lot of emotion attached to their properties. We have found that understanding the emotional side of real estate transactions can mean the difference between making the deal or missing out on an opportunity.

Writing an offer

Now that you are going to write an offer, you still have some decisions to make. The first is what kind of format to use. Because you will be signing a legally binding contract, this decision is an important one. The process of trying to reach an agreement on price and terms with a seller can vary from state to state, and even within some states. Part of your education process will be to learn the specific procedures used in your area. Generally, offers are made in one of three ways:

1. Having an attorney draw up a contract of sale

2. Using a standard preprinted contract supplied by your agent (often called a deposit receipt)

3. Using a simplified letter of intent

Unofficially...
The best transactions are the ones in which everyone comes away feeling as if they won. Winning means getting what you want. Getting what you want depends on clearly defining your motivation as well as the seller's and finding the best way to satisfy both person's needs.

An offer via your lawyer

Although the purchase of a piece of property usually is one of the most important financial decisions in our lives, an attorney rarely is used to draw up the initial contract. This probably stems from the fact that it often takes many counter-offers before parties come to terms. It can get fairly expensive to have an attorney draw up and review what sometimes amounts to countless contracts.

This does not mean you should not have an attorney review your transaction before it becomes binding. As part of your initial research on real estate, you should ask around for referrals of good attorneys. It is best if you can find one who specializes in real estate. He or she might charge more per hour, but a specialist usually will be able to give you a quick answer, which is what you need after you have negotiated a deal.

Attorneys primarily are used in the purchase of larger properties with complicated financing and intricate leases. You will definitely want to have an attorney review your documents in the following situations:

- There are many complicated changes to the preprinted contract.

- There are complicated leases on the property.

- The seller is carrying the financing using an unusual format such as a land contract, AITD, or lease-option.

- You need the seller to subordinate the financing to a new loan in the future.

- There are potential title problems.

- There are potential problems with easements, hazardous waste, or issues with the city.

> Each transaction is different. Choosing how I will make an offer depends entirely on who I am dealing with on the other end.
> —Sandra B., real estate agent

If you sense any potential need for a review of the contracts by an attorney, you will need to have a contingency in your original offer. It should look something like this:

> "This offer is contingent upon review and approval of the final agreement by the buyer's attorney. The buyer's acceptance of the purchase contract is contingent upon this approval."

This clause puts the seller on notice that, even though you have come to agreeable terms, the agreement will still need to be reviewed and approved by your attorney. As your deals and the properties you buy get bigger and more complicated, you might want to include this type of clause in all your offers.

Moneysaver
A contingency clause requiring review and approval by an attorney will ensure that you get your deposit back if the attorney finds the deal unsatisfactory.

Preprinted sales contracts

In most real estate transactions, deals are put together using preprinted sales contracts provided by the agents. If you are using an agent who is a Realtor®, the contract probably will have been drafted by the state or the national association with which the Realtor® is affiliated. We (the authors) are located in California, so we use the forms provided by the California Association of Realtors®. These contracts have been drawn up by attorneys with the goal of equitably protecting the interests of each party in a real estate transaction.

If you are using the preprinted forms, make sure you use the form designed for the type of property on which you are making an offer. Look for the following types of forms:

- Residential (homes and condominiums)
- Residential (1–4 units)
- Income property

- Commercial and industrial

- Exchange forms

- Lease with an option to buy

The goal of each of these contracts is to include all the necessary clauses so you and your agent can make offers without having to hire an attorney each and every time. However, this can be a binding contract if the seller accepts your offer. Therefore, include a provision that it is contingent upon your attorney's approval.

Letter of intent

Many sellers get scared off when they receive offers written on preprinted purchase contracts. This is because these contracts often are lengthy and always are complicated. For this reason, many offers to buy begin with a much simpler format known as a letter of intent. A letter of intent is meant to be a simple, straightforward expression of the buyer's desire to purchase a particular piece of property. It outlines how much he is willing to pay and the kinds of terms for which he is looking.

By eliminating all the legal mumbo-jumbo, the principals can find out quickly whether they can put a deal together. Sometimes the fact that the agreement is not meant to be legally binding allows the parties to concentrate on working out the important issues that solidify a transaction. It would be a good idea to have your attorney draw up a standard form you can use again and again. Here is an example of a letter-of-intent format:

Some sellers who are not familiar with letters of intent might not take your offer seriously if you use one, so be sure your agent warns the listing agent beforehand. In fact, have your agent fax him a blank

Bright Idea
If you are using a preprinted form and you find that it contains language you don't like or that does not apply, don't worry. There is a solution. Simply cross out the part you disapprove of, initial the change, and write in what you want.

LETTER OF INTENT TO PURCHASE REAL ESTATE

This letter covers the basic price and terms under which the undersigned,

_____ (buyer), agrees to purchase the property located at _____ .

PURCHASE PRICE:_____

DOWN PAYMENT:_____

FINANCING:_____

CONTINGENCIES:_____

ADDITIONAL TERMS:_____

_____

PURCHASE AGREEMENT: Within three days of acceptance of this basic agreement, buyer and seller agree to formalize their understanding by completing and signing a standard purchase contract and receipt for deposit.

This letter is written with the understanding that no party will be bound by any of the terms of this agreement unless and until the standard form mentioned above covering all the foregoing matters and such additional considerations as any of us deem appropriate has been executed by both parties.

This letter of intent shall expire on ____/____/____ .

_____   _____

BUYER   SELLER

_____   _____

DATE   DATE

letter of intent in advance. This way, there won't be any surprises if he is not familiar with this kind of agreement.

The good-faith deposit

No matter which method you use to make an offer, you still need to decide how much of a good-faith deposit to include. That is, how much money are you going to put down as an initial deposit on the property? There is no law that says you need to include a deposit at all, but the idea of a good-faith deposit has evolved into an integral part of the offer process.

The deposit serves two functions. Psychologically, it plays into the old adage, "Put your money where your mouth is." If you want the property, putting your money on the line makes a powerful statement to the seller. Second, it puts some money at risk after the due diligence is completed.

Once you put up a deposit, the issue becomes who will hold the money. Unless you specify otherwise in your offer, the check usually becomes the property of the seller. As you can imagine, this might cause some problems if the deal goes sour and you want your money back. Therefore, you must always address this issue when you write your first offer on the property. There most likely will be a custom in your area that addresses this issue, but here are a couple of general guidelines to keep in mind:

1. There is no need for the seller to cash your check until you have a basic agreement in place. It's a good idea to write into your offer that the "deposit is to be held uncashed by the Agent until the offer is accepted by the seller

> **"**
> As a property owner, I prefer to get offers written on preprinted forms rather than a letter of intent. I know that lots of investors like them, but for me, a letter of intent doesn't carry the weight that a formal contract does.
> —Chris Y., investor
> **"**

and communication of that acceptance has been made to the buyer.

2. When it comes time to cash your check, it is best to put the funds into the hands of a neutral third party. Your purpose in doing this is to protect your money until the transaction closes. Many states have escrow companies and title companies that assist in closings and will hold the funds in their trust accounts.

Once an agreement is negotiated, the due diligence, or "free-look," period begins. This period of time allows you to do an interior inspection and a thorough analysis of the property and any other contingencies without risking any of your deposit. (the next chapter is devoted to this subject in its entirety.)

If you decide not to buy after the free-look period has expired, most contracts are written so that you will forfeit your deposit. This is one reason why sellers usually want large deposits. They want it to be big enough that you feel committed to the deal. It could cost them a lot of time and money if you back out at the 11th hour because you find something that looks better down the street.

Specific performance

When buying property, you need to make sure you are taking the game seriously. If you decide to back out of the purchase after the due diligence period without good cause, the seller can sue you for specific performance. If you get sued for specific performance and a court rules for the seller, you will be ordered to complete the purchase under the terms to which you originally agreed. To avoid the possibility of this expensive litigation, many contracts

Watch Out!
Make sure your deposit is a credit towards the purchase price. In other words, if you are paying $200,000 for a property and a $5,000 deposit accompanies your offer, then $195,000 should be due at closing.

offer buyers and sellers an opportunity to agree to liquidated damages.

Liquidated damages

The idea behind a liquidated damage clause is to let the parties decide ahead of time what the amount of the damages will be in the event of a dispute. In a real estate transaction, damages are the money forfeited by the buyer in the event the buyer fails to complete the purchase. Remember that this does not refer to the termination of the contract if one of the contingencies is disapproved of. This only applies when the buyer fails to close the transaction for any reason other than a contingency. In other words, the buyer just backed out. A typical liquidated damages clause will read something like this:

> "If the buyer fails to complete this purchase by reason of default of the buyer, the seller shall retain, as liquidated damages for breach of contract, the deposit actually paid."

In some areas, the amount of the deposit is limited to 3 percent of the purchase price if the property is four units or less. If the contract for a four-unit were $200,000, a buyer would have to pay a maximum of $6,000 to the seller for backing out of the deal as outlined in the contingencies in the purchase contract.

The proper way to present an offer

Let's say you find a property and you decide to make an offer. If your offer is way below the asking price and is not presented properly, you may insult the seller. Hurting his feelings is one thing, but having him tear up your offer and refuse to make a counter offer is an entirely different matter. The following scenarios will illustrate how to best present an offer at less than the seller's listed terms:

Case #1: An overpriced but "sweet" building

Facts: This four-unit is listed at $220,000. Your analysis indicates a value of $195,000, but you might even go to $205,000 due to the good location and condition of the property.

Presentation: To begin with, your agent insists that he present your offer in person to the seller. Once they are face to face, your agent first gives the seller some background on you and what your goals are in real estate with a prequalification letter from a lender. The agent lets the seller know that you have decided to make an offer on this property because you are impressed with the way the seller has maintained it. As a lead-in to the offer with the lower price, your agent reviews with the seller a thorough comparative market analysis of value based on other sales in the area. He includes copies of the MLS information and pictures of those properties, so there is no doubt in the seller's mind that the data is correct. The agent finishes the presentation with the following statement, "I would have brought you an offer at your listed price, but this is the value that was indicated by the recent sales in the market. It wouldn't do any of us any good to put a deal together only to have it fall through because the value couldn't be justified by the lender."

Watch Out!
You run the risk of losing out on a deal if you make a low-ball offer. Sellers are emotional about their properties. If you make them mad, they might refuse to sell to you altogether.

Result: The seller does not like the lower price but wants to sell. We get a counter-offer at $205,000 because "This property is in much better condition than the ones in the agent's market analysis." We gladly accept.

Case #2: Perfect building but the required down payment is too much

Facts: This four-unit is just what you want, and the asking price of $200,000 is in line with the market, but you can't afford to put 20 percent down, so you will need the seller to carry some financing. The listing, however, indicates that the seller wants all cash.

Presentation: Again, your agent presents the offer in person with the background on you and your goals. The presentation goes something like this. "The buyer has made you a full-price offer, which is rare in this business. This is because this buyer needs some extra help from you to complete the purchase. The buyer needs you to carry a small loan and would like you to consider two options. Option number one would be for you to carry the loan yourself. We believe that, if you discussed it with your accountant, you would find that there are great tax advantages in carrying a note. Not only will you save some taxes, the interest rate the buyer has offered is well above the current bank rates. The second option is that, at the outset, we would ask you to carry the note, but then we would look for an investor to buy it from you at a small discount. The buyer asks that you absorb the discount because his offer was full price and most buyers would have offered you less."

Result: The seller likes that you offered him full price and agrees to carry or sell the note and absorb the discount.

The important things to remember in presenting your offer are:

- Know the seller's motivation before writing an offer.

- Have a comparative analysis or an appraisal in hand to justify low offers.

- Your agent should insist on presenting your offer in person.

Bright Idea
Sometimes your agent will have to educate a seller about the benefits of carrying a loan. If he does, make sure he works the numbers out on paper so the seller can actually see how much money he can make by carrying.

- Have a prequalification letter from a lender if financing is needed.

- When presenting your offer, your agent should give the seller your personal history and should review the reasons why you want to buy the property.

Just the facts

- You must look at your real estate agent as the bridge to getting to your goals.

- Knowing the seller's reasons for selling will give you a marked advantage when writing an offer.

- A letter of intent is a great way to begin a negotiation and to eliminate hard-to-understand legalese.

- Your deposit usually is refundable during the free-look period and usually is not after that time has expired.

- You should structure your offer so that, when your agent presents it, it looks like you are accommodating the seller's every wish.

The Due Diligence Period

O nce you have a property under contract, it might seem as if the toughest part of the job is over. After all, you weeded through all the available properties in your market and finally found the perfect fit for your plan. You then made an offer, probably got a counteroffer, and might have made a counteroffer or two of your own. In the end, you successfully negotiated the purchase of your first piece of income property. As far as you are concerned, it's now time to get on with being a landlord.

Hold on, it's not quite that easy. You still have to make sure you get what you bargained for. In most cases with income property sales, you had to have agreed on price and terms without ever having seen inside any of the units. In addition, you have to make profit projections based on estimated operating data. You haven't been flying blind, but now that you've put your money where your mouth is and signed a contract, you get an opportunity to study the seller's books, review the rental agreements, and to inspect the interiors. The truth about your deal will either solidify it or set you free.

Due diligence and contingencies

Once you are under contract, you enter the due diligence phase of a purchase. The due diligence period is built around questions that have yet to be answered about the property. These questions were expressed in your offer as contingencies. A contingency is legally defined as a future event or condition upon which a valid contract is dependent. In other words, once you have an agreement in place, your contingencies put the seller on notice that you will be researching specific items pertaining to the deal. In addition, you will be making a final decision to buy based on that research.

The most important contingencies of your deal will be:

- Physically inspecting the property
- Reviewing financial details of the property
- Inspecting rental agreements
- Getting a seller's warranty
- Securing financing
- Obtaining clear title

After your research, if you determine that everything checks out okay, you then can go ahead and close your transaction as planned. If some hidden land mines pop up, however, you probably will go back to the seller and ask him to clarify or fix the problems you discovered. After all, if you go ahead with the deal with newfound knowledge of some problems, you will be getting less than what you originally had agreed to.

When you go to a seller and ask for some clarification or repair requests, a number of results could occur:

1. The seller could fix all the problems with no questions asked, and you close the deal as planned.

2. The seller could tell you that he will not correct any problems, and you could choose to cancel the deal.

3. The seller could tell you that he will not correct any problems, and you could choose to stay in the deal.

4. You and the seller go through a small renegotiation regarding any problem areas, you shake hands, and you close the deal as planned.

It is important to think of the due diligence phase as an extension of the original negotiation rather than as a "take it or leave it" proposition. With income property, many items of the decision-making process are left up in the air until your deal is made. When you get a chance to review them, they may or may not impact your decision to move ahead. Most of the things that come up should not be deal-breakers. Instead, they just need clarification or a little re-negotiation here or there. Most of the preprinted forms include a contingency clause that says:

> "If, during the time periods provided in this contract, the purchaser provides the seller a reasonable written disapproval of any item for which the purchaser has a disapproval right, the seller shall respond within
> _____days after receiving the purchaser's written notice. If the seller is unable or

Watch Out!
Be careful not to go back to the seller with a laundry list of repair requests. This is a red flag that you are a beginner, and it makes the seller think he might be better off cutting his losses and selling to someone else.

unwilling to make the correction, then the buyer has the right to cancel the contract."

This means that, if you encounter something unexpected during the due diligence period (like the discovery of a two-foot hole in the wall inside unit #4), you need to put it in writing and ask the seller to fix it. If he doesn't fix it or come to an amicable solution with you, you have a right to cancel the contract and walk away unscathed.

You must be reasonable

The key to getting a seller to comply with your requests is to be reasonable. Let's say you found a property and you came to terms with the seller. That first night you probably toasted to your future wealth with a bottle of champagne. Now the due diligence period is here, and it is time to do your interior inspection. What happens next? You get to see the units and panic sets in. The carpet smells and looks like it hasn't been vacuumed in a year, dirty dishes are overflowing from the sink, and laundry is lying everywhere. All of a sudden, you begin to think, "I would never live here. In fact, I want out of this deal!" The truth is, you probably are just nervous about the big step you are taking. Unfortunately, "buyer's jitters" are not reasonable grounds for the cancellation of a contract.

Timesaver
If you find yourself worrying about all the small details, you probably haven't done enough homework before making your offer.

If this happens, realize that the jitters are natural, especially for first-time buyers. Backing out of a deal because a tenant doesn't keep a nice house, however, or because you think the kitchen cabinets in unit #3 look dated would be considered by a court to be unreasonable. Contingencies are not designed to give you an easy out from a transaction. Their purpose is to protect you in case you come across an unforeseen material issue that can't (or won't) be corrected. Material, in this case, means something significant, not minor.

What's the magic word?

When you make an offer, it is important for you to word all the items on which you will be basing your final decision as contingencies. Most preprinted forms have contingencies structured correctly, but if you (or your agent) decide to add any clauses to the contract yourselves, you might make what could be a costly mistake.

Let's assume you have a nice four-unit under contract, but when you first looked inside the garage, you noticed that the floor in one corner looks like it isn't level with the rest of the floor. There isn't anything in the preprinted contract that directly applies to this situation, so you decide to add a clause that says, "As part of the exterior inspection, I will be checking the floor of the garage to see if it is level."

During due diligence, you hire a contractor to have a look at the garage. He does a quick survey of the elevations and confirms what you had thought. The lot in the left rear corner of the garage is lower on one side. He says that this area probably will flood during heavy rains, making it hard for the tenants to get into the two parking spots on the left side. It can be corrected, but it requires raising the grade of that corner of the lot and possibly the floor of the garage.

This is something you hadn't planned on. What's more, you consider a garage that will flood to be a significant issue that goes directly to the heart of the deal. You decide that, unless the seller pays to have the problem corrected, you want out. Unfortunately, the seller refuses to compensate

Unofficially...
Real estate agents are required to have a separate bank account to hold all deposits.

you or fix the problem, so you are forced to call the escrow office and call the whole thing off. The seller then informs you that he will be keeping your deposit because you defaulted on the contract. He says he let you inspect the floor as you wanted, but you never let him know that having the garage floor level was a contingency of the transaction. The end result is that the large deposit you made probably will be held in trust until the ensuing legal battle between you and the seller can be resolved.

This mess could easily have been avoided if you simply had written into the contract that your offer was contingent on the inspection and approval of the garage being level. This would have put the seller on notice from the outset that his response to your requests for a repair (if one were needed) would directly determine the outcome of the deal.

Some examples of proper wording for your contingencies might be:

- "This deal is contingent on the buyer's approval of the interior inspection."

- "This deal is contingent on the seller fixing the broken railing surrounding the front patio."

- "This deal is contingent on a licensed pest-control company determining that the property is free of termites and termite damage."

- "This deal is contingent on the seller filling the vacancy in unit #2 at $550 per month or more."

By wording your concerns this way, you will ensure that the outcome of the deal (and the safety of your deposit) hinges on satisfactory resolutions to your own contingencies.

Removing contingencies in order to move forward

We've discussed the importance of contingencies in protecting your rights in a real estate transaction. Before we review the most important contingencies in detail, let's discuss the ways to remove them. Removing a contingency means that the problem has been corrected so that the deal can proceed as planned. Most of the preprinted contracts require you to choose one of two methods for removing contingencies:

1. The active method of removing contingencies

2. The passive method of removing contingencies

Active method of removing contingencies

Simply put, the active method of removing contingencies says that, if you find a problem during the due diligence period, you need to put it in writing and deliver it to the seller. It also means that, once there has been an amicable solution to the problem, you need to put that in writing, too. Once you do, that contingency will be removed, and you will be one step closer to closing your deal.

Passive method of removing contingencies

The California Association of Realtors defines the passive method of removing contingencies in this way:

> "If purchaser fails to give written notice of disapproval of any item or of a cancellation of this contract within the strict time frames specified in this contract, then the purchaser shall conclusively be deemed to have completed all reviews and inspections of the documents and disclosures and to have made the election to proceed with the transaction."

Unofficially...
It is more work to remove all your contingencies in writing, but it forces all parties involved to pay attention to the details.

This simply says that written notice to the seller is not required. Instead, you need to negotiate a correction of the problem within the time periods specified in the contract; otherwise, the seller will deem your silence on the issue to mean that the contingency has been waived or removed.

Regardless of the method of removal, the time period is very important. When putting your transaction together, you must calendar any deadlines that have been agreed to. The goal of most sellers is to get this free-look period over as soon as possible and to find out whether you are "in" or "out." Your goal is to complete your reviews in a timely fashion and to either accept the property as you find it or go back and ask for clarification or an adjustment to the deal.

Finding out what is behind door #3

Two big contingencies usually get quick attention by buyers as soon as the due diligence period begins. These are:

- Inspection of the interiors
- Inspection of the overall physical structure of the property

Watch Out!
If the person you hire to do the inspection believes he also is going to do any repair work, he might look for things to do. He also might inflate his prices if he thinks he can get away with it.

These inspections usually are not as important as many novice buyers make them out to be. Because you have to make a deal before you actually see much of what you are bargaining for, however, the built-up anticipation often becomes of paramount importance. The contingency for the inspections should read something like this:

"This offer is contingent upon inspection and approval of the complete interior and exterior of the property. The buyer has the right to perform these inspections, tests, or studies

at the buyer's expense or to hire professionals of his choosing to assist in these investiga-
tions. The seller shall make the property
available for these inspections."

Most preprinted forms have an extensive list of
items that your interior and exterior inspections
might include. You don't necessarily have to do an
extensive check of each and every item, but the list
will help you decide which ones might be important
for the property you are buying. The items to consider in your property inspections are:

- The physical structure itself, plumbing, roof,
  appliances, electrical system, fixtures, heating,
  basement, attic, and so on
- Property dimensions, footage, lot size, bound-
  aries, age, permits, and so on
- Sewer and water systems
- Zoning, building restrictions, city inspections,
  and so on
- Geological conditions
- Adequacy of parking
- Neighborhood conditions, adequacy of ser-
  vices, hazards, and so on

Professional inspections

There are two ways to perform a property inspection. You can either hire a professional property
inspector or do it yourself. We recommend that,
unless you have expertise in construction, it is best
to hire a professional. The peace of mind you get
from a professional's opinion will be well worth the
small expense. You should be able to find a reputable property inspector by looking in the Yellow
Pages. (We have included a professional property

Moneysaver
Reduce the cost
of your
inspections (and
any other service
you require) by
negotiating with
the inspector.
Almost everyone
expects you to
haggle over
prices, so don't
disappoint them.

inspection report on the example property at 1800 Mariposa Lane in Appendix E.)

As of the printing of this book, the property inspection business is in its infancy, and most states are just beginning to work on guidelines and licenses. The most important thing is that you find an inspector who is affiliated with a local or national organization of building inspectors. If you are unable to locate one of these professionals, find a local contractor that has experience with the type of building you are buying.

Do-it-yourself inspections

Even though you might hire a professional inspector, you also should do your own inspection of the property at the same time. A professional inspector is going to determine and note the condition of every aspect of the property. He might find that the systems work fine, but your job is to take his information and couple it with your own judgment to make determinations about potential upgrades or repairs you will need to make in the future. This information will let you know how accurate your estimated budget was for maintenance. This will be important in establishing a long-term budget for replacements, which we will discuss in Chapters 15, "The Big Picture of Management," and 16, "So What's Stopping You?"

It is important for you to sketch the layout of each unit. Knowing the size, the general floor plan, and the amenities will help you determine its future rentability compared to the competition. You also should use a checklist to make the job easier. Here is a checklist that you can use for yourself. Feel free to add to it or adapt it as necessary to meet your own needs.

> ❝
> I have always accompanied the inspector on his tour. That way, I can take notes and ask questions while he's inspecting the property.
> —Matt K., investor
> ❞

ADDRESS_____

UNIT #_____

CONDITION:	BAD	AVERAGE	GOOD
Paint			
Drapes/Blinds			
Vinyl Flooring			
Kitchen Cabinets			
Kitchen Counters			
Stove			
Refrigerator			
Dishwasher			
Garbage Disposal			
Faucets			
Sinks			
Doors			
Windows			
Heater			
Water Heater			
Air Conditioner			
Bathroom Cabinets			
Tub/Shower			
Shower Door/Curtain Rod			
Toilet			
Vanity			
Bedroom 1			
Bedroom 2			
Bedroom 3			
Closets			
Tenant			
Notes			

Bright Idea
You can use this same checklist with new tenants to inform them of the condition of the unit when they move in. When you give them a copy, make sure you get them to sign it.

Sometimes, inspections give you an opportunity to meet the tenants even before you take over ownership. It is natural that, once you meet them, you will begin to form an opinion about whether they fit into your overall plan for the property. Make sure you couple your first impression with a few months of property ownership before you make up your mind. First impressions can be deceiving.

The exterior inspection

As opposed to interior inspections, when you should get in and out with as little intrusion to the tenants as possible, you can take all the time in the world for your inspection of the exterior. This inspection is critical. If there's a big problem that you miss in the due diligence period, you could get stuck footing the bill. As you walk around the property, take notes on everything you see. Jot down notes about rusted railings, peeling paint, overgrown landscaping, fire escape access, gutters, downspouts, and anything else you see.

You also should make a rough sketch of the lot and the layout of the building as well as any structures on the property such as garages or driveways. This kind of diagram will make it easier for you to give directions to contractors or potential tenants throughout the tenure of your ownership. You should label the location of items such as:

- Water meters
- Gas meters
- Electric meters and breakers
- Furnace or boiler
- Water heater
- Shutoffs for all utilities
- Shutoffs for all equipment in the building
- Pool equipment room
- Drain clean-outs
- Sprinkler system controls
- Cable TV panels
- Layouts of the units

- Garages, carports, or space numbers
- Tenant storage units
- Laundry rooms and laundry utility meters

Seller's warranty and maintenance responsibility

After you complete the inspection of the condition of the property, there are a few additional things you can do to ensure that you will get what you bargained for.

If available in your area, you should get a real estate transfer disclosure statement. These disclosures essentially outline the seller's knowledge, or lack thereof, about the property. By making the seller fill out a transfer disclosure as a contingency of the deal, it forces him to think about most aspects of the property and to make written representations about those aspects. If you have trouble finding this disclosure, contact the Department of Real Estate in your state and ask for one or have your attorney draw one up.

Along with a transfer disclosure statement, you should get the seller to give you a warranty about the condition of the property as of the date of your inspection. This also should include a stipulation that the seller is to maintain the property in that condition until closing. This warranty should read something like this:

> The seller warrants that on the date of the inspection of the property:

1. There are no known leaks in the roof.

2. The tub and shower enclosures and pans are free of leaks.

3. All plumbing, electrical, heating, and air conditioning systems are operative.

> **66**
>
> If I can meet the seller at the inspection I try to establish a rapport. I also ask if we can communicate after escrow in case I have any questions about the building. In my experience, most sellers are willing to be helpful.
> —Jeremy L., investor
>
> **99**

4. All appliances that go with the property are operating properly.

5. All screens will be in place and any broken or cracked glass will be replaced.

6. The property in its entirety will be maintained in substantially the same condition until the closing as it was on the date of the inspection."

Many sellers will want you to purchase the property in "as is" condition. This is a legal issue you might want to discuss with your attorney. If it is a property you really want, and the price and terms were right, you probably are safe in doing this as long as you get a signed transfer disclosure statement from the seller. In doing this, your goal is to protect against the cover-up of a known problem by the seller. If you have a signed transfer disclosure and you discover a problem later that the seller knew about, you probably are in a good position to hold him liable.

Inspecting the books and records

One of the most important inspections is the inspection of the books and records of the operations of the property. Your purchase agreement should have a contingency that reads something like this:

"This offer is contingent upon inspection and approval of the records of income and expenses of the property. The seller warrants that these are the income and expenses used by the seller in completing state and federal tax returns. Expenses are to be for the prior 12 months of operations and should include copies of the actual bills for all utilities, city fees and licenses, property taxes, insurance, service contracts, and any other bills associated with the operation of the property for the prior 12 months."

It is important for you to see the actual bills rather than an operating statement or even the schedule from the seller's tax returns. Many part-time investors are not very consistent in the way they handle their books for tax purposes, whereas the actual bills tell you exactly what's happening with the operations of the property. From this data, you will be able to see how close your projections are to the actual operation of the property. If you are off, it might be that you can spot a problem. We will elaborate on this contingency in more detail in Chapter 14, "Managing the Expenses."

Inspecting rental agreements

As part of your review of the income and expenses of the property, you need to get copies of all the current rental agreements as well as the original applications filled out by the tenants before they moved in. You also should ask for a summary of any delinquent rents and a detailed payment history of each tenant. Though you won't be in a position to do anything about the data you get, the information will give you a strong idea of who will survive the storm and who will not.

Verification of terms

As a new landlord, you legally are required to honor any leases signed by the previous owner. One problem that can come up after a deal has closed is any special arrangements made between the tenants and the former owners. Even though you've seen the rental contracts, that doesn't mean there aren't other verbal agreements that the seller failed (or forgot) to disclose to you. To avoid inheriting any

Bright Idea
If you have trouble determining when a tenant began his tenancy, check the electric meters when you do your inspection. If the tenant pays for his own electricity, the meter might verify the move-in date.

problems, it is a good idea to have the seller help you get estoppel certifications from all the tenants before closing. This gives you a current signed statement verifying the main points of the rental agreement. If there are any agreements in the minds of the tenants, this is their opportunity to mention them or forever hold their tongue. See the following page for a sample estoppel certification you could use.

Service contracts

Along with your inspection of the operating details of the property, you also should review any service contracts currently in place. These might include any of the following:

- Laundry equipment and service
- Pest control
- Boiler or furnace maintenance
- Garbage and trash disposal
- Pool or spa maintenance
- Intercom or alarm systems
- Elevators
- Superintendent, porters, and doormen
- Cable TV
- Water treatment systems
- Gardening and landscaping

Many of these services are under long-term contacts, and breaking these agreements could cost you a bundle. Make sure you at least review them with representatives from each company, however, so you know what terms you will be living with.

Changes during escrow

Your closing might take some time (usually because you are waiting for financing to come through), and

1. Unit number _____

2. I have a month-to-month agreement/lease (circle one) and pay $_____ per month rent.

3. The last rent I paid was for the month of _____.

4. My security deposit is $_____.

5. My last month's rent is $_____.

6. The appliances I own are: (check all that apply)

   stove_____ refrigerator _____

   washer_____ dryer_____

   other_____

7. The names of the other tenants on the agreement or living in the apartment are _____.

8. I do have a pet_____.
   I do not have a pet _____.

9. Other agreements I have are _____.

10. Any problems relatd to my tenancy are _____

    _____

    (Write "none" if applicable)

Signed _____

Date _____

Watch Out!
Check the applications of any new tenants the seller finds during the escrow period. Sellers have a tendency to fill last-minute vacancies with less-than-qualified tenants.

it is important that the seller not make any material changes to the property without notifying you. You should have a clause that gives you the right to review and approve any material changes the seller wants to make during escrow. Remember that a material change is anything considered to be significant. The changes you should be concerned with are:

- Renting or leasing a vacant unit
- Beginning legal proceedings on a nonpaying tenant
- Changing the terms of any existing rental agreement or lease
- Making changes to any existing service contracts
- Any material change in the condition of the property

Lining up your financing ducks

Make sure specific details about the loan you are trying to obtain are contingencies. A typical financing contingency might look like this:

> "This offer is contingent upon the buyer obtaining and qualifying for a new first loan of not less than _____, payable at $_____ per month including interest at _____% (fixed/adjustable, circle one) amortized for _____ years, all due in not less than _____ years. Loan fees not to exceed $_____. Maximum adjustable interest rate to be _____%. Additional terms:
>
> _____.
>
> Buyer agrees to act diligently and in good faith to obtain the above financing."

If you notice how this contingency is worded, you will see that it is designed to protect you regarding all the important aspects of your loan. One line says that you will obtain a new loan for no less than a certain amount of money (you fill in the blank). By having this line, the clause protects you in case a lender refuses to loan you all that you need. Another example is the line that stipulates when the loan is due. If you write in that it will be due in 30 years but the lender will only give you a loan for 10, again you are not bound. Finally, there is a line that protects you from being hit up for loan fees that exceed the amount you budgeted.

Getting clear title

Once you have opened escrow, you should receive a title report, a title opinion, or some type of chain of title for your review. Any of these reports will let you know whether there are any recordings against the property that might adversely affect your plans. It is not uncommon to have federal or state tax liens, local property tax liens, or judgments that have been recorded. Most of these items can easily be rectified before closing. Nonetheless, you must have a contingency that requires the seller to give you clear title. A typical title contingency might be

> "The seller shall provide at the seller's expense a preliminary title report for the buyer's review and approval. At closing, the seller shall provide the buyer with title insurance and shall transfer title, free and clear of all liens. Unless otherwise agreed to in this agreement, title shall be free of other encumbrances, restrictions, easements, or other rights or conditions that are of record or known by the seller."

Watch Out!
Contingencies have time limits set for their completion. If you are not able to complete your due diligence by the time they expire, ask for extensions and get any new agreements in writing. If you fail to notify the seller that your loan approval is going to take a few extra days, the deal may go awry.

Moneysaver
Title insurance is one of those items that usu-ally gets paid according to the norms and cus-toms of the area. In some areas, the seller pays; in others, it's the buyer's responsi-bility. Regardless of the custom, you can always ask the seller to pay for title because it can only save you money. The worst he can say is "no."

Most title reports or opinions do not cover boundary issues, city zoning, or building issues unless they are recorded against the title. For that reason, if you have any concerns about property lines, fences, or where a structure is built, you might need to hire a surveyor or a civil engineer to answer these questions for you. If you have any zoning or building-code concerns, you need to check with the local departments that handle those issues.

Other contingencies

Years ago, when offers were made to purchase real property, the preprinted form was only one page long. Today, in California, for example, that same form is nine pages long, and it includes enough con-tingencies and disclosures to fill a small book. These agreements have evolved due to hard lessons learned in the courts and the desire in the real estate profession to provide full disclosure. Real estate agents have a fiduciary responsibility, which is the highest duty of good faith under the law, to pro-vide as much information as possible. These forms and disclosures help jog everyone's memory on the important issues in a transaction.

Space prevents us from reviewing all the current issues we see in these agreements. This chapter has touched on the major issues and contingencies that should concern you. The following list, however, contains some others to consider:

- Agency disclosure
- Smoke detector and water heater compliance
- Natural hazard disclosure
- Environmental hazards
- Environmental survey
- Lead-based paint

- Earthquake safety
- Military ordnance locations
- Tax withholdings
- Americans with Disabilities Act
- Pest control

You probably will be doing business with a real estate agent who is a Realtor®. This means he is affiliated with the National Association of Realtors® in his state. If this is the case, it would be in your best interest to use the preprinted forms he provides that correspond to the type of property you are buying. These forms will cover all the specific issues you need to be concerned with in your area.

Finally, you might want to get the assistance of an attorney to review your transaction. An attorney who specializes in real estate should be familiar with the preprinted contacts and will be able to quickly and economically review the important points.

Just the facts

- Many 270sactions require some extra give and take once the due diligence period begins.
- Contingencies are not designed to give you an easy way out; they are there to protect you from unforeseen material problems.
- You always should hire a professional inspector to check out any real estate purchase you are considering.
- Insist on seeing at least 12 months' worth of income and expenses before you make your final decision to buy.
- Make sure that obtaining sufficient financing and clear title are worded as contingencies of your deal.

"
At one property we were considering, the inspector pointed out that the acoustic ceiling might contain asbestos. The seller refused to pay to have it removed let alone tested, so we decided to walk away from the deal.
—Kirk M., investor
"

Property Management Essentials

PART VI

GET THE SCOOP ON...
The first things to do after you close escrow ▪
How to determine the market's vacancy rate ▪
Sure-fire techniques for finding new tenants ▪
Getting your unit rent-ready ▪ How to keep
your tenants happy and your units full ▪
Raising the rent

Managing the Tenants

Y ou have just closed your deal, and sweat is beginning to form on your brow for good reason; now is when the real work of owning property begins. It's time to take over management of the building and begin the job of running your new business. We know that closing your first escrow and taking on this new challenge can be a daunting if not terrifying prospect, especially when you think of dealing with vacancies, bounced rent checks, and late night phone calls about overflowing toilets. Fear not, this chapter is for you. Here you will get a jump-start on some key tenant-managing techniques before you ever close on a property.

Just closed escrow, now what?

It might sound trite, but this really is a people business. Many investors tend to focus on the money and forget that the way you make money is by keeping your customers happy, just as you would in any other business. In real estate, you have two customers to worry about. One is the person who will ultimately buy your building when it comes time to sell. You don't need to worry about him for a while. The second customer is the one you need to concern yourself with now because he is the customer that is going to make you rich. He is your tenant.

Meet and greet the tenants

After you close, you need to meet your new tenants right away (provided you haven't hired a management company). Either mail them a letter or post one on their door introducing yourself. Let them know that you would like to meet with them personally and that you will be calling in a day or so to set up an appointment. This request always brings up a tenant's worst fears. He thinks you're going to raise his rent (which you might), tell him to shape up or ship out (which you might), or tell him you want his first born child (which you don't). In truth, all you want to accomplish is to gain the tenants' trust, review any concerns or problems they might have, and if they are on month-to-month tenancies, get their signature on a new rental agreement.

There are both benefits and risks to getting to know your tenants personally. For the most part, you should keep your contact with tenants on a strictly business level. This way, if their child gets sick or they get laid off from their job, you will be able to ask for rent without guilt. There are a few steps you can take to protect your privacy. They include:

1. Picking up the rent in person or having it mailed to a post office box or other place of business.

2. Setting up your post office box before you purchase. This way, your address will not show up on any recorded documents or utility bills.

3. Having an unlisted phone number and caller ID blocked.

4. Never giving out your home address to anyone who lives at the property. This includes resident-managers and superintendents.

5. Getting either a voice-mail service or a pager to answer ad calls and emergencies. This way, you can stay available but still protect your privacy.

When you get this new agreement signed, you can discuss with the tenants how you want rent paid. This will be one of your first management decisions. If it is common practice in your area for the rent to be paid on the first of the month, that should be your policy as well. You might, however, end up making some concessions on this issue, especially if tenants you inherited had a different arrangement with the former owner due to a payday issue. If you decide that these are tenants that you would like to keep for a while, you should continue to honor their former arrangement. In the future, you will be able to exclude tenants that cannot pay on the day you want rent paid.

A policy on checks

It is a fact of life that tenants bounce rent checks. Now that you are a landlord, this problem affects you. Therefore, you need a policy regarding the acceptance of checks for rent. Have a firm rule that, if a tenant bounces a rent check, you no longer can accept personal checks from him, and he must now pay his rent by either cashier's check or money order. His bank will probably charge him for this, but this is a business and it isn't your problem. You also should be wary of allowing your tenants to pay cash for rent. Besides the inherent bookkeeping problem it poses, accepting cash can make you an easy target for a robbery. Finally, you should have a

Bright Idea
If you ever have to go to court with a tenant, it makes it much easier if your name is on their rental agreement rather than the former owner's. Although the former contract is binding, it will look better in the eyes of a judge to have your name on a new one.

reasonable late payment policy. Make sure the tenants know that you expect them to pay a late fee and any bank charges if and when they pay their rent beyond the agreed upon due date.

Change the utilities

During escrow, you should have received information about who does regular maintenance work on your building and the names of the local utility companies. Call all these people right away and let them know you are the new owner. In fact, you should call a week or two in advance to make sure none of the utility companies need deposits for the new service. It would be an ominous beginning if the utilities were turned off the very day you took over.

Get some insurance

Before your loan was funded, you were most likely required to purchase insurance for the building, but you also should consider buying insurance that covers your manager and the workers that come on the property. Most states require employers to carry workman's compensation insurance on their employees. You might not think you have any employees for your modest four-unit building but, in the eyes of the law, maybe you do. The guy who cuts your grass, the plumber who fixes the broken garbage disposals, and the tenant who shows the unit for you from time to time all will probably be considered employees by a court of law if they get hurt while working on your property.

The workman's compensation insurance laws are not very forgiving. For that reason, you should check with your insurance agent to see whether your existing policy covers these casual workers. If not, you need to get a policy to cover them. One way around the law is to only use contractors who can

Moneysaver
Consider buying comprehensive general liability insurance (CGL). It can cover most of the cost of a legal defense as well as any damages you might have to pay as a result of a lawsuit.

prove they have their own workers' comp insurance. The flip side of using only these types is that they usually charge the most because they pay all the fees and obtain all the licenses for the work they do.

The Apartment Owners Association wants you

One of the best organizations you can join at this time is a local apartment owners association. If there isn't one in your own community, see if you can find one in the closest major city. Experienced apartment owners and professional property managers usually run these organizations. Their purpose is to give help to other owners and managers. Most have monthly newsletters that will keep you up-to-date on current events and changes in your market. They also carry advertisements for contractors who can give you help when you need it. In addition, many associations will supply you with various forms you might need, and some have access to credit reports to check out potential tenants. Some associations even give seminars and classes on property management and specific classes for resident-managers. These are all well worth attending.

Get to know the neighborhood

The next order of business is to get to know the competition. You probably did some investigation already, but now you need to take some additional notes about the neighborhood and the buildings around yours. Get yourself a small notebook in which to write. Things to note include:

- The number of units in the surrounding buildings
- The number of properties on the surrounding streets
- Phone numbers from "For Rent" signs

- Amenities in the other properties
- Rental rates and terms on the vacancies
- The overall condition of the streets
- The location of the local police (get to know them)

Use this notebook to keep track of the facts you learn about the streets and buildings that surround your property. Don't try to do this in one day; the idea is to just begin the process. This is a working notebook that you can keep under the seat of your car, so it doesn't have to be anything fancy. The primary goal of your notes is to get a broad overview of the properties in your neighborhood. Additionally, these notes will be invaluable when it comes time to make decisions about your own property in the future.

The first thing to note is how many units are in the surrounding buildings. By knowing this number, you can determine the vacancy rate and will thus be able to monitor changes in vacancy trends. The easiest way to estimate the number of units is to just count the number of mailboxes you see. It is not necessary for you to be 100 percent accurate; you just want a general estimate of how many units are out there. Once you know the number of units, you can estimate the vacancy rate by counting the number of "For Rent" signs in the neighborhood and then dividing that number by the number of mailboxes. Your calculation will look like this:

$$\frac{\text{Number of "For Rent" Signs}}{\text{Number of Mail Boxes}} = \text{Vacancy Rate}$$

Know that this method of determining the vacancy rate is an inexact science. It should be close enough, however, to help you determine a general vacancy rate at a given time.

Giving the reigns of control over to management

Although you might want to turn properties over to management right after you purchase them, it is best to manage your first buildings yourself. We know, however, that this is not always practical for every investor. If you do opt for management, the key to doublechecking their effectiveness is to "manage the managers." The best way to do this is to always be aware of what the market rate for the rent should be.

It is easy to do a rent survey. The best way is to pretend you are a prospective tenant. Whenever you see a rental sign in your neighborhood, jot down the phone number and call. Make sure you ask all the pertinent questions that any prospective tenant would and then note the details in your notebook:

- How much is the unit renting for?

- How many bedrooms and bathrooms are there?

- What is the square footage of the apartment?

- What amenities are included?

- Do they accept pets?

- Can you see inside the unit?

By routinely doing this exercise, you will have plenty of ammunition to guard yourself against a complacent management company. It is very easy for them to turn in good numbers if they never raise the rents to their full potential. This is a business, however, and your cash-on-cash return depends on

Watch Out!
Make sure your management company calls you first when they think major repairs need to be done. It's not uncommon for a management company to call an expensive plumber when a plunger could have fixed the problem.

them selling your product for the correct price (the rental rate). Your tenants will never complain if your rents are too low, and they probably won't ever move either. Keep in mind, however, that when it comes time to sell or refinance your building, this lower-than-market rent will directly affect the value of your building.

Losing tenants

As a landlord, you will wear many hats. The very day a tenant gives you notice that he is moving out is the day you put on your salesman's hat; it's now time to market your rental to someone new. The first thing you should do when you get notice is to find out why he is leaving. Maybe there was a job transfer or perhaps he wants to move his children to a different school district. In these instances, there is nothing you can do. Sometimes the move might be directly related to other tenants in the building or to the way you run the show. If that is the case, your ears should perk up.

It is said that "one bad apple can ruin the whole bunch," and one bad tenant in this day and age isn't any different. You will find that most residents will not complain about a neighbor for fear of some kind of retaliation. They often will just decide to move out to get away from a bad situation. The same is true for maintenance issues that go unattended. Rather than complain, many tenants will just find another place to live where the owner takes care of things. If you ask your tenants why they are moving, it might be as simple as, "The building on the corner of 5th and Elm has cleaner laundry facilities." It's hard to take, but it's a wake up call that you have fallen behind the competition.

Unofficially...
If a new tenant moves in right after an old tenant leaves, it isn't considered a vacancy. Instead, it is called a turnover. A vacancy refers to units that are left unoccupied and are not producing income.

Finding new tenants

The key to filling your apartment as quickly as possible lies in doing the right kind of advertising for the soon-to-be-available unit. The major methods are:

- Posting rental signs or banners
- Offering a referral fee to existing tenants
- Holding an open house
- Posting fliers at local businesses
- Placing ads in the local papers
- Sending direct mail to tenants in similar buildings
- Registering with rental agencies
- Contracting with a management company

Your decision as to how little (or how much) advertising you need will be based on the vacancy rate in your neighborhood. Usually, the lower the vacancy rate, the quicker the unit will fill and the less effort will be needed to fill it.

Remember that your goal is to fill the unit so there is no lost rent. If you wait until the current tenant has vacated to do any advertising, you probably will lose a month of rent. The secret is to start your advertising campaign the day you get notice from the tenant that he is moving. Even if the market is strong and you only need a sign out front to attract someone, get it up right away. The sooner your rental is on the market, the better chance you'll have to get the best selection of future tenants. You don't want just a replacement tenant; you want the best-qualified tenant currently looking for a unit.

Put up a sign

Nice signs and banners out front are a great way to find people. We have seen hundreds of attractive properties over the years that advertise their vacancies with cheap looking, poorly worded, plastic signs just stuck in a front lawn. This is hardly the message you want to convey about your property. Instead, take a bit of time to make a legible sign that shows you care about your building. It doesn't have to be a Picasso, and it doesn't have to cost much, but it should show that you care about your property.

Don't forget that the sign should have enough information so potential tenants can decide whether the unit could work for them. The important information is:

- Size
- Cost
- How to see it
- Who to call for more information

If you have a two-bedroom for $550 a month, your sign should say something like this:

> Large 2-bedroom, $550.
>
> Open house Sat. 11 a.m. to 2 p.m.
>
> Call 555-2345 for more info
> or see manager in #3.

Many people won't bother to call if you don't list the size or the price. Others might be seriously looking, but you don't want them to waste your or the manager's time if they can't afford your unit or if it is the wrong size for them.

Post a flyer

Posting a flyer about your rental works well, too, especially if you are close to a commercial center that has a community bulletin board. In this case, make a nice flyer with a photo of the property and some tear-off tabs at the bottom that have the address and phone number of your building. More often than not, the flyer will stay on the board even after you have filled the vacancy. This is a great way to get the word out about your great building.

Offer a referral fee

Offering a modest referral fee to existing tenants is another great way to attract new tenants. It is less expensive than other paid methods of advertising, and by having your current tenants refer their family, friends, or co-workers to you, you have a high probability of finding compatible people that might stick around for a while. Make sure you make it clear that they only will get the referral fee if you rent to the person they referred. You're not offering money for just a list of names.

A bang for your advertising buck

If you need to pay for advertising, make sure you keep track of the calls you get, especially if you are placing ads in several different papers. By doing this, you will learn two things:

1. Which papers produce the greatest number of calls

2. What works and what doesn't when it comes to writing rental ads

Before you run an ad, check the newspaper and review the ads that other owners are placing. Notice which ads catch your eye and which do not. You will see that the size of the ad isn't always the most important feature. Instead, what is said in the ad is the most important thing. When placing your ad, try to list the key features about your property. Limit

Moneysaver
The most expensive papers aren't always the best choice for your advertising dollar. In a lower economic area, an ad in a throw–away-type paper might indeed draw more calls than an ad in a paper that the prospective tenant has to buy.

the "sale job"; instead, give enough facts to give people a reason to visit your property. A sample ad for that two-bedroom unit might be:

> $550/mo. lrg 2 bdrm, very clean. Laundry room, private patio, enclosed garage.
> 333 Center St. Open house Sat. 12–1 p.m. Manager in #3. For appointment call 555-2345.

Showing your unit

Having the unit available to show at the hours potential tenants are looking is the most important aspect of this process. The easier you make it to view your vacancy at hours when prospective tenants are looking, the better your chances of getting the best tenant. Generally speaking, prospective tenants will be out looking for apartments in the early evenings and on weekends, primarily Saturdays. These are the times that you or your manager needs to be available for a showing.

Beginning landlords always ask, "Can I show a unit before the current tenant moves out?" The answer is yes, sometimes. Most rental agreements have, or should have, a clause that allows you to enter the unit with 24-hour notice. This gives you the right to show the unit to a prospective tenant. Make sure you don't abuse the right, however. We have found that most tenants are very helpful when it comes to organizing convenient times to show their units. As always, if you treat your tenants well, the odds are good that they'll do the same for you.

You also should know that most states have laws permitting you to enter and show a unit to a prospective tenant—even if it is not in the rental agreement—as long as you give 24-hour notice.

Cattle calls are great

One way to make it easy on both you and the tenant moving out is to hold an open house for your upcoming vacancy. Let all qualified prospects know that you will have the unit open on an upcoming Saturday from noon to 1 p.m. If they are interested in renting from you, this is when they should show up. As far as you are concerned, the more the merrier! This technique is the least intrusive on your current tenants, and it creates a great sense of urgency in your prospects because they see lots of other people looking at the same great rental.

Getting a unit "rent-ready"

The biggest stumbling block in getting a unit rented quickly is getting it cleaned and ready after a tenant moves out. The key to this job is finding out ahead of time what has to be done and lining up the proper people to do the work. When a tenant gives notice, you or your manager should meet with him and walk through the unit to see what needs to be done to get it ready for the next tenant. Things such as worn carpet, dirty walls, torn screens, and so on should be written down on your repair list. Doing this walk-through with the tenant will help prevent any disputes about keeping all or part of their security deposit.

Once you have a list to work from, you can schedule the work so it can be finished quickly. In most instances, many small items that need to be replaced can be purchased ahead of time such as switch plates, towel bars, light fixtures, and so on. This way, you will avoid any delays while waiting for your contractor or handyman to make a run to the hardware store to get a small item.

Watch Out!
You might not want to show a unit if it needs extensive work or if the tenant is a slob. Instead, you should show them the manager's unit as an example of what the vacancy will look like when they move in. After the messy tenant vacates, get in there immediately and make the unit sparkle again.

Bright Idea
From a business standpoint, the only form of discrimination you should practice is one based on a tenant's ability to pay the rent.

The hardest part of cleaning a unit often is completing the minor finishing touches that make a unit sparkle. The paint job gets done, but there is a missing switch plate. The new carpet is in, but it hasn't been vacuumed yet. The blinds aren't up yet, there's a half-empty soda in the refrigerator, and you have yet to put up a new shower curtain. All these things need to get done so you can start collecting rent again.

The goal is to get the unit completely finished as quickly as possible whether or not you have a new tenant ready to move in. Two points to remember are:

1. If you have tenants ready to move in, they usually want to move in as soon as possible so get the unit rent-ready as soon as possible.

2. If you don't have a tenant lined up, it is much easier to rent a unit that is clean and ready to move into.

Discrimination = bad business

Whether you are the manager of a 100-unit apartment complex or the owner of a small duplex, federal anti-discrimination laws apply to you as might several state and local ordinances. The federal Civil Rights Act and the Fair Housing Act prohibit landlords from discriminating on the basis of race, ethnic background, national origin, religion, and sex. The Americans with Disabilities Act (ADA) effectively prohibits discrimination against someone with a disability.

The law says that, if you are faced with two equally qualified tenants, it is legal to pick one over another for no other reason than you liked one better; there is nothing discriminatory in that. If you have a pattern of not choosing African-Americans, women, or other minorities, however, you leave yourself open to an expensive discrimination lawsuit.

Even if you are not discriminating, as a landlord, you should be equally concerned with the appearance of discrimination. If you have an apartment complex occupied only by whites, for example, you might appear to be discriminating even if you are not. The key to minimizing that risk is to set up objective, legitimate business criteria when looking for new tenants and to stick to them. What you must do is look consistently for such things as two positive references, stable employment, and a good credit history. Treat people equally and use the same criteria in every case. It might even be wise to write down your criteria and keep it on file. Above all, be consistent and document your reasons for denying someone a unit.

Rental agreements or leases

You have picked a new tenant, and now it is time to sign the rental agreements. It is advisable to use a rental agreement that you get from your apartment association because it will have all the proper protection clauses for both you and your tenant. Never use one of those preprinted forms you get at your corner stationery store. These forms usually are very general and lack the details that will protect you legally. On the other hand, the apartment association's form should cover most legal issues for your area.

You will find that local custom often will dictate the kind of tenancies you will have. In some areas, month-to-month agreements are preferred. In others, leases are more common. Each has pros and

> **"**
> We specifically write into rental agreements that each party is required to give the other 30 days notice to discontinue a tenancy.
> —Mike and Brandy M., landlords
> **"**

cons, so it might be wise to stick with the most common format in your area.

In addition, you should have any other necessary agreements ready for signature. Some properties, especially larger buildings, have tenants sign a list of house rules. Most states have required disclosures regarding lead-based paint and other environmental concerns. Finally, you should have an interior condition checklist for review by the tenant and you or the manager (adapt the checklist from the "Do-It-Yourself Inspection" section in Chapter 12 to meet your needs). Walk the unit and go over the checklist together. When complete, make sure you both sign it. This will eliminate most arguments over deposit refunds in the event you need to charge the tenant because of damage when they move out. This form should cover the following areas:

- The condition of the carpet
- The condition of vinyl and other floor coverings
- The condition of the paint
- Any holes in the walls
- The condition of the ceilings
- The appliances and their condition
- The condition of doors, windows, and screens
- The condition of carports, garages, and storage areas
- Keys and accessories (garage door openers)
- Other

Help from Uncle Sam

There are some special groups of tenants of which you need to be aware. Because many people in our society lack the ability to afford adequate housing, the government has several programs available that assist them in paying for a place to live. The most common program is through the office of Housing and Urban Development (HUD). This division of the government provides assistance to people who cannot afford a place to live. This original goal dates back to the Housing Act of 1949. The purpose of this act was to provide "a decent home and a suitable living environment for every American family."

Section 8 is the program under which this rental payment assistance is administered. Some cities get Section 8 assistance; others have an office that administers the housing assistance programs for needy families in the community. Individuals and families must apply to these organizations and be qualified to receive the rental assistance. If qualified, the applicants will have part of their rent paid by the program, and they will be responsible for the balance. In most instances, the tenant's share of the rent does not exceed 20–30 percent of their income.

The advantage of having Section 8 or voucher tenants is that a major portion of the rent is paid by the government. What's more, the government usually is very prompt in payment. Now that's the kind of tenant we all like.

Part of HUD's job is to establish the general market rent for various size apartments and houses in the community. This rent schedule becomes the top rent the tenants are able to pay including any subsidies by HUD. If you have rentals in an area with HUD subsidies, you should find the rent they set to be more than reasonable. These rental rates are based on the size of the unit, the utilities paid, the appliances provided, and so on.

Watch Out!
When choosing HUD tenants, it is important for you to do the same due diligence checking of their references as you would with any other potential tenant. HUD makes no guarantees concerning the tenants' ability to pay their portion of the rent.

One hurdle you will need to face with a HUD-assisted tenant is the inspection of your property by a HUD official. Their goal is to provide decent, safe, and sanitary conditions for the tenants. As long as the unit passes inspection, it will pass the program's requirements. The unit will need to pass inspection before the tenant moves in and will be re-inspected every year.

We say yes to pets!

Should you rent to tenants who have pets? We think so. Most landlords handle the problem by just saying no to pets. This might be the easiest solution but perhaps not the wisest.

When you buy your building, you will inherit a pet policy from the previous owner; he either allowed pets or he didn't. You now have to decide how it is going to work under your watch. Here are some reasons to consider for taking a tenant who has a pet:

- Because the general method of handling the pet issue is not to allow them, it makes it tough for someone with a pet to find a new residence. By considering these tenants, you will have a pool of grateful tenants to pick from.

- Pet owners generally stay in an apartment longer than non-pet owners because it is so tough for them to find a landlord who will take them.

Unofficially...
A landlord cannot legally prohibit an animal that is used to assist someone who is blind, deaf, or disabled.

- Most pet owners are willing to put down a large security deposit if you accept them as a tenant. If the pet damages the unit, you have the money to fix it after they move.

- You can command a premium rent from someone with a pet.

- Accepting tenants with pets is a good method of combating periods of high vacancy.

In these instances, it wouldn't be unreasonable to increase the security deposit 50 percent and add 10 percent to the rental rate. If you decide to consider pets, advertise your unit just that way: "Will consider pets, call to discuss." Finally, it is important that, if you rent to a tenant with a pet, you check their references thoroughly.

It's important to have the checklist previously mentioned (indicating the condition of the unit before the tenants and their pet move in). It will be invaluable if you need to withhold a security deposit to repair damage caused by the pet. You also should take pictures of the unit before they move in just in case you ever need to go to court.

Bright Idea
When considering renting to a pet owner, make sure you interview the pet as well. Their dog might be small now, but even Great Danes are small when they're puppies.

Keeping tenants happy

Once you have a building full of tenants, you need to keep them happy while making the most money for yourself. You know that your main goal from real estate is to make the most profit you can. To do this, you need to keep the customers content. Your customers are your tenants, and your ability to do this will be reflected in the bottom line.

The most important aspect of keeping tenants happy is being sure they are getting their money's worth from the dollars they pay in rent. This is the basic philosophy under which most businesses operate, but it is very easy to forget in the rental business. A restaurant works to put out the best product every time because, if the customer get a bad meal, he might not come back. Once a unit is rented, the customer (the tenant) stills needs to be catered to, just like a restaurant patron.

Timesaver
From the very
first meeting,
give your tenants
a clear sense of
your guidelines
and expecta-
tions. You should
let them know
what you will do
for them as a
landlord and
what you expect
from them as
tenants. This
way, you will
avoid setting
any false
expectations on
either side.

It is easy to buy a property, fix it up, fill it with nice new tenants, and then let it slip back to its old tired condition over time. This doesn't have to happen. If you want to have a sharp property with a great tenant base, fix it up, manage it properly, and keep the property up at all times. Remember that most restaurant customers don't complain about bad food; they just don't come back. With rentals, if you let the building deteriorate over time, the tenants will probably just find another place to live rather than complain.

Addressing tenant requests

The first rule is to take care of tenant complaints as fast as possible. Again, most people don't like to complain, so when they do, assume that the problem has been going on long enough that it is really starting to bother them. It's not your fault that they waited so long to call, but the customer is always right. In addition, it doesn't hurt to ask your tenants when you see them if everything is going okay. They might forget to mention that little leak under the sink unless you ask.

If you have a resident-manager or superintendent, it's a good idea to have some form of check system to be sure they are remembering to let you know about problems. A good way to handle that is to put a clause in your rental agreement about maintenance problems. Here is a sample of what it might say:

> It is the owner's goal to handle your maintenance problems as soon as possible. To assure that your request is processed quickly, please do the following. Promptly report any problems to the resident-manager. Follow this up

by turning in a written request when you make your next rent payment. Please submit any major upgrade requests to:

Rocha Properties

P.O. Box 444

Sacramento, CA 91234

At some point, your tenants might want big upgrades like new appliances or cabinets, but we recommend that you save any major changes for turnovers. That is, unless you have a great long-term tenant that you want to keep happy. On the other hand, items such as floor coverings, window coverings, and paint might in fact need refurbishing while your tenant is in the unit, and you should consider doing it.

Painting the digs

Painting is the kind of maintenance item that can cause problems when it is done, and it doesn't really have any value to you (besides keeping the tenant happy) because you will need to repaint when the tenant leaves anyway. Problems occur because painting is messy; therefore, there is a risk of damage to the tenant's property. For that reason, we recommend two alternatives to a request for you to paint the unit:

1. Offer to buy the paint and have the tenant do the work.

2. Give the tenant a credit for the amount you normally would pay for new paint, but have the tenant contract directly for the painting work themselves.

In both cases, you have removed yourself as far as possible from the liability from any damage.

Window coverings

Window coverings are the easiest request to fulfill because you usually can just have the drapes cleaned or order replacement blinds and then have them installed. These items will hold their value when the tenant eventually moves, and there is not much opportunity for liability. What's more, new blinds or clean drapes, are relatively inexpensive and will certainly add to the value of your rental.

Floor coverings

Requests for carpet can be handled in two ways. One way is to get the carpet cleaned professionally. The process is fairly inexpensive, and it has a couple of good benefits. First, it improves the appearance of the apartment at a nominal cost. Second, frequent carpet cleaning, especially using the steam-extraction method, actually prolongs the life of the carpet. The worst enemy of carpet is the dirt that works its way down to the base of the fibers. The traffic on the carpet then grinds this dirt against the fibers where they are connected to the base and destroys the carpet. It is fairly easy to clean the carpet in an occupied unit because there is no reason to move the furniture. After all, nobody walks on areas occupied by sofas and entertainment centers. You can have the tenant move all his small items into the kitchen or a bathroom.

Moneysaver
If replacing the carpet needs to be done but money is an issue, consider replacing it only in the living area and then just cleaning the carpet in the bedrooms.

If the carpet needs replacing, this will require a significant capital investment from you. The carpet will last for several years, of course, so the benefit of the improvement will not be lost on the one tenant alone. You also should raise the rent to help recover the cost. We recommend a three-year recovery period for new carpet. If the carpet replacement costs you $1,200, the monthly increase in rent can be calculated like this:

$$\frac{\text{Carpet Cost} \quad \$1,200}{\text{Recovery Period} \quad 36 \text{ Months}} = \begin{array}{l} \$33.33 \text{ Rounded to} \\ \$30/\text{Month} \end{array}$$

This is only a recommended amount. If you are in an area where rents are lower, you might have to give tenants a more modest increase so you don't lose them.

New vinyl or linoleum

It's tough to clean vinyl or linoleum beyond what you would expect the tenants to do on their own. If it needs replacing, you should make the decision based on your desire to keep the tenant in the building. This is another item that should last for many years, so it's not a wasted improvement. You usually can include a nominal rent increase with an expense like this. Use the preceding calculation to help you decide how much to raise the rent.

Raising the rent

Raising rents is always a sensitive issue with owners and tenants alike. The problem with most small property owners is they get friendly with their tenants, making the job of raising rents that much tougher. The bottom line, however, is that this is a business. Your cash-on-cash return and your building's ultimate value depend on the amount of your rents. Therefore, raising rents is a necessary evil.

The first secret to raising rents is to know what the competition is doing. If the competition is getting more than you are for comparable units, a rent increase is in order. Don't fret. You probably won't lose a tenant because of a rent increase, especially if you are only taking the rent to the new market rate for the area. Your tenants certainly will not be happy about it, but it would be too much work for them to move and pay the same rent down the street just to "get even."

The second secret to raising rents successfully is to be consistent. If you plan to raise rents on a regular basis, do it every year at about the same time. Most people that work understand a cost of living adjustment, so they will take regular modest increases in stride.

To ease the pain, consider doing something extra for the tenants when you raise the rent. We already have discussed specific increases for items such as carpet or new linoleum. It doesn't hurt to follow or precede the cost of living increase with some general or specific upgrades in the building. A general upgrade might be new furniture in the patio area or new doormats in front of the apartments. A specific upgrade could be to have all the outside windows washed, or you could have all the living room carpets steam-cleaned one Saturday morning. Even a $10 gift certificate to a local coffee house at holiday time would remind them what a great landlord you are.

The best way to get the message about rents to existing tenants in an increasing market is to prominently display the current rental rate on your "For Rent" signs. When existing tenants see apartments being rented at a much higher rate for anyone new coming in, they will be far less apt to object when they get their increases, especially if they are paying less than the market.

Just the facts

- As soon as you close, you need to get all your tenants' signatures on new rental agreements.

- You must make it a habit to do diligent research about the buildings and vacancies in your neighborhood.
- When a tenant gives notice, begin your marketing campaign that very day.
- Discrimination in housing is illegal.
- There are ways to offset the expense of fixing up a unit while the tenant is still there.
- Keeping rents at market rate will help maintain the value of your building.

GET THE SCOOP ON...
Methods of determining expenses before you
buy ▪ How to manage your books effectively ▪
The difference between fixed and variable
expenses ▪ Why a great handyman is worth his
weight in gold ▪ Proven techniques for keeping
utility costs to a minimum ▪ Making capital
expenses and turnovers economically painless

Managing the Expenses

W hen you put on the bookkeeper's hat,
you become the chief financial officer
of your company. As you know, CFOs do
not make the widgets. Their job is to stay on budget
and to make sure the profit margin is as good as it
can be. Without the CFO watching the money, over-
time costs run wild, workers knock off early, and
expense accounts spin out of control.

If you own 100 units, you know how difficult
being in charge of the books is. If you are just starting out with a four-unit building, however, managing your expenses effectively is really not too hard,
even for the novice investor. To understand how to
become proficient in this area, we have broken
down this chapter into the following three areas of
study:

1. How the property operates

2. How to keep the books

3. How to control the expenses

Learning how the property runs

Finding out how a specific property runs should take place before you ever close on a transaction. As mentioned in Chapter 12, "The Due Diligence Period," when you make an offer to buy, you should include a contingency asking for review and approval of all expenses related to the building. Reviewing the true costs in advance will not guarantee how the property will run for you, but it should give a reasonable facsimile. Items you need to see before you consummate a deal include:

- 12 months' worth of all bills for the operation of the building including, but not limited to, the following:
  1. Property taxes
  2. Property insurance
  3. All utility bills including water, trash, sewer, electric, gas, and so on
  4. City licenses and other city fees
  5. Any ongoing maintenance expenses
- Current rent-roll (list of all tenants and agreed-upon rents)
- Rental agreements and applications of tenants
- Copies of all service contracts (laundry, elevator, pool, boiler and heating oil, gardening, and so on)
- Copies of any furniture or equipment leases
- Copies of any major expense items over the last 12 months
- Copies of any guarantees in effect on major improvements

Add any items to this list that you or your agent feels is necessary, especially if you are buying in a

❝
My husband couldn't balance a checkbook if his life depended on it. In our business, he manages the tenants and I'm in charge of the money.
—Leslie R., investor
❞

location that requires upkeep that is out of the ordinary. In areas where it snows a lot, for example, it might be necessary to pay for snow removal in the winter to clear walkways or parking areas. In this case, you would need to see 12 months of bills for this expense.

Sometimes, however, sellers might refuse your request to see the expenses for reasons that are innocent enough. Perhaps he throws the bills away after he makes his payments. If this is the case, ask for copies of his canceled checks and then double-check these figures by talking to the people he wrote them to. If he is being honest in his dealings with you, he should be more than willing to comply. If he is unwilling to supply you with his expenses, however, you should move on to the next deal. The odds are good that he is hiding something.

You might think it would be easier to just ask the seller for a copy of his tax return and review the expenses that way, but this is a bad idea. A tax return may or may not give you accurate information. If a seller is having trouble controlling expenses and decides to sell, it would be easy enough to report fewer expenses to paint a better picture of the property. The best way for you to find out what is going on is to get copies of the actual bills and to study them.

Keeping the books

The least enjoyable part of your real estate job will be writing the checks and actually paying the bills. After all, you're doling out most of your rental income to others when you'd rather keep it for yourself and spend it as you like. Nonetheless, paying bills is a fact of life for any business owner. If you

Bright Idea
Utility companies usually are willing to cooperate with someone trying to get information about utility costs for a building. If you are pleasant, the odds are good that they will give you the information you need.

learn to do it efficiently, you can save yourself time, money, and aggravation along the way.

One checkbook and one checkbook only

The simplest system for keeping books is to have one separate checkbook that you use only for your real estate business. It might be tempting to mix your business and personal checking accounts, but we advise against it. Mixing personal checks and business checks creates a bookkeeping nightmare, especially come tax time.

You should use the larger style checkbook that has three checks per page. These checkbooks have a couple of advantages. First, they give you ample room to write notes regarding each check. Second, a big three-check-per-page checkbook does not lend itself to fitting in your back pocket. This will help reduce the chances of using money in this account for personal expenses. Another good idea is to see if your bank offers a "one write" accounting system. These checkbooks give you a carbon copy of all pertinent information.

This simple checkbook system will work just fine for most small properties. As your business grows and you get a second and then a third property, make sure you open new accounts for each one.

You also need to get a three-compartment filing folder in which to keep your records. These folders are available at any office-supply store. One compartment is for the bills that come in, one is for all your expense receipts, and the last is for your canceled checks, statements, and the checkbook itself. At the end of the tax year, this simple and organized system should help you put your tax return together fairly quickly.

Moneysaver
If you have a tendency to use cash, always make sure to get a receipt and then attach the receipt to your checkbook. Otherwise, you might miss out on the many expense-related write-offs you can claim at the end of the year.

The one-page spreadsheet method

You might want to use a spreadsheet to keep track of your finances. If so, we recommend that you buy spreadsheet paper with at least 20 lines per page and then copy the following list exactly as written down the lefthand side. This list is taken from the 1999 Federal Form E, which is the form you will use to file your taxes at the end of the year. The description for each expense item is worded exactly as the form reads. By keeping track of your expenses this way, you will have an easier time come tax season.

Income							
Rents Received							
Royalties Received							
Expenses							
Advertising							
Auto/Travel							
Cleaning/Maintenance							
Commissions							
Insurance							
Legal/Professional Fees							
Management Fees							
Mortgage Interest							
Other Interest							
Repairs							
Supplies							
Taxes							
Utilities							
Other							

Manual accounting systems

If the single-checkbook system is not working for you and spreadsheets are not sufficient, many manual accounting systems you can purchase will work

Timesaver
No matter how you choose to keep track of your expenses, make sure you organize your books to correspond with the format you need for filing taxes. Your accountant will thank you for it, and his bill will reflect that.

just fine. One of the best is called Property Management D-12 by Safeguard Business Systems. This system, and others like it, is based on a one-entry pegboard system. You keep two cards on each property. The first contains all the vital information you might need—tenants' names, important phone numbers, and so on. The second card is the ledger card. It is used to keep track of all the financial details of the property. These details include all money coming in and all money going out. With this kind of system, you can run all your properties out of one checkbook. The simple coding of the properties and the expenses enables you to develop the reports you need at the end of the year.

The modern method: computerized accounting systems

For those of you with computers, many simple spreadsheet and bookkeeping software programs are available. Most of these property management systems can handle multiple properties and can generate any number of customized reports. You can find these programs advertised in the flyers and booklets put out by apartment owners associations. You also should be able to find them at any office or computer supply stores, as well as via a search on the Internet.

Controlling expenses

There are many expenses associated with the running of a property, and keeping them within reason, even for an experienced investor, is an ongoing struggle. Expenses can be either fixed or variable. Fixed expenses do not fluctuate with rental income. Examples include insurance or property taxes. Variable expenses, on the other hand, increase or decrease with the rent level and the occupancy level of the building. Variable expenses include items such as property maintenance and utility costs.

Fixed expenses

There aren't too many fixed costs associated with income property, and this actually is good news. Because most expenses are variable, you can use your management skill to curtail costs. There are, however, a couple of big fixed expenses that you need to know how to approach. Your biggest fixed expense will probably be your loan payment, to which we devoted an entire chapter (Chapter 5, "Financing Your Investment.") Beyond your loan payments, your tax bill will probably come in a close second.

The tax man's share

Your property tax payment will be a large fixed expense. Even though taxes are not billed monthly, you should think of them as if they were and should set the money aside so you can pay them accordingly. This way, you'll have the funds available when it is time to make the payment.

Another way to ease the pain of having to come up with a large lump sum of money for taxes is to have your lender set up an impound account for you. An impound account is like a forced savings account. You pay your taxes into this account on a regular basis, and the lender makes your tax payment for you as it comes due. Some lenders even give you a break on your interest rate if you have an impound account because you are showing yourself to be a responsible borrower, and that is the kind of customer lenders like best.

The costs of protection

The other major fixed expense is property insurance. You pay insurance just once a year, but like

Watch Out!
It can be tempting to use money set aside for taxes for other purposes, but as you can imagine, this can cause major problems. In fact, most real estate loans include a clause that requires you to pay your taxes when due; otherwise, the lender can call your loan due and payable immediately.

taxes, you should set the money aside for this bill each month. In fact, if you have money impounded each month for your taxes, you probably can include the funds for your insurance in the same account.

If you shop wisely, you can save a lot of money on insurance. We recommend the following three ways to find savings:

1. Shop around and compare prices of major insurance carriers as well as independent brokers.

2. Vary the dollar amount of the deductible on losses.

3. Vary the dollar amount of liability coverage.

Be sure to get quotes from all the major carriers as well as several local independent agents because the rates will vary. You should repeat the process every year because rates change depending on the type of business the insurance companies want to attract. It is not uncommon to find cheaper insurance elsewhere even after a year or two of property ownership.

For an apartment or commercial building, you need to get a package policy. A package policy includes fire and extended coverage but does not include flood or earthquake coverage. Most package policies also include some type of loss-of-rents coverage. This is important to have because lenders will require you to make your mortgage payment even if the property is damaged and rent isn't coming in.

You also need to be aware of the co-insurance issue. Most policies have a clause that requires you to carry a certain percentage of the replacement cost of the structure; an average number is 90 percent. The clause says that, in the event you carry less insurance than this percentage, you become a co-insurer with the insurance company if there are any losses. Simply put, this means that, if you have a loss, the insurance company will pay their share, and you will have to pay yours. This can spell financial ruin.

If you do not properly insure your property for the correct replacement cost, the effect of a loss can be costly. If the cost to rebuild a property is $200,000 and you have decided to only carry $150,000 worth of insurance, for example, your share of a $25,000 loss due to a fire, assuming there is a 90 percent co-insurance clause, will look like this:

Unofficially...
Title is usually transferred between sellers and buyers when the property "records." Recordation is the moment when the transaction is filed with the county recorder's office.

Reproduction Cost	$200,000
90% Value	$190,000
Actual Insurance	$150,000

$$\frac{\text{Actual Coverage} \quad \$150,000}{\text{Repro Cost} \quad \$200,000} = 75\% \text{ Co-Insurance Rate}$$

Cost Of Fire Repairs	$25,000
Insurance Pays (75%)	× .75
Dollar Value	$18,750

Cost Of Loss	$25,000
Insurance Payment	–$18,750
Your Share Of Loss	$6,250

Note that this $6,250 is in addition to your out-of-pocket deductible on the loss. The theory is that you can lower the price of your policy by raising the deductible and by covering less of the value of the structure. This problem usually doesn't surface unless you have a loss. When it does surface, however, property owners and insurance agents invariably point the finger at each other.

When buying a home, this situation does not present itself very often because most of these policies have a guaranteed replacement clause. Apartment policies, however, are not usually structured that

Watch Out!
Make sure your insurance agent properly insures your building for the current replacement cost. Otherwise, you could get stuck paying a large sum of money if you file a claim and it turns out that you do not have enough coverage.

way. It is important that, before your agent sells you a policy, he goes out and measures the property to find out the true square footage. This way, he can accurately calculate the current replacement cost of the building. If the cost (by his calculation) means you will have to buy more insurance than the price of the property, which is not unusual, bite your tongue and pay it. You cannot count on the lender catching this problem (being under insured) because most only worry about enough insurance to cover their loan.

Other fixed expenses

Other minor fixed expenses can be associated with real estate such as pool service, pest control, and gardening costs, all of which you can take steps to control. The first thing to know is that these kinds of expenses usually save you money in the long run because they treat potential problems when they are minor, thus keeping them from becoming major. As with any other costs, shop around so you can get the best rates. Do not be afraid to switch services if you find one for a lower cost. Many times, your existing providers will lower their fees to keep your business if they find out you are considering changing companies.

Variable expenses

Many variable expenses come into play during the management of a property. Remember that a variable expense is one that changes; it will increase or decrease with the rent level and occupancy level of the building. Two keys to keeping variable expenses at a minimum are to make sure you shop around and to avoid hiring overqualified contractors for basic fix-it jobs.

Everyone needs a handyman

The best way to save money on variable expenses is to get a good handyman—someone who can do most of the minor repairs around the property but does not have the knowledge (or license) to do major repairs. This can mean the difference between paying $15 per hour verses $50 per hour. Another advantage is that a handyman can take care of more than one type of problem when he goes to the property. This will save you from paying specialized professionals a minimum fee just to show up.

Your savings could look like this: The plumber comes to fix a leaky faucet in unit #1 and the bill is $45. You get an electrician out to fix the broken light switch in the laundry room. His minimum fee for a service call is $65. Finally, you need to replace an interior door on unit #3, and your general contractor charges you $120 for the parts and labor. Total cost for all the work is $230.00.

Now let's contrast this with what it could cost for one handyman to do the same work.

Parts	
Faucet Washer & Seats	$2.50
Light Switch	$1.50
30" Door	$29.00
Door Handle	$9.00
Hinges	$6.00
1 Quart Paint	+$4.95
Total Parts	**$52.95**
Labor @ $15 Per Hour × 4 Hours	+$60.00
Total for Handyman	**$112.95**
Cost for Professional Contractors	$230.00
Cost for Handyman To Do Same Work	−$112.95
Savings By Using A Handyman	**$117.05**

It will take some trial and error to find a good handyman because most of the good ones are kept

Timesaver
Using a handyman to handle all minor repair work always will save you time. This is because you or your manager only has to meet one person at the property rather than one for every little job that needs attention.

pretty busy. Some advertise in local papers; others find work by word of mouth. One good place to find workers is at your local home-improvement center or hardware store because this is where handymen purchase their supplies and thus the employees get to know them as regular customers. Additionally, make it a point to visit larger buildings in your area that have resident-managers. They might know of a good handyman who is eager to make some extra money working on your building as well.

Become a bargain hunter

One basic but often overlooked method for reducing costs is to shop around. There is a vast difference in what various contractors charge and what parts can cost for your property. You do not need to get three or four bids for every job, but you should get in the habit of always shopping contractors and suppliers, even when you don't need anything done.

You will find that materials can be 50 percent of the cost of any repair job. Many retail stores advertise loss leaders. A loss leader is a product advertised at a reduced rate to bring customers in the door. You can save a lot of money on materials by seeking out advertised loss leaders and stockpiling things you will need along the way. When things need fixing, you will only have to pay a handyman for labor.

Water bills and water damage

A big drain on your wallet can be your water bill. Although you have no control over the price of water, you can control how much is used. Toilets are the worst culprits when it comes to water waste. The classic problem is a toilet in which the flapper valve no longer seats properly, and it allows a slow, almost unperceptible trickle of water to run day and night.

In communities with higher water costs because of supply issues, this can double or even triple your bill quickly.

Worn washers on faucets are another big water waster. As the washers in faucets age, they wear out and become brittle. This leads to small breaks that show up as annoying drips from the faucet. The problem is that tenants do not mind minor drips, and they usually will not want to bother the landlord because of one. This constant leak, just like the toilet, can drive your water bill sky high.

There are two other classic water-related problems that tenants don't tell you about until the damage is done. The first is a leak in the seal around the toilet. The seal only costs about $1.25, and your handyman probably would charge you less than $25 if you catch the problem early enough. If not, you will need to replace the subflooring and the floor covering and then fix the problem. The total cost would be upwards of $250.

The other problem is the caulking around the shower. As caulking ages and cracks, it allows water to migrate to the drywall or plaster outside the shower door. A tube of caulking costs about a dollar, but a wall repair can cost $50 or more. In addition, these leaks usually affect the flooring, and we've already seen what that can cost.

The most annoying and recurring plumbing problems are clogged toilets and drains. Unless you are smart, they invariably can cost you time and money again and again. Clogged drains and toilets fall into three groups:

1. Tenant-caused problem

2. Tree roots growing into the pipes

3. Mystery problems

> **"**
> When I first started out as a resident-manager, I wasn't very good at fixing things. But after watching electricians and plumbers and handymen do work at the property, I can now do most of the repairs myself.
> —Adam F., resident-manager
> **"**

Far and away, tenants cause most of the clogged drains and toilets, even if there is no way to know for sure. For that reason, you should have a clause in your rental agreement addressing this issue. Make sure tenants initials this clause so you both will have proof that they read and understood their responsibility. It should read:

> Tenant will pay for any drain stoppages caused by their own negligence. Owner will provide tenant with a copy of the bill showing the cause found by the plumber.

The second method of controlling water problems is to have a handyman or plumber do a checkup on your building once a year. Have him go through all the units, check all the fixtures, and make any necessary repairs. It will be well worth the expense. This also will give you a chance to check the units in general to see whether there are any other problems you need to address.

Finding a reliable drain-cleaning specialist who works 24 hours a day also is important. Their rates can vary, so do your shopping and check references. When you have picked a company, set up your billing account ahead of time because, inevitably, the stoppage will occur late at night or over the weekend. Make sure the worker understands to always write the cause of the problem on the bill (if it can be determined) because you can use this to collect from the tenant if he or she was at fault.

Finally, buildings with steam or hot-water heating systems are prone to leaks. Because these leaks often are at floor level and sometimes are behind radiator covers, they can go undetected. Tenants also fail to report such leaks because they tend to affect the apartment below more than the one with

"
I encourage my tenants to keep me informed of even the little things that need fixing. It's really not a bother because it allows me to save money by fixing problems before they get out of hand.
—Mari H., investor
"

the leak. Make sure you check these heating systems annually and keep them in proper working order.

Cutting down on electricity costs

If you are paying for electricity on your property, it probably is for the outside lights, garage, and the laundry room. You cannot eliminate these lights because they are needed for security, but you can work to cut down on your bill. To begin with, you should replace the current fixtures and install low-voltage florescent lights. These will save you money on the bill, and the bulbs actually last longer than the nonfluorescent bulbs. You also should put the lights on a timer so they do not have to run all night. For areas that are not used much, you should have motion-detection lights that only come on if movement is detected. Not only do they cut down on costs because they are not on very often, they also help prevent crime by scaring intruders away when they come on.

Nipping the gas bill

Usually, the only gas you will pay for is for the laundry room and sometimes for the hot water in the apartments. In the laundry room, you can do two things to cut costs. First, make sure there is an energy-saving blanket on the water heater. These fiberglass coverings go around the heater to provide insulation and can easily be installed by your handyman. The second way to save money is to always keep the thermostat on the heater at the lowest level. Most tenants only do laundry on the weekend or at night, so there is no reason to keep the water hot for all those extra hours when the equipment is not in use.

If you are paying for hot water in the apartments, make sure the heater has an energy-saving blanket as well. In addition, if the hot-water heater holds 100 gallons or more, it should be equipped with a recirculating pump. Recirculating pumps move the hot water through the pipes continually so that the apartments farthest away from the heater get hot water just as quickly as the apartments closest to the heater. Otherwise, the tenants farthest away will waste a lot of water (and money) waiting for the hot water to get to their unit.

Heating and air conditioning

In many areas of the country, the property owner provides heating and air conditioning for the tenants. This can be a significant expense. A couple of ways to keep these costs under control include:

1. Review 12 months of utility bills before you buy so you're sure the costs are reasonable for your area.

2. Have your heating and air conditioning units serviced regularly so they operate at maximum efficiency.

3. Keep thermostats set at the "Goldilocks" temperature, which means not too hot and not too cold. (Some communities mandate minimum day and night temperatures during cold months.)

Interior painting

Interior painting is a frequent expense of property ownership. One way to save money is to pick one color of paint for all your units and use it on all future paint jobs. Besides never having to worry about whether paint matches again, in many cases, it will allow you to just do touch-up painting when you have a turnover.

You usually can find lots of competing companies and individuals looking for painting work. You can either use professionals or, again, trim costs by hiring a handyman. The key point here is to check references for speed and quality of workmanship. A quick-and-cheap job will not save any money if your carpets are stained with paint and the windows all need to be cleaned of over-spray.

Carpet and floor covering

Carpet, if it is of decent quality, should last three years or more. The best way to help your carpet last is frequent and proper cleaning. If your tenants are not in the habit of paying to get their carpet cleaned, you should do it yearly and tack on the cost with their annual rent increase. They get something for the increase, and you add some life to the carpet.

You should pick carpet for your units just like paint. Pick one color and one brand and stick with it. Make sure it is a brand and color that won't be discontinued in a few years when you need it. If a unit has a bad stain, you usually can cut the stain out and patch it with some of the extra carpet you have lying around. If the stain is in a unit for which you don't have any extra carpet, take a piece from a closet to make the repair or take a 3 × 3 section from in front of the front door. You can always replace the closet with a remnant from any carpet store. The piece in front of the door can be replaced with vinyl, which will look fine. The idea is to make the repair and save having to replace the entire carpet because of one or two stains. Remember the bumper sticker, "Stains happen!"

Like carpet, vinyl and linoleum can take a beating, especially in the kitchen. The usual problem is

Timesaver
Be sure to tell your painters whether you will be putting in new carpet after they paint. If so, their preparation time will be cut down considerably.

Bright Idea
If you only need carpet in one or two rooms, consider buying used carpet. You sometimes can locate used carpet by talking to a carpet installer and telling him what you are looking for. Odds are, he would be more than happy to make a buck by selling you something he otherwise would throw away.

a tear or hole caused by a tenant dragging the refrigerator or stove across the floor. If the overall condition of the vinyl is decent, your handyman should be able to repair it by taking a small piece of existing vinyl from underneath the refrigerator or stove. This can be replaced with a 12" × 12" square that can be purchased at any hardware or home improvement center. Don't worry if it is not an exact match because the stove or refrigerator will be covering it.

Master-metered properties

Some properties are master metered. This means there is only one utility meter for all the units, and unfortunately, the landlord is the guy who gets stuck paying the bill. You usually find master-metered properties in areas where the buildings are older, and most are made up of smaller units containing singles and one bedrooms. To a novice investor, these buildings look attractive at first because the price compared to the income looks good. Once you factor in the added costs of the utilities, however, any initial attraction may quickly fade.

There are a couple of things you can do to cut costs on master-metered buildings. First, explore the possibility of changing the metering so the tenants pay their utility bills instead of you. This will require you to get some bids and then do an analysis to see whether it is worth the expense. Many older properties are in need of a wiring upgrade, and doing this at the same time might not add that much more to the price of just changing the metering. Gas, on the other hand, might be more costly to separate. Its value and feasibility will depend on the location of the stove and the heater.

The other method to cut costs on a master-metered building is to install energy-saving light

fixtures and appliances to each and every apartment. Long-life, low-voltage lights can save significantly on the electric bill. Installing modern stoves
and heaters also can save on gas usage while improving the appearance of your units. Many utility companies offer rebate programs to encourage these
upgrades. Some will even assist in the cost of
upgraded insulation, which will help cut down the
cost of heating.

High-cost capital expenses

Capital expenses are costs that cannot be written off
in full in the year you spend the money. The IRS
says that these are items that have a useful life of
more than one year or that increase the value of the
property. Some examples include:

- Carpeting

- A new stove or refrigerator

- New plumbing or a new roof

- An addition to the building

- New asphalt on the driveway

When you purchase your property, you should
make an assessment of all capital expenses and start
working on cost estimates for replacements. By
doing this from the get-go, you can start setting
some money aside each month so you will be able to
take the cost of the item out of operations rather
than out of your pocket. It wouldn't hurt to put
some of that money in a money market account or
even a certificate of deposit. Just make sure you
keep some money in reserve for emergencies.

The following capital expense budget is for our
four-unit example at 1800 Mariposa Lane. We have
estimated the time for the expense in months to

Watch Out!
The big problem
with master-
metered build-
ings is that ten-
ants in these
buildings have
no incentive to
turn off any of
the utilities. This
is because you
are paying the
bill and they
are not.

make it easier to calculate the monthly amount you should put aside from the cash flow:

Item	Months Until Replacement	Total Cost	Monthly Reserve
Carpet Unit #1	12	$400	$33
Carpet Unit #3	24	$700	$29
Paint Exterior	48	$1,500	$31
Replace Roof	60	+$3,000	+$50
Total		$5,600	$143

By budgeting for capital expenditures and setting aside money each month, you will be able to pay for the expense as planned feeling as if you'd been pick-pocketed every time a capital expense comes along. This is an ongoing process, so you will need to revisit your budget every year or so to add and delete items.

The major disadvantage of larger capital items is that the IRS says you must write off the expense over time, even though you spend the money in one lump sum. A new roof, for instance, might require a depreciation schedule that goes beyond the period you will be holding the property. For that reason, many investors prefer to repair major items in stages rather than doing it all at once and having to pay for the entire capital expense in one year. If your roof has four sections, for example, you might be better off repairing each section separately and expensing the cost in the year you do the work. This also might save on permit fees because many cities do not require a permit for a mere repair, but they would if you put on a whole new roof.

If you are purchasing a property as a fixer-upper project, you will be doing the same kind of budget. The difference is that you will be including the costs in your initial capital requirements rather than in your future capital budget. Most properties will need some kind of capital budget unless they are new or recently upgraded. At a minimum, you should be setting aside money for floor and window coverings because they are the most frequently changed items.

Handling tenant turnovers

The last and least desirable yet ongoing expense of a property is the turnover. Unfortunately, turnovers come with very short notice, usually 30 days or less. What's worse is that tenants do not care if you had earmarked their rent money for something else or had a vacation planned for the very weekend they give notice. When it is time to move on, they do. The key to making turnovers as emotionally and financially tolerable as possible is having a plan in place before they happen.

You should develop a turnover budget for each apartment or each size apartment in your property. By having this budget and cost breakdown ahead of time, you will know what items to order and which subcontractors are needed the minute someone gives notice. The budget might look like this:

Moneysaver
As long as you stay within legal limits, don't be shy about asking tenants for a sizable security deposit. If they take care of the unit, they probably will get a good portion of it back. If they do any serious damage, you'll have the money to make it rent-ready for the next tenant.

TURNOVER BUDGET—2 BEDROOM, 800 SQUARE FEET

Carpet	75 Yards	$600
Vinyl	125 Square Feet	$125
Carpet Cleaning		$60
Painting	Off White #6800	$225
Blinds	7 Windows	$105
General Cleaning		$75
Accessories And Misc.		+$50
Total		$1,240

Just the facts

- Insist on seeing all income and expense statements before you buy.

- Any bookkeeping system you choose should correspond with IRS tax forms to make filing your taxes easier.

- Use impound accounts to help save for property taxes and insurance payments.

- A good handyman is essential to a successful real estate operation.

- You must budget in advance for capital expenses and turnovers.

GET THE SCOOP ON...
What "curb appeal" is and why you must have
it ▪ How to manage the common areas of your
building ▪ The truth behind security systems ▪
Why you need a resident-manager ▪ The best
way to structure a manager's salary ▪ Getting
the most out of professional property
management ▪ How to dramatically increase
your profits by doing an interior upgrade

The Big Picture of Management

O nce you become an income property owner, you are in charge of your own small business. It feels great to puff up your chest and tell everyone you know that you own a wonderful piece of property. Unless it's raw land, however, you have to work at it just like any other business. As a real estate investor, the business you chose is the renting of apartments. Your goal now is to keep the units full and to get the highest rent per square foot possible.

The allure of "curb appeal"

It has been said that the clothes make the man. The same holds true for your rental property. The first impression from the street will be the one to which potential tenants respond. If your building doesn't show well when prospects drive up, the odds are good that they will probably just keep on going.

Timesaver
When placing ads to fill your vacancies, make sure they are factual and list the most positive aspects of your rental. Also be sure to say how much the unit's rent is. This will help reduce calls from people who can't afford your apartment.

The most important sales tool you have as a property owner is your building's "curb appeal." Curb appeal is how inviting your building looks from the street. To get the best tenants and command the highest rent, you want to have the nicest building on the block. When a prospective tenant drives up, you want him to think, "Wow, this is where I want to live!"

An identity all your own

The first thing a prospect will see when he drives up is the front elevation of your property. The front elevation is the view as you approach the building. It is a combination of the paint, landscaping, and identity of your property. These aspects combine to create a theme for your building.

If you think about it, most large apartment complexes have an identity or theme all their own. This begins with having a sign out front with the name of the property on it. This kind of attention to detail can work for large and small units alike. Have a nice wooden sign made up with a catchy name for your building etched into it. If your building is on Mariposa Lane and has nice landscaping, why not call it "Mariposa Gardens"? This special touch will help create the kind of identity people like. Just make sure no one else in the neighborhood is already using the name you've chosen because this could cause confusion.

Hearty plants and a mowed lawn

Landscaping is another important aspect of the curb appeal of your property. There is nothing appealing or attractive about a drab lawn surrounding a square-shaped building. You don't need to spend a fortune on landscaping, however, to spruce up your investment. Simply buying some low-maintenance plants and shrubs will make your property stand out from your neighbors.

A good way to plan a project like this is to drive around and look at buildings and homes that have landscaping you like. If you take photos of the ones that catch your eye, you can later review them with the employees of your local home-improvement center and have them help you work up a plan for your property that will be affordable and attractive. Another option is to contact the owner or resident-manager of the buildings you like and ask who did the landscaping.

Automatic sprinklers and outdoor lighting

It is worth the initial extra expense to install an automated sprinkler system after you buy. It will pay for itself the first time your manager goes on vacation and your landscaping lives to tell about it. Another nice addition to the outside of your building is a low-voltage lighting system. These are very reasonably priced and will add a lot of class to the curb appeal of your property at night. Many prospective tenants see your property for the first time after they get off work, and this kind of lighting really makes a property stand out from the competition. This lighting also can reduce the potential for crime and lawsuits, making it an even smarter investment.

A fresh coat of paint

The exterior paint of your building also is key to making a great first impression. Your building's color choice can either date it or make it. Once again, while driving around, look at color combinations that stand out on properties similar to yours. Take pictures and keep track of the addresses in case you want to try to match the colors for your

Moneysaver
Make sure to landscape with low-maintenance plants that are hearty. Having shrubbery that won't die easily will help keep your hard-earned money where it belongs...in your pocket.

own property. A word of caution, however: Before you order a couple hundred gallons of paint, get a pint of the color (or colors) you plan to use and try it out on an inconspicuous wall to see how it will actually look. Just as new clothes often look better on the mannequin in the store, new paint sometimes looks completely different on your building. Also, check to see whether there are any zoning restrictions on exterior colors. Some towns and historical districts have strict regulations.

The front entrance and lobby

Keep the front entrance to your property looking sharp. In fact, because this is such a high traffic area, the lobby should always be kept spotless. Pay your gardener or manager a few extra bucks to make sure it is cleaned regularly. As for the lobby area, put some effort into making it look attractive, too. A couple of pieces of furniture, a few silk plants, and some pictures will do wonders. You also can carpet or tile this entrance to enhance its appeal. Your current tenants, as well as any potential new ones, will surely appreciate it.

The common area

Bright Idea
Make a point of driving around the neighborhood and seeing how your competition takes care of their properties. Are they doing a better job than you are? If so, they will attract the good tenants and the high rents you desire.

Another area that needs regular maintenance is the common area of a property. Even in smaller buildings, areas that aren't rented still need attention. One of the most visited areas that often goes unattended is the laundry room. This area should be kept locked and well-lit. Your tenants need to feel safe if they have to do laundry in the evening. Keeping the laundry room clean also is important. Health and legal concerns could arise if your laundry room isn't kept up.

If your laundry machines are provided by an outside laundry contractor (which is very common), make sure they regularly service them and keep the exteriors clean. Have them post a sign in the laundry room so the tenants know how to get in touch with them if something goes wrong with a machine. This information also should be spelled out in your rental agreement so the tenants know you are not responsible for the laundry machines.

You should have your own posted list of laundry room rules including:

- Laundry room hours: 8 a.m. to 10 p.m.
- Contact Mr. Machine at 1-800-555-5678 for problems.
- Residents, please clean up after use.
- For your safety, please keep door locked at all times.
- Never leave children alone in laundry room.
- Please report any water leaks to manager immediately.

Your laundry room should have a trash can and (if there is enough room) a table so your tenants can fold their clothes. If you have a table, you'll want a couple of inexpensive folding chairs; otherwise, people will sit on the table, which might break or collapse under them. It's also important to have nonslip floor covering because water leaks are common in laundry rooms. You don't want a tenant with an armload of laundry to slip and fall because the floor was wet. A wet floor in a laundry room is a lawsuit waiting to happen.

As for trash areas, they often get dirty and litter-strewn if not attended to regularly. Because these areas often are out of the way, you should make sure they are well-lit and secure. You also should consider having a window that peers into this area so

Watch Out!
Beware of tenants who monopolize the laundry machines. You don't want to lose good tenants because they consistently have a problem finding an empty washer or dryer.

tenants can see if anyone is in there before they go in. Recycling bins should be clearly marked.

Parking concerns

Parking areas are another location that often gets overlooked. The way you maintain this area depends on whether you have open parking, garages, carports, or a subterranean parking structure. Regardless, the first thing to do is to paint numbers on the spots and assign them to your tenants. You should do this even if you have open parking. Nothing starts feuds quicker in a building than someone parking in another person's parking space. Assigning spots will help eliminate any potential conflicts.

Any extra parking spaces (over and above the ones assigned to your tenants) can be used for two things:

1. They should be made available to tenants who need more parking (for an extra monthly fee, of course).

2. You should have spots available for guest parking. If there aren't any rules governing guest parking in your area, one guest space for every four units is a good rule of thumb to live by.

Your parking area should have a sign that says you have the legal right to remove any nontenant cars from tenant spots. Your tenants will appreciate this. Most cities require posting a sign that cites the corresponding vehicle code and a phone number to call if a car is towed.

Parking rules should be spelled out in your rental agreements and also be posted in the parking area. They should include:

■ Only park in designated areas

■ Guest parking in assigned areas only

- No storage in assigned parking spots
- No storage of flammable or dangerous materials
- No car washing in parking area
- No auto repairs or oil changing in parking area

Driveways and parking surfaces should be properly maintained and serviced. Your tenants see these areas every day, and they are part of the overall appearance of your building. If you fix small cracks and holes as they occur, it will save you a major expense later on. Your best tenant with the nice car might just move out because of the holes in the pavement and the dingy driveway you didn't maintain.

Security gates and entrance systems

In recent years, more and more parking areas have some type of security gate or system. In addition to the cost of the gates and the equipment that runs them, you have codes, cards, or clickers to worry about. At best, they keep out the guests that would normally park in the spots marked "No Parking." In truth, these systems do little to discourage car break-ins or car thefts, but they do give potential tenants a sense of security. Nevertheless, it is not wise to advertise "secure parking" because you might be held legally liable if your tenants suffer a loss.

The same thinking that goes into security gates also applies to security entrance systems. When you advertise an amenity such as a security entry system as a way of inducing a tenant to rent your property, it can easily create additional legal liability for you if those systems fail. Often enough, they do fail, and it is the tenants who cause the failures. They forget their keys, they lose their clickers, or they have to make several trips with packages so they prop the security door open and somehow harm the system.

Unofficially...
Security gate systems provide a false sense of security, and most landlords agree that they are not worth having.

Regardless of how it happens, it happens. Unfortunately, you need an expensive specialist to do the repairs. A lawsuit resulting from a failed security system could bankrupt you.

Locks and keys to worry about

Many tenants make extra keys for their apartments and take old keys with them when they move. It would be a disaster if a former tenant gained unlawful entry to a current tenant's unit. For this reason, you must either change locks or, at the very least, make sure you rekey each unit after every turnover.

It is not advisable to leave extra sets of keys with a manager unless you know him extremely well. Even then, there is some risk involved because an intruder could break in to the manager's apartment, take the keys, and have access to all the other units. Instead, if you keep all extra sets of keys, you probably won't have to worry about your manager ever being accused of taking anything from any of your tenants.

Maintenance and repairmen

Many maintenance and repair people will need access to your units. It is important for you to use reputable companies that are bonded and/or insured. Never give a key to a repair contractor to use unsupervised. A situation like this simply has too great a potential to create liability for both of you when the tenant starts to complain about missing jewelry, money, CDs, or television sets. If at all possible, let the tenant and contractors set the appointment for repair themselves.

Window security

Security for your windows also is important. If the windows in your units have any type of locks, you must make sure they are always working properly. In some urban areas, security window bars are common.

Timesaver
It is best if tenants are home when repair work is done. This way, they can communicate the problem they have and can keep an eye on their belongings. If the tenants cannot be home, it is imperative that someone you trust stay with the repair contractor at all times while he is completing his work.

These bars can indeed keep intruders out, but they also can make it nearly impossible to escape in the case of a fire or another emergency. For that reason, window bars, especially in bedrooms, all should be equipped with quick-release mechanisms. Furthermore, make sure you check the building codes to make sure you meet current standards. Again, your potential legal liability for these items is enormous if they fail.

Bright Idea
Keep trees and bushes trimmed and away from ground floor windows. They can inadvertently offer an intruder a place to hide when trying to open a window.

Security summary

Security is a major issue for most tenants, and it should be for you as well. There are two major points to remember regarding security:

1. If you advertise that your building is a "secure building" either in print-ads or in what you say, although it becomes part of the inducement for people to rent your units, it also becomes part of your contract and can create a lot of additional liability on your part.

2. It is imperative that you quickly repair any security-related items that are broken including door locks, security doors, window locks, window bars, and security gates. Delays in making these repairs can ruin you financially.

Your management team

Unless you're Superman, you probably will need the help of others to help you manage your properties. In the beginning, you most likely will use the services of a superintendent or a modified resident-manager. This person is a tenant who helps out on occasion. From there, you might go with a paid resident-manager. Eventually, you might even want to turn your buildings over to a professional property management company.

Manage the first one yourself

We strongly advise that you manage your first property yourself. This experience will be invaluable to you, especially when it comes time to hire resident-managers, superintendents, and property management companies. The most important skill you will learn from managing the first one yourself is the ability to understand and communicate with your customers effectively. It is very easy to forget that tenants are customers. Without them, you could not make any money in this business. The more absent you are from contact with them, the less you understand them.

A resident-manager or superintendent

The duties of a resident manager can vary greatly. Large apartment complexes or buildings have full-time resident-managers who get a rent-free apartment and a salary for managing the property. Some are even professionally trained and are usually in high demand. Your first resident-manager probably won't need these kinds of credentials.

Most buildings, even small ones, can use a resident-manager. This person will serve as your eyes and ears when you're not there. He can call you if there is a problem and can show the apartments to potential new tenants when there is a vacancy. For this level of assistance, you should give him slightly reduced rent and an additional flat fee if he assists you in renting a unit. A situation like this is good for you and is good for him, too.

As a rule of thumb, the resident-management fee you are going to pay should be about 5 percent of the gross income of the property. At 1800 Mariposa Lane, the income is $550 per apartment for a monthly total of $2,200. You wouldn't pay someone to manage themselves, so the fee would be 5 percent of the rent on the remaining three units, which is $82.50 per month ($1,650 × 5% = $82.50). You could structure the deal so you give the individual a rent reduction of $50 every month and then an additional fee of about 10 percent of the cost of any rental he helped with. This would give the person an additional $55 ($550 × 10% = $55.00) on top of their monthly $50 rent reduction. Though the person made $105 this month, ($50 rent reduction plus $55 for helping to rent a vacant unit), there will be other months when there won't be any rentals to help with, so he'll only get the $50 rent reduction. In the end, the person will end up averaging around the $82.50 proposed target per month.

For this small level of management, you will not need a big list of rules for this person to follow. The manager should call if he knows of a problem, should look out for the building, and occasionally will help out on a rental.

An involved resident-manager

When you own larger properties, it becomes necessary to have a more involved resident-manager. In these larger properties, the manager can perform more duties for you, so a more organized system of directing his efforts is necessary. You should create a list of tasks for the resident-manager to accomplish each month. This should be in writing and should be signed by both you and your manager. It is important for the compensation to be spelled out for the work you expect. As a general rule, it is best to have a small basic salary with duties listed for that amount. Offer an additional flat fee on top of the salary for any other tasks you want completed.

Unofficially...
Many cities and states have rules that require you to have a resident-manager for a certain number of units. Check with your local city or county government to find out the rules in your area.

It helps to express all the tasks in terms of hours and to use an hourly wage to arrive at the flat fee for the task. The reason for this is that, from a practical standpoint, most of the salary on smaller property just goes to a reduction in what the manager pays in rent. If you only give a flat fee, the person gets used to paying this lower rent and has no incentive to do a good job on the various other things that should get done around the building. By separating the various tasks, the implication is that someone else can do them if the manager decides he does not want the work.

With any management job such as this, you have to start with a budget and then assign the work and the hourly wage based on that budget. Let's assume you have a 20-unit building, and the units rent for $600 each. This means a monthly gross of $11,400 ($600 × 19 units = $11,400) not counting the manager's apartment. Using the rule of thumb of 5 percent, the management fee should be $570 per month ($11,400 × 5% = $570). Remember, you should assign a reasonable hourly wage for duties you want the manager to accomplish. If we assume an hourly wage of $8.50, this equates to about 67 hours per month ($570 ÷ $8.50 = 67).

The following is an example of the kind of tasks you might expect from your manager:

Management Duties

Collect Rent from Tenants	3 Hours
Bring Rent to Owner	1 Hour
Be Available for Tenants	30 Hours
General Cleaning of Grounds	7 Hours
Clean Decks and Laundry Area	8 Hours
General Maintenance	18 Hours
Touch Up Painting	
Light Gardening	
Minor Repairs	
Total Hours	67 Hours

Now the manager has some guidelines as to the amount of time expected for the salary you are paying. In reality, he probably won't be putting in nearly this much time on all these tasks, but this type of list will serve as a reminder of just how much he is receiving for this job as compared to a regular job. If you find that cleanup isn't getting done or that the manager is complaining about doing the repairs you requested, you can hire someone else to do the work and adjust the salary accordingly.

Managing the big buildings

When you graduate to larger properties, you will have to fine-tune your management control system. At this high level of investing, you should have written policy manuals, reporting systems, and formalized meetings to review the operation of the property. We don't have space in this book to properly cover this level of management, but we have recommended several books in Appendix C that should be helpful.

Professional property management

Most owners, at some point in their investment careers, decide to turn their properties over to professional property management companies. You might choose to do this to spend more time with your family because the demands of your regular job have increased, or maybe you just want "out." Whatever the reason, there are a number of realities about professional property management companies of which you need to be aware.

The most important reality is this: You probably will never find a company that will do as good a job as you did. It is not that they do not want to do a good job or that they do not have the capability of

> **"**
> The best property manager I ever had was a married couple. He was handy and worked during the day. She was a stay-at-home mother who didn't mind looking after things at the building while her husband was away.
> —Neil C., investor
> **"**

doing the job. The fact is simply that you could not afford to pay them to work your properties as you would. We say this with the assumption that you have worked your way into management. You bought that first four-unit building years ago and now have five properties totaling 65 units. You have done it all and can do it all, but now you just want to kick back for awhile.

Remember that the management company is in business to make a profit. You will be paying a fee based on the scheduled rent of your property. This typically is 5 to 7 percent of your gross rents, though it might be higher in some areas. For this fee, the company has to pay its office staff to do your accounting, pay its field staff to oversee the property, and make a profit.

There are a couple of things you can do to get the most for your money. First, don't pick a company because they have a fancy office or an attractive brochure stating how good they are. What you really want from management is three things:

1. Units rented at the market rates

2. As little vacancy as possible

3. Expenses controlled and on budget

Ask around before you pick a company. Your real estate agent should be able to make some suggestions. The best source will be to check the companies managing in the area around your properties. Most management companies put signs on the properties they manage, so you should be able to find a few companies that way. Try to get the names of some of the owners of properties managed by the companies you are considering and then go talk to them. It will take some extra work to hunt down the owners using the sign method, but you will get the most unbiased opinion that way.

After you have narrowed the field down to a couple of choices, make an appointment and go talk to the person in charge of new business. Once you have listened to the sales pitch, you will want to focus in on the philosophy of management to which the company adheres. Ask some specific questions so you know how much effort will be devoted to hands-on management. These questions should include:

Watch Out!
Do not get owner referrals from the management companies themselves. They no doubt will pick the ones who will give them the most favorable review.

- What is their management fee?

- Are there any extra charges for showing rentals or going to court on evictions?

- What kind of advertising do they do for vacancies?

- What is the typical cost of cleaning a vacant unit?

- How long does it take to make a vacant unit rent-ready?

- What are their business hours?

- Who covers rental calls on the weekends?

- What types of reports will they give you?

- When are the reports mailed each month?

- What is their policy on slow or nonpaying tenants?

- What kind of training does their staff have?

- Do the owner and/or manager own property themselves?

- Does anyone check up on the repair work done by the contractors they use?

- What dollar amount of expense needs owner approval?

- Is the repair approval amount negotiable?

- Is there a problem if you regularly visit your property to check on their performance?

By the time you have enough property to need a full-time management company, you will be able to add many questions to this list.

After you have interviewed the managers of these companies as well as the other owners that use them, a prime candidate should emerge. Make sure you feel comfortable with the person who runs the operation. You both should share a common philosophy of management.

After you have picked a company and are getting ready to turn your building over to management, you should then go over the operation of your property the way it has been running for you. The historical data will give the new manager a target to work toward. During this transition, you should expect some of your expenses to increase because of the contractors the company uses, but you should discuss this with the person in charge and budget accordingly. Now is when you should be setting some profit goals so that the company knows you expect them to earn your business. Their "years of experience" should show up on your bottom line.

Managing the manager

We say that "managing the managers" is the key to keeping your empire running smoothly. It's pretty easy to turn your property over to management and then sit back and wait for the checks to roll in. Josh Billings, a 19th-century American humorist and real estate agent, said it best when he coined the phrase, "the squeaky wheel gets the grease." When it comes to property management, this couldn't be truer.

Unofficially...
The more time you personally spend with your property management team and the more positive feedback you give them for a job well done, the more personal attention they will give your property.

For the first three months, you should probably meet with the management team once a month to make sure the transition goes smoothly. After that, you should meet quarterly to discuss the performance of the properties and to review any problems, potential problems, or changes in the foreseeable future. At least one meeting per year should include a trip out to the property with the head of the company to review the overall condition.

These meetings will be extra work for the management company and the staff, so keep this in mind. Don't waste their time. Have an agenda, review what you need to, and let them go back to work. Remember, management is a thankless job. Don't forget to let them know when they are doing a good job.

Upgrading the interiors

At some point in the life cycle of your property, you will need to upgrade the interior of your units. Although the existing fixtures still work, they look tired and worn, and you know that another coat of paint would be about as effective as an adhesive bandage on a major head wound.

Rental properties always get in this condition quicker than single-family homes because the people who live in them don't have an ownership interest. Unfortunately, most property owners are in such a hurry to fill their vacancies that they tend to do the minimum when fixing up units between tenants.

When you begin to notice that you are unable to attract the high-end rents your competitors are getting, it is time to assess your building and determine whether an upgrade to the units is in order. It probably is.

Timesaver
This kind of a
rehab effort must
start with dili-
gent research on
your part. You
first must visit
the properties
commanding the
higher rent per
square foot and
see what they
have that you
don't. This will
give you the
overall feel of
these properties
so you can
assess whether
you, too, will be
able to command
similar rent.

As an example, let's assume you currently are averaging $.80 per square foot on your apartments, and you have noticed that similar properties in better condition are regularly getting $.95 per square foot. Your four units average 800 square feet each and your building is in an area where the capitalization rates are 8.5 percent. By upgrading, you will be able to increase your rents to match those of your competition. Even though this will increase your annual expenses some, it still gives you a net increase of $.10 per square foot. The potential profit from an upgrade looks like this:

New Rental Rate	$ .95 per square foot
Existing Rate	−.80 per square foot
Expense Increase	−.05
Potential Increase	$.10 per square foot

Unit Size	800 Sq. Ft.
# Units	× 4
Total Footage	3,200

Total Footage	$3,200
Increased Rent	× .10
Monthly Increase	$320
Yearly Increase	$3,840

Remember, with the capitalization method, we divide the net income by the capitalization rate to estimate value. If we apply this formula to our increased income, we get an estimate of the new value as follows:.

$$\frac{\text{Increase Rent} \quad \$3,840}{\text{Capitalization Rate} \quad .085} = \$45,176$$

As you can see, $45,176 in value appreciation and $3,800 in annual cash flow are both sizable increases that might make an interior upgrade worth your efforts.

Unlike a home remodel, it usually is not practical to add rooms or bathrooms to a rental property. Instead, you should look at the "finish" of the apartments from the walls out. If it is financially feasible, it's wise to remove everything in your units down to the drywall and begin your upgrade project from that point.

The following list covers items to rehab from the least expensive to the most expensive:

Interior Rehab Checklist
- Floor and window coverings
- Wall and ceiling finish
- Electrical outlets and switches
- Moldings and trim wood
- Closet and interior doors and hardware
- Front and rear door and hardware
- Kitchen and bathroom plumbing fixtures
- Bathroom vanity or sink, medicine cabinet, and toilet
- Bathtub and/or shower
- Kitchen appliances
- Kitchen cabinets and layout
- Heating and/or air-conditioning system

Floors and window coverings

Floor and window coverings are ongoing maintenance items, but in the case of a rehab project, they need to be redone with an eye to the overall look you are trying to achieve. It's relatively painless and inexpensive to change drapes to mini-blinds or to put in new linoleum, and these additions can make a huge difference.

Timesaver
It pays to do your homework before you start on a project of this magnitude. A major upgrade might increase your property's value and cash flow, but you might find through your research that an upgrade actually would not be worth the time, effort, and expense.

Walls and ceiling finish

The walls and ceilings of your units are a good place to start a property makeover. You will find that the paint, trim, and moldings all suffer because of tenant turnovers followed by many quick repainting jobs over the years. This phase of a makeover usually includes some updating of the look of these finishes. Older moldings might need to be removed for a cleaner, simpler finish. The ceilings might have the old-style "cottage cheese," but a plain flat finish is now the preferred look.

This does not have to be too costly because a handyman-level contractor usually can do this type of work. It is preferable to remove all the trim molding even if only some of it will be replaced because the paint buildup really shows in these areas. You might need some special help with the ceilings because some of the older "cottage cheese" finishes have asbestos in them and need a special contractor for removal. After the preparation work is complete, your normal painting contractor can give you the new finish you desire.

In older buildings, years of painting oil-based paint over calcimine results in a permanently peeling ceiling. The only solution is to scrape down to the plaster or to drywall over the ceiling. Drywall is quicker and less painful.

Bright Idea
Pick one brand of paint and one uniform color to use in all your rentals. This way, you will never have to worry about whether the paint matches.

Electrical outlets and switches

If you go to the trouble of refinishing the walls, it is advisable to put in new electrical outlets, switches, and face plates as well. Nothing looks worse on a newly painted wall than an electrical outlet that has an old, painted cover plate. You also should replace and update the light fixtures. Most major home improvement centers have great selections of lighting at very reasonable prices. Make sure you save the brand name and style information of your new fixtures for future reference.

Open a new door

The doors of apartments seem to suffer greater abuse than those in most homes. This is because numerous coats of paint and lock changes over the years naturally take their toll. Remember that the first thing a prospective tenant sees is the front door of your vacant unit. If the door looks clean, your new prospect will see right away that you are the kind of landlord that takes pride in his rentals. This might just lay the groundwork for him wanting to rent from you. Remember, these front doors also are an integral part of the overall appearance of the exterior of your property. It ruins the effect of the thousands of dollars you spent to paint and landscape the exterior if you have a conglomeration of new and old exterior doors with mismatched knobs and hardware. You also might add brass kick plates to keep down scuff marks from shoes holding the doors open.

Bathroom upgrades

Bathroom upgrades can provide a significant improvement in the look of your unit. What's great is that they do not have to cost as much as you might think. The simplest upgrade is a new medicine cabinet and light fixture. If there is a shower in the bathtub, a new shower enclosure is nice, too. You also should install low-flow shower heads. They're cheap, easy to install, and will save you money on the water bill.

The next upgrades might be to replace the sink, vanity, and toilet. These items can cost a bit, so shop wisely. Because they are all necessary items, however, they usually are worth the expense.

Timesaver
Go ahead and change any worn out or damaged outlets or switches once you repaint. This way, you will not have to return to the unit to fix a dead outlet when your tenant moves in and begins to complain.

Moneysaver
Many cities offer
rebate programs
that reduce the
cost of new low-
flush toilets for
your units. This
savings, com-
bined with
cheaper water
bills, makes this
upgrade well
worth it.

Many older apartments still have their original toilets. Although they might work fine, they do not have the efficiency of modern, water-saving units. Most of your water and sewer costs come from the use of the toilets in your building. Therefore, the new low-flush toilets now available will provide a permanent savings once installed.

The final item in the bathroom, and potentially the most costly to upgrade, is the tub or shower. You should know that it is usually a major expense to remove an ugly, old, cast-iron or plastic tub unit and install a new one. For this reason, we generally do not recommend doing this kind of upgrade. Luckily, a coating process is available that can give your old tub the appearance of a new one at a substantially lower price. This process is not permanent, but it should last years and can be touched up as needed to keep the new look. Ask your local home improvement expert for guidance.

A beautiful new kitchen

Upgrading a kitchen usually costs a bundle. A common problem with older kitchens is that they are located in separate rooms and have doors closing them off from the rest of the apartment. In some areas, a more open kitchen is desired. The idea is that a breakfast bar–type opening to the living area adds an open and homey feel. If this can be done without any major structural modifications by just opening up a wall, it probably is worth the effort.

Kitchen cabinets, counters, sinks, and stoves

It usually is not cost-effective to put new cabinets in the kitchen. Assuming the kitchen has a workable layout, there are two options you should consider. The least expensive, but most labor intensive, option is to take all the cabinet doors off, take the drawers out, and do a very thorough job sanding them and the base cabinets. You then can get your painter to prime and paint the cabinets and drawers. This takes a lot of time and effort, but the finished product should look great.

The other option is to install new cabinet doors and drawer fronts and just refinish the base cabinets. This costs more, but you can achieve the most up-to-date style this way. You can get prices for the doors and drawer fronts at most large home-improvements centers and local cabinet shops. In either case, wait until the cabinets are finished to install the new hardware.

If you are updating the cabinets, it probably is a good time to repair or replace the counters, too. If the counters are made of Formica, they can be replaced or resurfaced with a process similar to the one used on bathtubs. Your bids will determine which process you decide on. If the counters are made of tile, it can be more costly to do an upgrade. One way to save is to have new tile put directly over the old tile. This can be done by using a special additive with mastic-type glue designed for setting tile on tile.

Along with the new counters and cabinets, it might be time to install a new sink and faucet. If you are not tearing out the countertop, however, it might not be practical to replace the sink. Instead, consider using the same refinishing system recommended for the bathtub. You then can replace the faucet, and everything will look new again for a reasonable price.

The last items in the kitchen are the stove and vent fan. If you have the old freestanding-style stoves

Moneysaver
When replacing faucets, it usually is best to also replace the supply lines and the angle stops. This will save you money in the long run.

Bright Idea
It is wise to do your exterior upgrade first and then upgrade the interiors one at a time as tenants move out.

in your units, you might consider upgrading to the built-in or slide-in type. They will give your kitchen a great look and should give you years of trouble-free service. You can sell the existing stoves, and this might pay a good portion of the cost of the new ones. If you have vent hoods over the stoves, go ahead and change these to match the color of the new stoves.

Summary of your interior upgrade

For the most part, you now have a "new" apartment. This will attract the best tenants who are willing to pay premium rents for a great place to live. Keep in mind, however, that your expensive interior upgrade will all have been for naught if you have yet to do any upgrades outside. Tenants who will pay premium rents for upgraded units will not even stop to see them if the exterior of your building does not grab their attention from the street.

You should test the market one unit at a time to help determine the correct rent for your upgraded apartments. You might find that the market rent is actually higher for your units than your original rent survey indicated. If you get a lot of interest in the units and more than the usual number of interested applicants, your rent might be on the low side. If this happens, you can raise the rent some on the next upgraded unit to again test the interest level. It is not unusual to have a large pent-up demand for nicer apartments in markets that have been stagnant for several years. Unless there is a wave of new construction in the area, this demand is not usually seen.

Just the facts

- Your property must grab a potential tenant's attention from the street.

- Landscaping does not have to cost a bundle to achieve your desired effect.

- To limit your liability, make sure your tenants adhere to the rules of your common areas and parking facilities.

- To avoid manager complacency, structure financial incentives into his contract.

- Staying in touch with your professional property management team will help to ensure that they do a good job for you.

- Do some market research to make sure an interior upgrade is worth the expense.

Facing Your Fears

PART VII

GET THE SCOOP ON...
Three proven methods for combating negative
cash flow ▪ The economy and how it affects
your choices ▪ The fear of losing your shirt ▪
Why lesser areas make for better investments ▪
Property management solution ▪ Your
retirement realities

So What's Stopping You?

Chapter 16

The first thought that creeps into people's minds when they consider investing is, "The entire market is going to collapse the day I make my move." If this mirrors your thinking, know that you're in good company. In fact, that very idea has crossed the mind of every investor (including the authors) who has ever risked a nickel at anything.

It would be a terrible shame, however, if your fear kept you from doing what you know could change your life. You see, there usually is as much risk from inaction as there is from action. By not acting, you might forever be stuck in the 9-to-5 rat race. For that reason, this last chapter is dedicated to addressing the most common fears about investing. Our goal is to help you get over the hump, if in fact there still is one to get over.

Fear of negative cash flow

We've touched on negative cash flow a couple of times, but let's attack it again and put this beast to

Moneysaver
Think about any negative cash flow from your real estate investments as the equivalent of the money you invest in life insurance and retirement packages. It is a savings plan for the future.

bed once and for all. As you know, negative cash flow exists when your income can't cover your expenses. That's a problem no one wants to have. Here are three good techniques used to combat negative cash flow:

1. Apply the right formula to determine how much you can afford to pay for a property and still stay positive.

2. Convert money normally used to purchase equity into money to offset any initial negative cash flow.

3. Manage a negative building into profitability.

Apply the right formula

As you learned in Chapter 3, "Elements of Return," the amount of money you put down on a property directly correlates to how much cash flow you will receive. To determine the maximum you can pay for a property and still break even, you need to do a little math. We'll use the following abbreviations in these equations:

G.M. = Average gross multiplier in your area

I = Current market interest rate

N.I.P = Net income percentage

D.P.P. = Down payment percentage

Don't worry, these calculations are easy as long as you take them one step at a time. The first thing to determine is your net income percentage (N.I.P.). Your N.I.P. is determined by first subtracting your gross expenses from your income and then divide that number by the gross income as follows:

Gross Income – Gross Expenses = Net Income

$$\frac{\text{Net Income}}{\text{Gross Income}} = \text{N.I.P.}$$

Once you know your net income percentage (N.I.P.), plug that number into the following formula to find out your down payment percentage (D.P.P.):

$$\text{D.P.P.} = 1 - \left(\frac{\text{Net Income}}{\text{G.M.} \times \text{I}} \right)$$

As an example, let's say your net income percentage is 75 percent. Let's also suppose that the average gross multiplier in your area is 9.00 times gross, and the current market interest rate is 10 percent. Plug these numbers in as follows:

$$1 - \left(\frac{.75}{9 \times .1} \right) = .17$$

As you can see, to avoid going negative, your down payment must be at least 17 percent of the purchase price. To determine how much you can afford, apply this formula:

$$\frac{\text{Available Down Payment}}{\text{Down Payment Percentage}} = \text{Maximum Purchase Price}$$

For example, if you had $35,000 to invest, your maximum purchase price (to avoid going negative) would be calculated as follows:

$$\frac{\$35,000 \text{ Available Down Payment}}{.17 \text{ Down Payment Percentage}} = \begin{array}{l}\$205,882 \\ \text{Maximum} \\ \text{Purchase Price}\end{array}$$

As you can see, a building costing no more than about $205,000 should keep you in the black.

By applying these calcualtions, you can minimize having to dip into your pocket to pay expenses. We

say "minimize" because increased vacancy, reduction in market rent, or unanticipated expenses in
the future could affect you negatively. Of course,
increased occupancy or rents and lower expenses
will be to your advantage.

Use cash to offset the negative

A second technique is sometimes used to manage
cash flow. In this example, we'll assume you have
found a property that is priced higher than you can
finance using the break-even formula in the preceding section. You believe that with better management you can increase your gross income. The good
news is that the owner of this property will carry the
loan and accept a down payment which is less than
the cash you set aside for your purchase. This will
allow you to purchase the property and keep a sizable reserve in your bank account. You have $35,000
set aside for this investment. The facts are as follows:

Price:	$250,000
Down:	$25,000
Gross Income:	$25,000
Expenses:	$6,000
Loan:	$225,000
Loan Payment @ 10% interest only	$22,500 per year

Operating Summary

Income:	25,000
Expenses:	−$6,000
Loan Payments:	−$22,500
Net Negative Cash Flow:	−$3,500

As you can see, the negative cash flow is $3,500
per year. This comes to about $292 per month
($3,500 ÷ 12 = $291.66). Remember that your cash
investment is $10,000 less than you originally had
budgeted ($35,000 to invest less $25,000 down payment = $10,000). The idea is to use some of these

Unofficially...
For the most
part, our tax
laws—both state
and federal—
compensate us
for negative cash
flows. We are
returned for
every dollar lost
a percent of that
dollar equal to
our combined
state and federal
top tax bracket
levels.

cash reserves to offset the negative until you can turn the building around. Many properties that have absentee owners or buildings that have been in the same hands for many years are the ones that best fit this bill. That is, there is a possibility to increase the rental income with careful management.

For these owners, their real estate is secondary to the rest of their lives. Once the property they own performs adequately, they tend to ignore it as an investment. They don't raise rents or make any changes for fear they will need to get more involved in the day-to-day operations. In these instances, tenants with low rents hesitate to bother the owner, and owners keep the rents low so they won't be bothered.

Manage your property to riches

The most effective defense against negative cash flow is the ability to recognize a potentially good business opportunity, to negotiate its purchase under reasonable terms, and to manage it into profitability. This is the method most frequently overlooked by beginning investors, yet it is the method of choice for investors who have been around awhile.

The following are some characteristics of a property that will allow you to buy it for a good price and then turn any negative into a positive fairly quickly:

- **Lower-than-market rents:** You find a building where the price looks very good but the rents are low. Negotiate the price based upon the lower rents and then raise the rents to market rate. Once your rents are up, the value of your building goes up as well.

- **Excessive operating expenses:** Many owners, especially absentee owners, fail to control their

Watch Out!
This technique should be reserved for properties that show strong evidence that you can generate a positive cash flow within a year. Properties that have rents well below market usually are the ones that would fit this bill.

> The low rents on the last building I bought allowed me to get a good buy, but they also gave me negative cash flow in the beginning. I did some minor upgrades and then raised the rents a bit. I haven't been negative since.
> —Melinda K., investor

operating expenses. By locating owners whose expenses appear too high, you might be able to negotiate a significant price reduction. Once you take over, follow the guidelines laid out in Chapter 14, "Managing the Expenses," to lower costs and increase your cash flow and the property's value.

- **Debt service costlier than market:** Many owners put their buildings on the market because the cost of their financing is too high. For whatever reason, they are unable or unwilling to refinance their debt, so selling seems to be the only alternative. With your down payment and good credit, you can rescue them. Your reward should be a substantial reduction in price.

With minimal work, you should be able to turn any negative cash flow problem into a positive "cash cow" in a reasonable amount of time.

Fear that this isn't the "right time" to invest

So you don't think this is the right time to invest, huh? A close observation of the last 35 years would reveal that not one of those years passed without potential real estate investors feeling that it would be advantageous to wait for better times. This illustrates, however, a significant misconception about real estate investing. As far as real estate goes, the only unprofitable investments in the last 35 years were the ones that never closed escrow.

The truth is that profiting from real estate investing has little to do with the economic climate at the time you buy. Of course, the economy surely should be examined with any investment you make, but you must understand that it is not the main factor in determining whether you will get rich in real estate. Let's blow up the belief that there is a mystical "better time" to buy out there. Let's see how a property you purchase might perform over an extended period of time using the following facts:

- Purchase Price: $100,000
- Down Payment: $10,000 (10%)
- Annual income: $10,000
- Annual expenses: $2,500 (25% of gross income)

Now let's examine value appreciation in a couple of ways:

1. If the property goes up in value a modest 3.5 percent in one year, it increases $3,500. That is a 35 percent return on your down payment. One question, where are you going to find an investment vehicle that will pay you 35% on your money?

2. If your expenses increase 5 percent because of inflation and you raise your rents only 7 percent to help compensate, you would have an operating expense increase of $125 per year and an income increase of $700 per year. This would give you a $5,757 increase in net income per year. Again, where are you going to find an investment that will do that for you?

We believe that the soundest way to circumvent the notion that tomorrow will be a better time to invest than today is to:

1. Develop a small investment plan with attainable goals.

2. Absorb a reasonable amount of knowledge about real estate investing.

3. Get started by buying your first property.

Unofficially...
The rate of appreciation for investment property in Southern California has averaged more than 7.5 percent per year for the last 35 years.

Fear of losing your money

By now, you probably realize that real estate is the answer, but you've still got one nagging fear—you're afraid of losing your money. This is because this investment will probably represent the biggest financial move of your life. Tapping into your savings and investing the fruits of years of hard work is nothing if not unnerving, even under the best of circumstances. This fear usually comes from two things:

1. The lack of a plan of attack

2. A lack of knowledge about the product in which you are investing

We believe that having a well-thought-out business plan will give you the direction you need to run your real estate business effectively (see Chapter 9, "Building an Investment Plan"). As for your education, there are many sources from which to learn about real estate investing including:

- Lots of great books on the subject (see Appendix C, "Recommended Reading List").

- Community college courses taught by teachers with real-world experience.

- Practical property-management seminars offered by your local apartment owners association.

- Weekend and evening seminars given by authors and lecturers. Along with the chance to purchase their books and tapes, these individuals usually have plenty of good information and ideas to share.

You might ask, "How can I be sure I won't lose my money?" The best way is to make sure you buy your property at fair market value. Remember that fair market value is defined as "the price a reasonable

Moneysaver
Never volunteer to put more money down than the seller requires. Instead, put down the minimum amount of money necessary and then let the bank buy the rest of the property for you.

buyer would pay a reasonable seller for a property that has been on the market for a reasonable period of time." One way to determine fair market value is to get the property appraised before you buy. Two common sources for appraisals are:

1. **Investment real estate agents**: Appraisals from agents generally are free and are a good way to learn about value in general.

2. **Professional property appraisers**: These appraisals cost a bit of money, but they are worth the expense for the piece of mind they will bring.

The bottom line is that most investments have some risk. When you begin to think about venturing into a new world of investing, having some concerns is normal. The key is to do enough study and research that you feel comfortable with the investments before you buy. By having an appraisal done, you are tapping into the mind of an expert. This will further increase your comfort level for a particular property.

Fear of tenant and management hassles

Many people balk at investing in rental property because they are afraid of the headaches that come with property management. In general, smaller buildings (one to four units) tend to have fewer management hassles than larger ones. At the most, you'll have four units to worry about. In time, you'll be able to manage them with your eyes closed.

One solution is to hire professional property management to do the job. There are plenty of reputable companies out there, and for a small fee, they will manage your building for you. Remember, however, by hiring someone other than yourself,

> 66
> Property management doesn't cost, it pays!
> —The Stevenson Group, property managers
> 99

you are giving the reigns of control of your investment over to a third party. Professional property management companies can be good but should come recommended by other investors or an experienced real estate professional.

If, however, it is against your fiscal religion to pay for management, and managing tenants is the hurdle that is keeping you from investing, you might want to consider a different route—investing in commercial and industrial buildings. What's great is that these properties frequently rent on a triple-net basis. Remember that a triple-net lease means the tenants are responsible for all operating expenses and the upkeep of the property. During the term of the lease, the tenant would run the building as if it were his own. Additionally, your interaction with the tenants would be significantly reduced as compared to an investment in residential real estate.

Fear of bad and low-income areas

One of the truly great mistakes made, especially by beginning investors, is thinking in terms of "pride of ownership" rather than "profit of ownership." In truth, just as many substantial fortunes have been made in low-income areas as in high-end areas and usually for a much smaller initial investment.

When talking to beginning investors about the kind and location of property they would like to buy, the answer they give is almost always the "best property" in the "best location" with the "best tenants." It rarely is articulated in this concise a fashion, but boiled down, that's what they want. Furthermore:

- By "best property," they mean a property they would be willing to live in or better.

- By "best location," they mean something comparable to their own neighborhood or better.

Unofficially...
The profits to be made from investing in residential real estate dwarf the return from many other investments. One reason is to compensate investors for the time and effort necessary to manage it. You may be able to get a 4 to 6 percent return on your money in a passbook savings account, but try retiring on that.

■ By "best tenants," they mean themselves or better.

In theory, these goals are well and good. Unfortunately, you probably couldn't afford to repurchase your own home let alone buy units in your neighborhood today. You might be surprised to learn that the "best" property in the "best" location only rarely makes the best investment. For starters:

1. You will pay a premium for such a property.

2. The seller will want the best terms for himself.

3. The economics of operation will be considerably less attractive.

On the other hand, lesser buildings located in a less desirable location often will have just the reverse effect:

1. Prices will be favorable.

2. Terms will be negotiable.

3. The operating costs of the building will be within reason.

4. Lower down payment options often are available (better leverage).

5. Sellers sometimes will carry some of the financing at good terms.

6. It is usually the area that is least affected by recession.

Unfortunately, when most investors think of property in less desirable neighborhoods, the word "slum" creeps into their thoughts. They think it's going to be a hassle managing "those kinds of tenants." Actually, nothing could be further from the truth. Most of the people renting in less affluent areas are good people. They might not be as financially fortunate as others,

Bright Idea
If it's positive cash flow you're looking for, low-income areas will provide you with plenty of it. Though these areas require considerably more hands-on management, you will always get more building for your buck than you can in upscale neighborhoods.

Bright Idea
One sensible approach is to make your fortune in less prestigious properties and then trade your equities into more desirable properties for your retirement years. You'll probably own the Taj Mahal one day, just not yet.

but they work hard to raise a family and would like the nicer things in life if they could afford them. The truth is that tenants in these areas usually really appreciate all the little things you might do to make their home nicer. Conversely, the tenants in the best areas expect it and then some.

Though we're not advocating that you buy in the worst neighborhood in town, we are suggesting that you find an average area in between the best and the worst. This is where the money is made. Working class areas seem to be the least affected during recessionary periods. One reason is that these tenants seem to be the last to lose their jobs, and if they do, government safety nets such as welfare and Section 8 programs are available to help with housing.

Fear of rocking the boat

Most people never think much about their retirement until it is staring them in the face. This is because, during their most productive years, their lives are very comfortable. So comfortable, in fact, that there doesn't appear to be any need to worry about retirement. Any money that would be spent on investments would take away from enjoying the current pleasures in life. As they say, "Why rock the boat?"

The problem is that, as we grow older, our financial burdens often get heavier. For one thing, we are less able to perform for ourselves those things necessary for our daily existence, and we need to begin to purchase such services. Furthermore, more and more people are taking on the responsibility of caring for aging parents. The costs of this kind of care can be staggering. And finally, it is not unknown for parents to have the additional burden of financially helping their children as the children begin to build lives and careers of their own.

Before you convince yourself that you are financially comfortable now, you'd better be sure your net worth today plus all projected retirement income will meet your retirement needs. The earlier in your career you face this issue, the better your chances are for an enjoyable retirement. To do this, you need to find out what you need to preserve your current lifestyle.

We'll refer to this level of income as the minimum security level. What we're talking about here is a level of income for you and your family that is independent of your efforts. It will be a combination of Social Security, any retirement plans, and other investments you may have.

Several factors should be considered when defining your minimum security level. Two of the most important are:

1. Present and future material needs for you and your family

2. Present and projected economic conditions such as inflation, recession, and the cost of capital and their potential effects on your retirement

Once you have a good idea of your minimum security level, you need to determine whether you'll have enough assets at retirement to sustain it. If not, you should begin investing now in a plan that will guarantee this level of security as soon as possible. Investing until that level is reached is the key to a secure retirement. Most people need to generate about 70 percent of their preretirement income to maintain their same lifestyle.

"
I wasn't sure what I'd need to fund the kind of retirement I wanted. I was lucky. A friend recommended a financial planner who was able to help. He charged me for his time rather than a commission on what he could sell me.
—Bill B., computer specialist
"

As you analyze your finances, remember that we are talking about a level of income that just maintains your current lifestyle. This means you can pay your bills, feed the family, and take one or two vacations a year, but that's about it. When you were working, you spent five days a week and 49 or 50 weeks a year at your job. Now you won't have to go to work, but you won't have any money to do anything else either. That's why it's called the "minimum" security level.

If you want to truly enjoy all that free time, you'd better decide how you want to spend your retirement years and what it's going to cost. Then you'd better take a hard look at what you're going to have to do to amass enough assets to fund this retirement. If you do this early enough in your life and get the boat rocking, you might truly be able to enjoy your retirement.

The only thing to fear is fear itself

The hardest part of anything new is just getting started. That's because human beings are great at making excuses. We've heard every excuse there is for why someone shouldn't invest, whether it's the economy, credit card debt, or the new baby that's due in June. Whatever the reason, many people who could be financially set today are instead cheating themselves out of what could be a better life.

With all due respect to *The Late Show,* here are the top 10 excuses we have heard for not investing in real estate.

10. I'm waiting for a better time to invest.

9. The negative cash flow will swallow me whole.

8. I have to pay off my credit card debt first.

7. Managing the property will be too hard.

6. I need to buy a house before I invest in rental property.

5. I'm waiting for a good deal to come my way.

4. The economy isn't right.

3. I'm waiting for interest rates to drop.

2. My brother-in-law lost a bundle this way.

And the number one reason people wait is…

1. I can't do a thing until Elvis shows up.

In all seriousness, the most valid reason anyone could have for not moving forward is that they just don't understand what this game is all about. Fair enough. If that's what's stopping you, we applaud you for putting the brakes on. Experience has shown that, if you proceed without adequate knowledge, the results could be disastrous.

If, at this point, you find yourself still struggling, here is what we suggest:

1. Reread this book (but slower this time).

2. Read someone else's book on this subject.

3. Find someone who understands the value in real estate investing and get them to explain it to you.

Do what you have to do to get this knowledge, but get it one way or another. Someone is collecting rent on all those small apartment buildings in your town. It could be you.

Your plan of attack

Merriam-Webster's dictionary defines an entrepreneur as "a person who organizes and manages a business undertaking, assuming the risk for the sake of profit."

We'd venture to say that there hasn't been a successful entrepreneur yet who hasn't stumbled a bit

Moneysaver

Ask your investment real estate agent to give you data on how property has appreciated in your area during the last 20 years. Compare this information to that of other investments and the return they provided. See for yourself whether real estate investing would be in your best interest.

along the way. The key is that they've dusted themselves off, stepped out of their comfort zone, and kept working at something they believed in. That is the real ticket to success. You might make some mistakes along the way, but real estate is a forgiving investment. By applying what you've learned here, any mistakes you might make should be easily overcome.

Let's review the game plan we've laid out together:

1. **Learn**: Your best guarantee of success is to never quit educating yourself about this business. There are enough books, classes, and seminars on the subject to keep you in school until the day you decide to turn your business over to the next generation. Some will teach you a lot and some only a little, but all education stimulates you to keep thinking deeper about your business.

2. **Research**: Along with learning about real estate in general, you need to learn about your specific real estate market and the way it performs in your area. Your goals must be to become an expert on what property has done in the past and what it is doing today. By doing diligent research, you will ensure that you are choosing the best properties to reach your goals.

3. **Plan**: Planning is the key to being successful in any business. Real estate is no exception. When you have a plan for your future, you create the road map toward financial security. Investing without that plan is like taking a trip to Twig without a map. The probability of success in either case is remote. Without a plan, you're

Timesaver
Do your learning and research at the same time. This way, you can apply your education to the actual market.

never quite sure which properties are right for you. Without a map, you wouldn't even know where Twig was (pssst... Minnesota).

4. **Invest**: Now it's time to pick that first property and make a purchase. You have educated yourself on what and where to buy, and you have identified the kind of property you need to satisfy your investment plan goals. You will next use due diligence to make sure the property you have found meets all your criteria.

5. **Manage**: Once you have acquired your property, you take over as the manager. Your long-term plans will be put aside, and you will now be involved in the day-to-day operational goals for your business. You will work to increase your income, to keep the expenses under control, and to meet profit expectations. In time, you will be able to move on to bigger and better buildings.

And finally

In this guide, we have attempted to give you as much of the inside scoop on real estate investing as possible. We believe that, if you apply the principles we've laid out here with a concerted effort to keep educating yourself, great success will follow. Our hope is that we have motivated you to take control of your destiny. It's time for you to take some risks, and it's time for you to reap the rewards.

This is the place where we would normally wish you good luck, but we know you don't need it. Instad, we wish you good fortune.

Martin Stone & Spencer Strauss

Just the facts

- Proper management is the savvy investor's solution to negative cash flow: Increase income, lower expenses, improve financing costs.

- Lack of adequate knowledge is the real reason people hesitate to invest in anything.

- Real estate can produce a profit in both good and bad times.

- If the day-to-day hassles of property ownership are keeping you from investing, turn it over to a management company.

- Less affluent economic areas can offer greater potential for profit.

- Without proper planning, a comfortable retirement might be out of the question.

Glossary

acceleration clause   A clause in a loan that requires the loan to be paid off in the event of an occurrence such as unauthorized transfer of title.

accommodator   A neutral third party that assists in completing a delayed exchange. The accommodator usually is a corporate entity.

active investor   An IRS classification for a real estate investor who materially participates in running a property.

adjustable-rate mortgage (ARM)   A loan in which the future interest rate might change, with that change determined by an index of rates. The frequency and amount of change are limited by the mortgage contract.

adjusted cost basis   For the purpose of computing capital gains or losses, this refers to the original purchase price plus closing costs paid at the time of purchase plus the cost value of improvements done while the property was held less all depreciation claimed.

adjusted gross income   The income from a piece of property after any adjustments are made for other income or rental losses.

adjusted sale price   The price of your property after deducting the costs of sale.

agent   One who represents another, called the principal, in dealing with third persons.

all-inclusive loan   This is a loan that incorporates several loans. The borrower makes one payment on the all-inclusive loan, and the person receiving that payment pays on the underlying financing.

amortization   The repayment terms of a loan—including the required principal and interest—based on the interest rate and the period of time allowed to pay down, or amortize, the loan to zero.

annual depreciation allowance   The deduction you can take on your income tax against earnings to recapture the cost of the structures on your property.

annual expenses   All the costs you must pay to operate your property.

annual percentage rate (APR)   A term used in the Truth in Lending Act. It represents the total cost of credit—including interest, discount points, origination fees, and loan broker commission—as a percentage of the amount financed.

appraisal   The process of estimating current market value of a property.

appreciation   Increase in value due to any cause.

"as is"   When you buy a property "as is," the seller is not making any warranties or guarantees about its condition.

assumption   A loan feature providing that the borrower can allow a future buyer to take over payments on the loan as well as responsibility for repayment.

average return on equity (AROE)   Each year you own a property, you can calculate the return on the equity for that year. If you add these up for several years and divide by the number of years, you get the average.

balloon mortgage   A mortgage that has one large payment due at the end of the loan.

balloon payment   The outstanding balance due at the maturity of a mortgage or loan

bank repossessions   Property that has been taken by the lender because of the owner's failure to meet the terms and conditions of the loan.

basis   The cost of the building on your property, plus improvements and fixtures, that can be depreciated but not claimed as deductions. This is calculated as original cost plus capital improvements less depreciation.

board of Realtors®   An association of Realtors® in a given town or district.

boot   An IRS term for taxable proceeds from a sale other than cash.

building cost tables   Tables that show the current cost to build structures in various parts of the United States.

buyer's agent   The agent who locates the buyer and brings an offer to the seller.

cap   A limit on the amount of increase a lender can impose under the terms of an adjustable-rate mortgage. The annual cap specifies the maximum annual increase, and the lifetime cap specifies the overall increase the lender is allowed to pass on to the borrower.

capital expense   The outlay to purchase any asset with a useful life of more than one year. (The tax treatment for such an expenditure allows the asset to be "capitalized," which means its cost is deducted over its useful life according to the applicable depreciation method rather than an expense in the current period.)

capital gains   The profit you make on an investment.

capitalization of income   A valuation method achieved by dividing the net income of a property by the capitalization rate of that kind of property.

capitalization rate   The percentage return you get by dividing the net income from a property by the price of a property.

cash flow   The amount of money received from rental income each month less the amount paid out in mortgage payments, the purchase of capital assets, and the payment of any operating expenses. Cash flow is not the same as profit because it includes nondeductible payments.

cash-on-cash return   The cash profit from an investment divided by the cash invested to buy the investment.

chain of title   A history of all titles to a piece of real estate, beginning with the original transfer from government to private ownership and ending with the latest document transferring title.

clear title   A title held without disputes concerning ownership or liens against the property. All liens are agreed to, identified, and not in dispute.

closing   Takes place when the buyer takes possession of the property and the seller gets the proceeds from the sale.

co-insurance   A clause in an insurance policy that says the property owner will assume some of the liability for any loss.

collected rent   Amount of rental income actually collected.

commercial loans   Any loan not classified as a residential loan, usually on five units or more.

commercial property   Nonresidential property operated for business use.

commission   An agent's compensation or fee for negotiating a real estate or loan transaction, usually a percentage of the transaction amount.

common area   Space not used and occupied exclusively by tenants such as lobbies, corridors, and stairways. In a condominium, the property in which a unit owner has an undivided interest.

comparables (comps)   Properties that are similar to the property being considered or appraised.

comparative analysis   A method of appraisal in which selling prices of similar properties are used as the basis for arriving at the value estimate. This also is known as the market data approach.

compound interest   Interest paid on the original principal and also on the accrued interest.

compound interest algorithm   A mathematical formula used to calculate the percentage return when the profits from an investment are reinvested over a given period of time.

condominium   A form of property ownership that combines absolute ownership of an apartment-like unit and joint ownership of areas used in common with others.

condominium association   A condominium's governing body to which every unit owner automatically belongs.

constructive receipt   An IRS term that means the IRS will tax you as though you had received monies even though you might not have been in physical possession of them during that tax period.

consumer price index A figure constructed monthly by the U.S. Bureau of Labor Statistics that weighs products by their importance and compares prices to those of a selected base year, expressing current prices as a percentage of prices in that base year.

contingencies Terms in a contract that qualify the agreement by stating that, for the deal to go forward, one side or the other agrees to meet certain conditions. Typical contingencies include completion of inspections and qualifying for financing.

contract for deed A method of financing a property. It is similar to an all-inclusive trust deed or a mortgage.

conventional loan A loan not underwritten by a government agency.

cost basis Your basis for calculating the capital gain on a property you own.

damages Financial compensation awarded to a person who was injured by another.

debt coverage The comparison between the net income of a property and the loan payments on the property.

debt service The total of the monthly payments on a property.

deduction An expense of property ownership that can be written off against income for tax purposes.

deferred maintenance Ordinary maintenance that is not performed and that negatively affects a property's use and value.

delayed exchange An IRS-approved technique for completing an exchange of equity to postpone taxes. Also called a "Starker" exchange.

demand appreciation Appreciation in value related to an increase in the desire to possess the property.

Department of Veterans Affairs   The federal government agency that administers GI or VA loans. Previously known as the Veterans Administration.

depreciable improvements   The value of the structures on a property that the IRS allows you to depreciate.

depreciated value   The value that remains after deducting the depreciation from the cost base for a property.

depreciation   As an appraisal term, this means loss of value due to any cause.

depreciation allowance   The dollar amount the IRS allows you to deduct each year from the earnings from a property.

dual agency   A situation in which one agent represents both sides in a transaction.

due diligence   The effort made to study and research a property and all the components of a purchase before you make the final decision to purchase.

earned increment of value   That part of the increase in a property's value attributed to the efforts of the owner.

easements   A right to use the land of another for a specific purpose.

encumbrance   Anything that burdens or limits the title to a property such as a lien, easement, or restriction of any kind.

energy-saving blanket   An insulating pad placed around an appliance such as a water heater.

equity   The portion of real estate you own. In the case of a property bought for $200,000 with a $133,000 mortgage owing, the equity is the difference, or $67,000.

equity growth from appreciation   The increase in a property's value because of the effects of inflation.

equity growth from loan reduction   The increase in the owner's equity in a property from the payoff of the financing.

escrow   The process of completing contractually required steps (such as obtaining financing, completing inspections, paying and transferring funds) and of checking and clearing the title to the property to ensure that all liens have been identified and are satisfied before closing.

estoppel certifications   Agreements usually signed by the tenants of a property outlining the terms of their tenancy.

fair market value   The price a reasonable buyer will pay a reasonable seller for a property that has been on the market for a reasonable period of time.

Federal Housing Administration (FHA)   An agency created by the National Housing Act of 1934 to provide a home-financing system through federal mortgage insurance.

fiduciary   A relationship founded in trust and legally requiring loyalty, full disclosure, full accounting, and the application of skill, care, and diligence.

fixed expenses   The regular recurring costs required in holding a property, such as taxes and insurance.

fixed-rate loan   A loan in which the interest rate will not change during the contract period as a matter of contract.

fixer-upper   A property requiring repairs, either structural or cosmetic, to gain its full potential market value.

foreclosure   A court action initiated by the mortgagee for the purpose of having the court order the debtor's real estate sold to pay the mortgage.

fully amortized   Refers to a loan that is completely paid off when all the payments are made.

GI loan   A guaranteed loan available to veterans under a federal government program administered by the Department of Veteran's Affairs. It also is called a VA loan.

good-faith deposit   A deposit presented by the proposed buyer at the time an offer is made. If the buyer's offer is accepted and the contract is later breached, the good faith deposit may be forfeited.

gross lease   An agreement in which the tenant pays an agreed-upon rent and the owner pays all the expenses associated with operating the property.

gross multiplier   A factor used for appraising income-producing property. The multiplier times the gross income gives an approximate property value.

guaranteed replacement clause   A clause in an insurance policy whereby the policy will pay to replace a damaged property regardless of changes in valuation or the cost of the replacement.

hard money loans   Loans made by nonconventional lenders. They usually have high interest and high fees.

highest and best use   The use of a property for the most profitable, efficient, and appropriate purpose, given the zoning and other restrictions placed on the land.

impound account   A trust account in which funds are held, usually by a lender, for the payment of property taxes and insurance premiums required to protect the lender's security. These amounts usually are collected with the note payment.

improvements   Any structure or addition to a piece of raw land.

index   One of the components used to calculate the interest rate on an adjustable-rate loan.

in-fill project   A construction project in an area where most of the land already is developed with structures.

inflation   An economic condition occurring when the money supply increases in relation to goods. It is associated with rising wages and costs and decreasing purchasing power.

inflationary appreciation   Refers to the value of a product increasing due to inflation taking place in the economy.

installment note   The name of the note carried by a seller of a property that gives the seller special tax benefits.

installment sale   The sale of a property in which the seller carries an installment note.

interest-only loan   A loan for which no amortization is required and the entire principal balance is due at maturity.

invest   To commit money or capital in business to earn a financial return. The outlay of money for income or profit.

land sales contract   Another name for a conditional sales contract. The buyer takes possession. The seller retains the title until all conditions are met.

landlord   The owner of real estate who rents property to another.

leverage   The use of borrowed money to purchase an investment that realizes enough income to cover the expense of the financing with the excess accruing to the purchaser.

liability   Penalty for failure to act in a manner as prescribed by law.

lien   An encumbrance on a property for the payment of a debt or obligation.

linear regression analysis   A mathematical formula for calculating the best-fitting line through a series of points on a graph or chart.

liquidated damages   A definite sum of money to be paid under a contract in the event of a breach of the contract.

listing   A contract authorizing a broker to sell, buy, or lease real property on behalf of another.

management fixer-upper   A property with management problems that need to be corrected.

margin   The number added to the index of a loan to get the final interest rate of the loan.

market analysis   The process of placing a property in a specific space market and then evaluating it by those market standards.

master-metered properties   A property that only has one meter for the utilities.

Modified Accelerated Cost Recovery System (MACRS)   The IRS system for determining the depreciation schedule for capital items.

mortgage   A contract that makes a specific property the security for payment of a debt.

mortgage over basis   When the amount of the loan on a property exceeds the cost basis of the property.

mortgage relief   When a taxpayer sells a property for which the mortgage (loan) balance exceeds the cost base.

Multiple Listing Service   An association of real estate agents and appraisers that pools listings, shares commissions on a specified basis, and provides data for agents and appraisers in preparing market evaluations and appraisals of real property.

"neg-am" loans   Loans in which you have the option to pay a lower payment than is needed to pay all the interest due.

negative amortization This takes place when the payments on an adjustable loan are not sufficient to pay all the interest due. In this case, the loan increases by the amount of the unpaid interest.

negative cash flow The condition in which payments are greater than receipts.

"no-neg" loans Loans in which the payment will always pay all the interest due on the loan.

nonrecourse loan Loans, usually long-term mortgages, for which no partner, limited or general, assumes personal liability. In most cases, the debt is secured by the property itself.

offer The proposed terms of a contract in real estate. An offer is put forward and must be accepted by the other side before a contract can exist.

operating expenses Periodic expenditures necessary to maintain a property and to continue the production of effective gross income.

opinion of value letter A letter that expresses an opinion of value but that is not a complete appraisal.

package policy An insurance policy that covers more than one type of loss.

passive investors An IRS term that refers to someone who is limited in the deductions that can be claimed against earnings.

point One percent of the loan amount; an additional charge added on by a lender as a fee assessed for getting the loan. Points also are called loan fees.

positive cash flow A situation in which cash receipts are greater than cash payments.

preliminary title report A report by a title company that gives all the basic title information, usually given at the opening of an escrow.

prepayment penalty A clause in a note that provides for a monetary penalty in the event of an early payoff of the note.

private mortgage insurance (PMI)   Insurance to protect lenders from loss on a loan. This usually is required when the loan-to-value ratio is over 80 percent.

property management   A service profession in which someone other than the owner supervises a property's operation according to the owner's objectives.

raw land   A parcel of land or acreage not zoned for any specific purpose or a parcel of land that is zoned but that lacks basic services and, thus, is not yet buildable.

Realtor ®   A trademark name of the National Association of Realtors ® (NAR). Members using this title agree to conduct themselves according to a Realtors' Code of Ethics, and they are subject to the rules of the association. Some jurisdictions make a distinction between Realtors ® (who must be licensed as real estate brokers) and Realtor-Associates (who hold sales licenses). Others designate all their members as Realtors ®.

recordation   A system by which documents concerning title and other legal matters are collected in one convenient, public place, commonly the county recorder's office. Documents properly recorded constitute constructive notice of the contents of the documents.

recovery period   Under depreciation rules, the number of years over which depreciation is claimed.

rent   Money paid (or sometimes services rendered) for use and occupation of a property.

rent control   Laws enacted on a city-by-city basis that dictate the amount of rent landlords can charge tenants.

rent survey   A survey done to find out what other owners are charging for rent in a given area.

rental agreement   An agreement between a landlord and a tenant that sets forth the terms of a tenancy.

reproduction cost   The cost to rebuild a property today.

residential loans   A loan on a residence or residential units up to and including four units.

resident-manager   An agent of the owner of a building who is employed on a salary to manage the property in which the manager resides.

RESPA   The Real Estate Settlement Procedures Act, a federal law that ensures that buyers and sellers in certain federally related residential real estate deals receive full disclosure of all settlement costs so they can shop around for settlement services.

return on equity (ROE)   A percentage of return calculated by dividing annual net income by equity.

return on investment (ROI)   Interest or profit from an investment.

Schedule C   The schedule used to report income and expenses from an investment property for tax purposes.

scheduled rent   The current rent scheduled for all the units in a building.

seasoned financing   Any loan over a year old.

second position   A loan recorded after another loan.

Section 8   The federal government's principal medium for housing assistance. It was authorized by the Housing and Community Development Act of 1974, which provides for new construction and rehabilitation.

seller's agent   The agent who enters into a listing contract with a seller, agreeing to find a buyer and to represent that seller's interest in negotiating a contract.

short sale   When someone sells a property for less than what is owed on the property.

slumlord   A slang term used to describe the owner of a building in which overcrowding and deterioration are evident.

specific performance   A doctrine of contract law by which a party can be compelled by the court to perform as agreed.

speculating   To enter into a transaction or venture in which the profits are conjectural or subject to chance; to buy or sell with the hope of profiting through fluctuations in price.

Starker exchange   A type of tax-deferred exchange that got its name from the court case with the same name. Also called a delayed exchange.

straight note   A note with only one payment at which time the amount of the loan and the interest are paid.

tax benefits   The tax savings from property ownership.

tax shelter   An investment with paper losses that can be used to lower one's otherwise taxable income. In other words, the tax loss from the tax-shelter investment is a write-off against regular salary or other income, therefore "sheltering" that income.

tax-deferred exchange (1031 tax-deferred exchange) A method of deferring capital gains by exchanging real property for other like-kind property.

tenant   A person who pays rent to occupy or gain possession of real estate.

three-party exchange   A tax-deferred exchange that involves three different parties.

title company   A company that specializes in establishing the title to real property including identification of all existing liens on the property. The title company issues a title insurance policy insuring that all liens have been disclosed at the time of closing.

title insurance policy A special form of insurance issued by a title company to insure the buyer against any undiscovered liens on the property. The coverage is paid by a single premium during escrow, and it remains in force as long as the buyer owns the property.

title opinion An analysis of the chain of title of a property in a state where the property owner keeps all the original deeds.

title report A report that discloses all matters of public record that affect a piece of property.

transfer disclosure statement A form filled out by the seller of a property to disclose any knowledge the seller has about the property.

triple net leases A type of lease in which the tenant not only pays rent but also might pay for property taxes, insurance, and property maintenance.

turnover When one tenant moves out of a property and another moves in. This usually means no loss of rent.

unearned increment of value An increase in the value of property not brought about by the owner, due primarily to the operation of social forces, such as an increase in population.

up-leg property The larger property in a tax-deferred exchange.

U.S. Department of Housing and Urban Development (HUD) A government agency established in 1965 to provide federal assistance in planning, developing, and managing public housing.

useful life For tax purposes, this is the period of time over which you must depreciate a property. As a general concept, this is the period of time that a property is expected to be functional.

utility   A public service such as gas, water, or electricity.

vacancy rate   The average percentage of units vacant in a given market area.

value   The worth or usefulness of a good or service expressed in terms of a specific sum of money.

Value appreciation   An increase in the value of a property due to any cause.

variable expenses   Expenses on a property that tend to be different each month or pay period.

Veteran's Administration (VA)   *See* Department of Veterans Affairs.

zoning   Any restriction on the use of real property within a given area.

Resource Guide

National

National Association of Realtors®
430 N. Michigan Ave.
Chicago, IL 60611
www.realtor.com

Alabama

Alabama Association of Realtors®
522 Washington Ave.
Montgomery, AL 36104
334-262-3808
www.alabamarealtors.com

Alaska

Alaska Association of Realtors®
741 Sesame St., Suite 100
Anchorage, AK 99503
907-563-7133
www.alaskarealtors.com

Arizona

Arizona Association of Realtors ®
255 E. Osborne Rd. #200
Phoenix, AZ 85012-2327
602-248-7787
www.aaronline.com

Arkansas

Arkansas Realtors ® Association
204 Executive Ct. #30
Little Rock, AR 72205
501-225-2020
www.arkansasrealtors.com

California

California Association of Realtors ®
980 Ninth St. #1430
Sacramento, CA 90020
916-444-2045
www.car.org

Colorado

Colorado Association of Realtors ®
309 Inverness Way South
Englewood, CO 80112
800-944-6550
www.colorealtor.org

Connecticut

Connecticut Association of Realtors ®
111 Founders Plaza, Suite 1101
East Hartford, CT 06108-3296
860-290-6601
www.ctrealtor.com

Delaware

Delaware Association of Realtors®
9 E. Lookerman St. #305
Dover, DE 19901
302-734-4444
www.delawarerealtor.com

District of Columbia

Greater Washington Commercial Association of
Realtors®
1818 N. St. NW, Suite T-50
Washington, DC 20036
202-887-6213
www.gwcar.org

Florida

Florida Association of Realtors®
P.O. Box 72505
Orlando, FL 32872-5025
407-438-1400
fl.realtorplace.com

Georgia

Georgia Association of Realtors®
3200 Presidential Dr.
Atlanta, GA 30340
770-451-1831
garealtor.com

Hawaii

Hawaii Association of Realtors®
Realtor Building
1136 12th Ave., Suite 220
Honolulu, HI 96816
808-737-4000
www.hawaiirealtors.com

Idaho

Idaho Association of Realtors ®
1450 W. Bannock St.
Boise, ID 83702
208-342-3585
www.idahorealtors.com

Illinois

Illinois Association of Realtors ®
P.O. Box 19451
Springfield, IL 62794-9451
217-529-2600
www.illinoisrealtor.org

Indiana

Indiana Association of Realtors ®
P.O. Box 50736
7301 N. Shadeland Ave.
Indianapolis, IN 46250-0736
317-842-0890
indianarealtors.com

Iowa

Iowa Association of Realtors ®
1370 NW 114th St. #100
Clive, IA 50325
515-453-1064
ialiving.net

Kansas

Kansas Association of Realtors ®
3644 SW Burlingame
Topeka, KS 66611
800-366-0069
www.kansasrealtor.com

Kentucky

Kentucky Association of Realtors®
161 Prosperous Pl.
Lexington, KY 40509
606-263-7377
www.kar.com

Louisiana

Louisiana Realtors® Association
P.O. Box 14780
Baton Rouge, LA 70898
225-923-2210
la.realtorplace.com

Maine

Maine Association of Realtors®
19 Community Dr.
Augusta, GA 04330
207-622-7501
www.mainerealtors.com

Maryland

Maryland Association of Realtors®
2594 Riva Rd.
Annapolis, MD 21401
800-638-6425
www.mdrealtor.org

Massachusetts

Massachusetts Association of Realtors®
256 Second Ave.
Waltham, MA 02451
781-890-3700
ma.living.net

Michigan

Michigan Association of Realtors ®
P.O. Box 40725
720 N. Washington Ave.
Lansing, MI 48901-7925
800-454-7842
www.mirealtors.com

Minnesota

Minnesota Association of Realtors ®
5750 Lincoln Dr.
Edina, MN 55436
612-935-8313
mn.living.net

Mississippi

Mississippi Association of Realtors ®
P.O. Box 5809
Brandon, MS 39407
601-932-9325
ms.living.net

Missouri

Missouri Association of Realtors ®
2601 Bernadette Pl.
Columbia, MO 65205
573-445-8400
mo.living.net

Montana

Montana Association of Realtors ®
208 N. Montana #105
Helena, MT 59601
406-443-4032
www.mtmar.com

Nebraska

Nebraska Realtors® Association
145 S. 56th St.
Lincoln, NE 68510
402-488-4304
nebraskarealtors.com

Nevada

Nevada Association of Realtors®
P.O. Box 7338
Reno, NV 89510-7338
775-829-5911
www.nvrealtors.org

New Hampshire

New Hampshire Association of Realtors®
115A Airport Road
Concord, NH 03302
603-225-5549
www.nhar.com

New Jersey

New Jersey Association of Realtors®
295 Pierson Ave.
Edison, NJ 08818
732-494-5616
www.njar.com

New Mexico

Realtors® Association of New Mexico
P.O. Box 4190
Santa Fe, NM 87502
603-225-5549
nm.living.net

New York

New York Association of Realtors ®
130 Washington Ave.
Albany, NY 12210
518-463-0300
www.nysar.com

North Carolina

North Carolina Association of Realtors ®
2901 Seawell Rd.
Greensboro, NC 27407
336-294-1415
www.realtor.org

North Dakota

North Dakota Association of Realtors ®
1120 College Dr. #112
Bismarck, ND 58501
701-258-2361
nd.living.net

Ohio

Ohio Association of Realtors ®
200 E. Town St.
Columbus, OH 43215-4648
614-228-6675
www.ohiorealtors.com

Oklahoma

Oklahoma Association of Realtors ®
9807 N. Broadway
Oklahoma City, OK 73114
405-848-9944
www.oklahomarealtors.com

Oregon
Oregon Association of Realtors®
693 Chemeketa
Salem, OR 97308
503-362-3645
or.realtorplace.com

Pennsylvania
Pennsylvania Association of Realtors®
4501 Chambers Hill Rd.
Harrisburg, PA 17111-2406
717-561-1303
www.parealtor.org

Rhode Island
Rhode Island Association of Realtors®
100 Bignall St.
Warwick, RI 02888
401-785-3650
www.riliving.com

South Carolina
South Carolina Association of Realtors®
P.O. Box 21827
Columbia, SC 29221
803-772-5206
screaltors.com

South Dakota
South Dakota Association of Realtors®
120 N. Euclid
Pierre, SD 57501
605-224-0554
www.sdrealtor.org

Tennessee

Tennessee Association of Realtors®
P.O. Box 121149
Nashville, TN 37212-1149
615-321-0515
www.tarnet.com

Texas

Texas Association of Realtors®
P.O. Box 2246
Austin, TX 78768-2246
512-480-8200
www.tar.org

Utah

Utah Association of Realtors®
5710 S. Green St.
Murray, UT 84123
801-268-4747
www.utahrealtors.com

Vermont

Vermont Association of Realtors®
148 State St.
Montpelier, VT 05602
802-229-0513
www.vtrealtor.com

Virginia

Virginia Association of Realtors®
10231 Telegraph Rd.
Glen Allen, VA 23059-4578
800-755-8271
www.vareltor.com

Washington

Washington Association of Realtors®
504 E. 14th Ave., Suite 200
Olympia, WA 98507-0719
360-943-3100
www.warealtor.com

West Virginia

West Virginia Association of Realtors®
2110 Kanawha Blvd. East
Charleston, WV 25311-2205
304-342-7600
www.wvrealtors.com

Wisconsin

Wisconsin Realtors® Association
4801 Forest Run Rd., Suite 201
Madison, WI 53704-7337
608-241-2047
www.wra.org

Wyoming

Wyoming Association of Realtors®
P.O. Box 2312
Casper, WY 82602
307-237-4085
wy.living.net

Canada

Real Estate Institute of Canada
5407 Eglinton Ave. West, Suite 208
Toronto, ON M9C 5K6
800-542-7342
www.reic.ca

Recommended Reading List

Investing

Hicks, Tyler G. *How to Make Big Money in Real Estate in the Tighter, Tougher '90s Market.* Prentice Hall, 1992.

Miller, Peter G. *Successful Real Estate Investing: A Practical Guide to Profits for the Small Investor.* Harper Perennial, 1995.

Neal, H. Roger. *Streetwise Investing in Rental Housing: A Detailed Strategy for Financial Independence.* The Panoply Press Real Estate Series, 1994.

Pivar, William H. *Real Estate Investing from A to Z.* McGraw-Hill, 1997.

Thomsett, Michael C. and Jean Freestone Thomsett. *Getting Started in Real Estate Investing* (2nd Edition). John Wiley & Sons, 1998.

Vollucci, Eugene E. and Gene Volluccci. *How to Buy and Sell Apartment Buildings.* John Wiley & Sons, 1993.

Whitney, Russ. *Building Wealth: From Rags to Riches With Real Estate.* Simon & Schuster, 1995.

Woodson, R. Dodge. *Profitable Real Estate Investing: Making Big Money, Finding the Right Properties, Investing on a Shoestring.* Real Estate Education Co., 1999.

Landlording

Goodwin, Daniel and Richard Rusdorf. *Landlord's Handbook: A Complete Guide to Managing Small Residential Properties.* Dearborn Trade, 1999.

London, Lawrence and Lawrence L. Stevens. *Landlording As a Second Income: The Survival Handbook.* Madison Books, 1998.

Milin, Mike and Irene. *How to Buy & Manage Rental Properties.* Simon & Schuster, 1988.

Robinson, Leigh and David Patton. *Landlording: A Handy Manual for Scrupulous Landlords and Landladies Who Do It Themselves.* Express, 1997.

Reference

Cummings, Jack. *The McGraw-Hill 36-Hour Real Estate Investing Course.* McGraw-Hill, 1993.

Cummings, Jack. *Real Estate Finance & Investment Manual.* Prentice Hall, 1997.

Cummings, Jack. *The Real Estate Investor's Answer Book: Hundreds of Money-Making Ideas for Today's Market.* McGraw-Hill, 1994.

Friedman, Jack P. *Dictionary of Real Estate Terms* (4th Edition). Barrons Real Estate Guides, 1997.

Friedman, Jack P. and Jack C. Harris. *Adjustable Rate Mortgages.* Barrons Educational Series, 1993.

Gadow, Sandy and Dave Patton. *All About Escrow and Real Estate Closings.* Escrow Publishing, 1999.

Hoven, Vernon. *The Real Estate Investor's Tax Guide.* Real Estate Education Co., 1998.

Strauss, Steven D. *Landlord and Tenant (Ask a Lawyer).* W.W. Norton & Co., 1998.

Tyson, Eric and Ray Brown. *Mortgages for Dummies.* IDG Books Worldwide, 1999.

Ventelo, William R. and Martha R. William. *The Art of Real Estate Appraisal: Dollars and Cents Answers to Your Questions.* Dearborn Trade, 1992.

Sample Real Estate Investment Plan

Property
1800 Mariposa Lane

Prepared for
The Unofficial Guide™ to Real Estate Investing

Prepared by
Martin Stone & Spencer Strauss

BUCKINGHAM   INVESTMENTS
333 Richmond St. Suite 10
El Segundo, CA   90245
PHONE: 310-322-8343
FAX: 310-322-4050

www.buckinghaminvestments.com

Contents of the Plan

Financial Goal for the Plan

Summary of the Investment Plan

Financial Overview of the Beginning Property

Tabular Presentation of Year, Value, Equity, and
    Income

Tabular Presentation of Year, Cash Account, and
    Tax Account

Year-by-Year Financial Detail of the Plan

Financial Goals for the Plan

1. Final gross equity position in the property of $431,000.00

2. Potential of an annual installment sale income of $40,300.00

3. Hedge against inflation during the entire period of the plan

4. Minimize negative cash flows during the entire period of the plan

5. Schedule operating expenses for professional property management

Real Estate Investment Plan
Summary

This 10 year real estate investment
plan was prepared for:

The Unofficial Guide to Real Estate Investing
The plan maintains a 30-percent average levered
return to achieve a final gross equity position of
$518,797.00 in 9 years. During the last year of the
plan, an installment sale is made. The cash down
payment received from the sale is only that amount
of money required to pay federal and state taxes due
and to bring the cash and tax accounts to positive
balances. The balance of the sale price is loaned to
the buyer and is evidenced by a note, secured by a
trust deed, bearing interest at 10 percent.

After the installment sale, the investor will have
$49,395.00 in annual interest income from the note
and cash account balance. The plan assumes the
following:

1. A 5 percent annual value appreciation rate,

2. A 3 percent annual increase in income
   collected, and

3. A 2 percent annual increase in operating
   expense costs.

PROPERTY FINANCIAL PARAMETERS ARE:

Purchase Price	$220,000.00	Equity	$30,000.00
Monthly Income	$2,200.00	Monthly Expenses	$660.00
Account Balance	$0.00		
1st Td & Note		**2nd Td & Note**	
Loan Amount	$190,000.00	Loan Amount	$0.00
Interest Rate	9.00%	Interest Rate	0.00%
Years of Loan	30.00	Years of Loan	0.00
Monthly Payment	$1,450.00	Monthly Payment	$0.00
V.A. Rate	5.00%	Income Increase	3.50%
Vacancy Rate	2.50%	Expense Increase	2.50%
Land Value	$66,000.00	Depreciable Imp.	$154,000.00
Annual Operating Expenses:			
Property Taxes	$2,640.00	Insurance Costs	$380.00
Licenses	$98.00	Utilities	$1,372.00
Management	$1,372.00	Maintenance	$1,029.00

Real Estate Investment Plan

MARKET VALUE, GROSS EQUITY, AND ANNUAL LIQUIDATED INCOME

Year	Market Value	Gross Equity	Income*
1999	$220,000.00	$30,000.00	$3,000.00
2000	$231,000.00	$41,300.00	$4,172.00
2001	$242,550.00	$53,177.00	$5,472.00
2002	$584,520.00	$58,452.00	$5,845.00
2003	$613,746.00	$91,126.00	$8,506.00
2004	$644,433.00	$125,572.00	$11,524.00
2005	$1,260,483.00	$126,048.00	$12,605.00
2006	$1,323,507.00	$196,508.00	$18,342.00
2007	$1,389,682.00	$270,788.00	$24,852.00
2008	$1,459,166.00	$349,107.00	$32,171.00
2009	$1,532,124.00	$431,694.00	$40,339.00

* The annual liquidated income is computed as follows: The property is sold using an installment sale, any cash in the cash account is added to the equity account, and finally, we assume you carry the balance at 10 percent interest.

The data in this analysis is approximate, should only be used with a Buckingham Investments agent, and is not a guarantee or warranty of investment return. Copyright©1990, J.R. Buckingham, El Segundo, CA 90245

Real Estate Investment Plan

CASH ACCOUNT, TAX ACCOUNT, AND NET OF THE TWO ACCOUNTS

Year	Cash Account	Tax Account	Net
1999	$0.00	$0.00	$0.00
2000	$420.00	$1,415.00	$1,835.00
2001	$1,543.00	$2,619.00	$4,162.00
2002	$0.00	$0.00	$0.00
2003	−$6,070.00	$5,075.00	−$995.00
2004	−$10,328.00	$9,535.00	−$793.00
2005	$0.00	$0.00	$0.00
2006	−$13,089.00	$9,500.00	−$3,589.00
2007	−$22,271.00	$19,000.00	−$3,271.00
2008	−$27,395.00	$28,500.00	$1,105.00
2009	−$28,306.00	$35,276.00	$6,970.00

The data in this analysis is approximate, should only be used with a Buckingham Investments agent, and is not a guarantee or warranty of investment return. Copyright©1990, J.R. Buckingham, El Segundo, CA 90245

YEAR OF THE PLAN IS 1999

Market Value	$220,000.00	Equity	$30,000.00
Cash Account	$0.00	Tax Account	$0.00

During-the-Year Values

Income	$26,400.00	Expenses	$7,920.00
Cash Flow	$420.00	Tax Rebates	$1,415.00
Amortization	$300.00	Appreciation	$11,000.00
Roe	44	Delta Roe	30

End-of-the-Year Values

Market Value	$231,000.00	Equity	$41,300.00
Cash Account	$420.00	Tax Account	$1,415.00

YEAR OF THE PLAN IS 2000

Market Value	$231,000.00	Equity	$41,300.00
Cash Account	$420.00	Tax Account	$1,415.00

During-the-Year Values

Income	$26,400.00	Expenses	$7,920.00
Cash Flow	$1,123.00	Tax Rebates	$1,204.00
Amortization	$327.00	Appreciation	$11,550.00
Roe	34	Delta Roe	14

End-of-the-Year Values

Market Value	$242,550.00	Equity	$53,177.00
Cash Account	$1,543.00	Tax Account	$2,619.00

YEAR OF THE PLAN IS 2001

Market Value	$242,550.00	Equity	$53,177.00
Cash Account	$1,543.00	Tax Account	$2,619.00

During-the-Year Values

Income	$27,324.00	Expenses	$8,118.00
Cash Flow	$1,852.00	Tax Rebates	$983.00
Amortization	$356.00	Appreciation	$12,128.00
Roe	29	Delta Roe	9

End-of-the-Year Values

Market Value	$584,520.00	Equity	$58,452.00
Cash Account	$0.00	Tax Account	$0.00

Tax Deferred Exchange Occurred in the Last
Quarter Of 2001
Trade Out Of:
Market Value = $254,678.00
Total Loans = $189,017.00 [Leverage: 74%]
Total Equity = $65,661.00
Accounts = $0.00

:::

Total "Out-of-Pocket" Exchange Transaction
Cost = $14,206.00

:::

Total Equity = $58,452.00
Accounts = $0.00
Market Value = $584,520.00
Total Loans = $526,068.00 [Leverage: 86%]
Trade Into: Exchange Property
[Costs: Sell – 3.0% Buy – 1.0%]   [Gm – 8.50 Va
Rate – 5.00%]
[Loans: 86.4 % First At 9.0%]

YEAR OF THE PLAN IS 2002

Market Value	$584,520.00	Equity	$58,452.00
Cash Account	$0.00	Tax Account	$0.00

During-the-Year Values

Income	$68,767.00	Expenses	$24,068.00
Cash Flow	−$6,070.00	Tax Rebates	$5,075.00
Amortization	$3,448.00	Appreciation	$29,226.00
Roe	54	Delta Roe	6

End-of-the-Year Values

Market Value	$613,746.00	Equity	$91,126.00
Cash Account	−$6,070.00	Tax Account	$5,075.00

YEAR OF THE PLAN IS 2003

Market Value	$613,746.00	Equity	$91,126.00
Cash Account	−$6,070.00	Tax Account	$5,075.00

During-the-Year Values

Income	$71,174.00	Expenses	$24,670.00
Cash Flow	−$4,258.00	Tax Rebates	$4,460.00
Amortization	$3,758.00	Appreciation	$30,687.00
Roe	38	Delta Roe	13

End-of-the-Year Values

Market Value	$644,433.00	Equity	$125,572.00
Cash Account	−$10,328.00	Tax Account	$9,535.00

YEAR OF THE PLAN IS 2004

Market Value	$644,433.00	Equity	$125,572.00
Cash Account	−$10,328.00	Tax Account	$9,535.00

During-the-Year Values

Income	$73,665.00	Expenses	$25,287.00
Cash Flow	−$2,376.00	Tax Rebates	$3,816.00
Amortization	$4,097.00	Appreciation	$32,222.00
Roe	30	Delta Roe	2

End-of-the-Year Values

Market Value	$1,260,483.00	Equity	$126,048.00
Cash Account	$0.00	Tax Account	$0.00

Tax Deferred Exchange Occured in the Last
Quarter of 2004
Trade Out Of:
Market Value = $676,654.00
Total Loans = $514,764.00 [Leverage: 76%]
Total Equity = $161,890.00
Accounts = $ 0.00

::

Total "Out-of-Pocket" Exchange Transaction
Cost = $36,489.00

::

Total Equity = $126,048.00
Accounts = $0.00
Market Value = $1,260,483.00
Total Loans = $1,134,434.00 [Leverage: 86%]
Trade Into: Exchange Property
[Costs: Sell – 3.0% Buy – 1.0%]   [Gm – 8.50 Va
Rate – 5.00%]
[Loans: 86.4 % First At 9.0%]

YEAR OF THE PLAN IS 2005

Market Value	$1,260,483.00	Equity	$126,048.00
Cash Account	$0.00	Tax Account	$0.00

During-the-Year Values

Income	$148,292.00	Expenses	$51,902.00
Cash Flow	–$13,089.00	Tax Rebates	$9,500.00
Amortization	$7,436.00	Appreciation	$63,024.00
Roe	53	Delta Roe	2

End-of-the-Year Values

Market Value	$1,323,507.00	Equity	$196,508.00
Cash Account	–$13,089.00	Tax Account	$9,500.00

YEAR OF THE PLAN IS 2006

Market Value	$1,323,507.00	Equity	$196,508.00
Cash Account	–$13,089.00	Tax Account	$9,500.00

During-the-Year Values

Income	$153,482.00	Expenses	$53,200.00
Cash Flow	–$9,182.00	Tax Rebates	$9,500.00
Amortization	$8,105.00	Appreciation	$66,175.00
Roe	38	Delta Roe	5

End-of-the-Year Values

Market Value	$1,389,682.00	Equity	$270,788.00
Cash Account	–$22,271.00	Tax Account	$19,000.00

YEAR OF THE PLAN IS 2007

Market Value	$1,389,682.00	Equity	$270,788.00
Cash Account	–$22,271.00	Tax Account	$19,000.00

During-the-Year Values

Income	$158,854.00	Expenses	$54,530.00
Cash Flow	–$5,124.00	Tax Rebates	$9,500.00
Amortization	$8,834.00	Appreciation	$69,484.00
Roe	31	Delta Roe	4

End-of-the-Year Values

Market Value	$1,459,166.00	Equity	$349,107.00
Cash Account	–$27,395.00	Tax Account	$28,500.00

YEAR OF THE PLAN IS 2008

Market Value	$1,459,166.00	Equity	$349,107.00
Cash Account	−$27,395.00	Tax Account	$28,500.00

During-the-Year Values

Income	$164,414.00	Expenses	$55,893.00
Cash Flow	−$911.00	Tax Rebates	$6,776.00
Amortization	$9,629.00	Appreciation	$72,958.00
Roe	25	Delta Roe	4

End-of-the-Year Values

Market Value	$1,532,124.00	Equity	$431,694.00
Cash Account	−$28,306.00	Tax Account	$35,276.00

YEAR OF THE PLAN IS 2009

Market Value	$1,532,124.00	Equity	$431,694.00
Cash Account	−$28,306.00	Tax Account	$35,276.00

During-the-Year Values

Income	$170,169.00	Expenses	$57,290.00
Cash Flow	$3,464.00	Tax Rebates	$5,256.00
Amortization	$10,496.00	Appreciation	$76,606.00
Roe	22	Delta Roe	3

End-of-the-Year Values

Market Value	$1,608,731.00	Equity	$518,797.00
Cash Account	−$24,842.00	Tax Account	$40,532.00

This analysis was generated by a Buckingham Investments Analysis Automated System.

It is to be understood that the computerized systems employed by Buckingham Investments are simulations only. As such, they are *what if* not *what is.*

The calculations used in the systems are accurate as to representing the true financial mechanisms that most investments in real property undergo. Therefore, the systems are quite accurate when the assumptions concerning the future values of certain significant parameters used in the systems also are accurate. Your participation in selecting these parameters is solicited and welcomed.

The significant parameters for which future values are predicted or assumed are:

1. Value appreciation rate

2. Rate of increase of rental income

3. Rate of increase of operating expenses

4. Vacancy rate

5. Loan interest rate increases

6. Competent level of property management

7. General assumptions such as your longevity, health, and the continuance of a stable political and economical order

You have considerable control over some of these parameters. Others are at the mercy of external forces.

Of course, continual updating of any analyses using the systems will guarantee greater accuracy.

When using the analyses generated by the systems as a plan, two major benefits accrue:

1. The plan is a measure of what you should do.

2. The plan is a measure as to how well your financial intentions are being executed.

The data in any analysis generated is approximate, should only be used with a Buckingham Investments representative, and is not a guarantee or warranty of return on investment.

It is distributed with the understanding that it is for planning purposes only.

*The following are the results of a
general building inspection performed at the
following location:*

1800 Mariposa Lane

Prepared exclusively for:

**The Unofficial Guide
to Real Estate Investing**

INSPECTION
REPORT

Inspected by:

J. Mark Roach
California licensed general contractor #556371

MARK 1
& SON
HOME INSPECTORS
www.mark1homeinspectors.com

1621 Loma Drive Hermosa Beach, CA 90254   Phone (310) 318-5634 Fax (310) 318-3172

GENERAL DATA / ACTION LIST   PAGE 1

REPORT # _1800 MARIPOSA LANE_

GENERAL DATA

Date _8-27_ 199_9_ Time of day _10_ : _00_ (am) pm
Current weather conditions _CLEAR_   Most recent rain was approximately _12 WKS_ ago
Other known factors_____ ☐ None
Type of property: ☐ Single family ☐ Duplex ☐ Tri-plex ☒ 4-unit ☐ 2 on lot ☐ Other _____
                  ☐ House ☐ Condominium ☐ Townhome ☐ Other _____
Current status: ☒ Occupied ☐ Vacant   Electricity: ☒ On ☐ Off   Water: ☒ On ☐ Off   Gas: ☒ On ☐ Off
Approximate age of structure: _20_ years old   Additions: ☐ Yes ☒ No ☐ Could not determine
Present during inspection: ☒ Buyer ☒ Buyer's agent ☒ Seller ☐ Seller's agent ☐ Other _____
Remarks: _____
_____

NOTE: All utilities must be on at the time of the inspection, if not,
we cannot determine the functional capability of that utility.

ACTION LIST
This space is for client/agent use.

NOTE: Read opposing page for further information, explanation and limitations.

MARK 1
HOME INSPECTORS

Stucco

It is normal to find minor stucco cracking. Cracking is caused by a number of things including normal aging, vibration, expansion and contraction, earth movement , settling etc.. Continued observation of the stucco and its condition is advisable. It is wise to keep such cracks grouted to prevent moisture from penetrating and undermining the material, especially on walls directly exposed to wind and rain.

Vents

Vent screens should be kept in place to prevent unwanted creatures from entering sub area or attic. Vents should be kept clear to allow proper ventilation.

Trim

Wood trim will be covered by the termite report. Proper paint seal and caulking should be considered normal maintenance to all wood on the exterior.

Chimney

Our inspection of the chimney and fireplace(s) is a surface inspection only. We *do not* use any device to determine condition. For full in-depth evaluation we strongly urge full inspection by a licensed contractor. We advise the installation of spark arrestors where they are not present, as well as keeping the inside flue area well swept to prevent fire hazards.

Utility shut-off

It is wise to communicate to all occupants of the premises, the locations of all utility shut-offs. Accordingly, it is also advisable to have a plan, in the event of emergency to shut off necessary utilities. We suggest a wrench be attached to the gas meter to facilitate immediate shut off of the gas system in the event of earthquake or other disaster.
NOTE: It is recommended that a main shut off be present and readily accessible for all utilities. For those utilities that have no main shut off, we recommend that one be installed.

EXTERIOR	PAGE 2

A-Construction

☒ Stucco : ☐ Minor cracking ☐ Excessive cracking ☐ Color coat separation

☒ Siding : ☒ *(circled)* Wood ☐ Wood shingle ☐ Aluminum ☐ Vinyl ☐ Asbestos-like shingle

☐ Composition lap ☐ Other _____

(✗) ☒ Intact ☐ Loose/broken/missing pieces ☒ Dry rot (See termite report)

☐ Brick : ☐ Minor cracking ☐ Excessive cracking ☐ Repair / maintainance suggested

☐ Mold / mildew : ☐ Minor ☐ Excessive

(✗) ☒ Foilage overgrowth noted ☒ Pruning suggested — LARGE TREE AT N.W. CORNER

B-Ventilation :

Attic vents : ☒ Eave vents ☐ Gable vents ☐ Top vents ☐ Side vents ☐ Turbines

☒ Screens present ☐ Screens missing ☐ Screens rusting out ☐ Other _____

Foundation vents : ☒ Present ☐ N/A on slab ☒ Screens present ☐ Screens missing

☐ Screens rusted / damaged

C-Trim :

☒ Eaves open ☐ Eaves covered ☒ Wood ☐ Aluminum ☐ Needs scrapping / painting

(✗) Facia Boards : ☒ Complete ☐ Incomplete ☐ Damaged ☒ Dry rot (see termite report)

Note: See termite report for condition of all wood

D-Guttering :

☐ Galvanized ☐ Plastic ☐ Other ☐ Partial only ☒ None ☐ Full of debris ☐ Rust noted

Downspouts : ☒ Complete ☐ Incomplete ☐ None ☒ System appears over-all functional ONLY

E-Chimney(s) :

Chimney #1: Location FRONT UNIT #1 ☒ Brick ☐ Metal ☐ Stucco ☐ Block

Spark arrestor present : ☐ Yes ☒ No ☒ Needed

Chimney #2: Location FRONT UNIT #2 ☒ Brick ☐ Metal ☐ Stucco ☐ Block

Spark arrestor present : ☐ Yes ☐ No ☒ Needed

(✗) ☒ Cracks : ☐ #1 ☒ #2 Separations : ☐ #1 ☒ #2

(✗) ☒ Caulk seal (at wall) needed: ☐ #1 ☒ #2 ☐ Deteriorated mortar : ☐ #1 ☐ #2

(✗) ☐ Loose brick : ☐ #1 ☐ #2 ☒ Cracking at chimney cap: ☐ #1 ☒ #2

☐ Flue liner : ☐ #1 ☐ #2 ☐ Could not determine : ☐ #1 ☐ #2

(✗) ☒ Chimney sweep needed : ☒ #1 ALL UNITS ☐ #2 ☒ Repair/further inspection needed : ☐ #1 ☒ #2

(✗) ☒ Suggest further inspection / repair by licensed contractor #2

Utility Shut-offs:

Water main shut off location: FRONT   Gas main shut off location: WEST SIDE

Electrical main shut off location: WEST SIDE   ☐ None (must turn off all breakers)

Remarks : CHIMNEY #3 - FRONT OF UNIT #3 - SPARK ARRESTOR NEEDED
     "   " #4 - "   "   "   "   "
CHIMNEY SWEEP NEEDED AT ALL CHIMNEYS

MARK 1 HOME INSPECTORS

NOTE: Read opposing page for further information, explanation and limitations.

Foundation

We can only comment on portions of the foundation readily accessible and visible, as the whole of this report is considered "general" in nature and we can only comment on the general condition of the foundation to the extent that we are able to observe it.

Bolting

In this Report, the structure is considered "bolted" if one (1) bolt is located in either the house or matching garage. We *do not* suggest that the bolting is sufficient or adequate in any way. We only refer to the fact that bolting does exist if we observe one bolt. For further evaluation of the adequacy of the bolting system or for a retro-fit of a non-bolted structure we recommend a licensed specialist be contacted for further consultation.

Floor System

It is common in older properties to show evidence of settling caused by a variey reasons such as normal earth settling, earth movement, expansion and contraction etc. Out-of-leveled floors can be re-leveled in most cases. It is advised that if you experience a significant change in levels of the floors that a licensed specialist be contacted to evaluate the cause. It is recommended that the ability of water collection close to the foundation be minimized, especially around hillside properties and properties within expansive soil areas.

Roof

If there is no evidence of active leakage it is assumed that the roof does not leak, however, a roof may begin leaking at any given time. It is our endeavor to make an accurate assessment of the current condition based on the visible character of the roof. Unless documented proof of repair exists, evidence of leakage must be considered a potentially active leak. It is recommended that an ongoing maintenance schedule be kept during the life of the roof to prevent future leakage. We *do not* walk on any roof unless there is ready access. In the absence of ready access roofs are observed from the perimeter.

We can comment only on the portions of the roof system that are readily visible. This report *is not* a roof certification. For roof certification a licensed roofing contractor should be obtained.

STRUCTURAL / ROOF   PAGE 3

STRUCTURAL

A-Foundation :

Type : ☒ Poured concrete ☐ Block ☐ Brick ☐ Cripple walls ☐ Other _____

☒ Raised foundation ☐ Slab ☐ Partial Raised ☐ Partial slab

☒ **Crawl space :** ☒ Able to inspect fully ☐ Unable to inspect fully ☐ Not fully accessable

☐ **Basement :** ☐ Full ☐ Partial **Crawl or basement floor :** ☒ Dirt ☐ Concrete

☒ Dry ☒ Clean ☐ Debris noted ☒ Moisture noted   Describe _SEE PLUMBING PG 5_

☒ **Foundation wall cracking noted :** ☒ Minor ☐ Major   Location _____

☒ **Settling :** ☒ Appears minor ☐ Appears excessive   Possible cause _____

FOUNDATION BOLTING : ☒ Bolting observed ☐ No bolting observed ☐ See "Remarks"

Location of bolt observed _SUB AREA_   ☐ Retro-fit work performed

B-Floor System:

☒ **Wood frame :** ☒ Floor joists _2 x 8_   ☒ Grade beam _4 x 6_

☒ **Pier post support :** ☒ Adequate ☐ Additional support suggested ☐ Pier posts leaning

☐ **Concrete stem wall support :** ☐ Appear solid/straight ☐ Leaning and cracking noted

☐ **Slab :** ☐ Feels/appears level ☐ Cracking noted ☐ Appears minor ☐ Appears major

☐ Slab covered and not visible ☐ Furniture and belongings prevent full evaluation

Remarks: ☐ Suggest further inspection by licensed foundation or structural contractor

NOTE: Read opposing page for further information, explanation and limitations.

ROOF

C-Type :

☐ Gabled ☒ Flat ☐ Hip

Material : ☐ Composition shingle ☒ Rolled composition ☐ Gravel/rock ☐ Wood shake

☐ Wood shingle ☐ Clay tile ☐ Concrete tile ☐ Slate ☐ Hot mop ☐ Metal

If sections vary in type, describe : _____

Approximate number of layers ___/___   ☐ Cannot determine

D-Condition :

Age : ☐ Appears newer ☒ Appears older ☐ Appears mid-life

☐ Extended life expected ☒ Limited life expectancy

✖ **Evidence of leak(s) :** ☒ Yes ☐ No

☒ Leaks _appear_ active ☐ Leaks do not appear active ☐ Cannot determine

✖ **Location of evidence of leak(s)** _UNIT 2 LIVING ROOM   UNIT 3 KITCHEN_

☒ Visible ultra-violet damage ☐ Split, warped, missing shingles ☐ Patching ☐ Bare spots

☒ Maintainance work needed ☐ Re-roof needed ☒ Roof certification needed

Remarks : ☒ Suggest further examination and/or repair by licensed roofing contractor

MARK 1
HOME INSPECTORS

NOTE: Read opposing page for further information, explanation and limitations.

Service

In most cases, maintenance of the lines that run from the power pole to the weatherhead are the responsibility of the local power company. It is advisable to notify the power company if wires are old, damaged or show wear and if branches and/or foliage obstruct the path to the pole.

Panel(s)

We do not remove the back plate(s) or dismantle any breaker or fuse panels which may exist. If fuse box panel(s) still exist we recommend that they be upgraded to breaker panel(s).

NOTE, If moisture or rust is discovered inside of the the breaker panel, it may indicate a need to reseal where the lines enter the property.

We recommend that all circuits are labeled to indicate their function.

System

We can only report on what we are able to see. Wiring and connections may vary and may be obstructed from view by walls, insulation, framing, personal belongings etc., and may be inaccessible during a general inspection. Wire splices, open junction boxes, damaged wire, worn wire, knob and tube wire, or any other sub-standard condition will be reported only if viewed. For a complete evaluation and exhaustive report of the electrical system, an evaluation by a licensed electrician is advised.

Plugs and Switches

We test a representative sampling of the wall switches and receptacles, We *do not* test all plugs and receptacles.

NOTE: We recommend that old, worn switches and ungrounded or two (2) pronged plugs be upgraded as needed.

It is recommended that Ground Fault Interrupter (GFI) recepticles be installed at all outdoor outlets and on outlets in wet areas such as bathrooms and kitchen counter areas. Consult a licensed electrician for local codes and requirements. GFIs should be tested monthly to ensure they are functioning.

ELECTRICAL SYSTEM	PAGE 4

A-Service: ☒ Overhead ☐ Underground   Line Condition: _OK_   Weatherhead condition: _ok_

Drip loop: ☒ Yes ☐ No   Number of lines _3_   Volts _240_

B-Panel(s): Main panel approximate capacity: _200_ amps ☐ Not labeled - unable to determine

Type: ☒ Breakers ☐ Fuses ☐ Futures _MAIN BREAKERS PER UNIT - 50 AMPS_

Main breaker: ☒ Present ☐ None   Main breaker capacity: _200_ amps

    Number of 110 volt circuits ___ @ ___ 15 amp and ___ 20 amp breakers

    Number of 220 volt circuits ___ @ ___ 30 amp ___ 40 amp ___ ___ amp

    Circuits labeled: ☐ Yes ☐ No ☐ Should be

    Grounding: ☒ Yes ☐ No ☐ Could not determine   _#4 HALL_

Number of sub-panels: _4_   Locations #1 _HALL_   #2 _HALL_   #3 _HALL_

Sub-panel #1 - _4_ 110 volt circuits _2_ 220 volt circuits   Circuits labeled: ☒ Yes ☐ No

Sub-panel #2 - _4_ 110 volt circuits _2_ 220 volt circuits   Circuits labeled: ☒ Yes ☐ No

Sub-panel #3 _#4 - 4_ 110 volt circuits _2_ 220 volt circuits   Circuits labeled: ☒ Yes ☐ No

C-System: Wiring type: ☒ Conduit ☒ Romex ☐ Knob & tube ☒ Obstructed/Unable to determine

Outlets: ☒ 3 prong ☐ 2 prong ☒ All plugs hot ☒ Did not test all outlets _— BY ATTIC INSULATION_

☒ Dead/ damaged outlet(s) location(s): ☐ None located _BROKEN WALL PLUG IN UNIT 2 ON NORTH WALL OF LIVING ROOM._

Wire splice(s) location(s): ☐ None located _1 LOCATED AT UNIT 3 GARAGE DISPOSAL. 1 LOCATED IN ATTIC OVER UNIT #1_

Open junction box(es) location(s): ☐ None located _SEVERAL IN ATTIC AND IN SvB AREA_

Reverse polarity located at the following outlet(s): ☒ None _____

Open ground located at the following outlet(s): ☐ None _2 RECEPTICLE HAVE OPEN GROUND ON EAST WALL OF GARAGE #2_

Switches: ☒ Appear functional ☐ Not functional ☒ Old and worn _SEVERAL_ ☒ Did not test all switches

Ground Fault interrupters(GFI): ☐ All tested operational ☐ Did not function properly

Describe: _____

☒ "GFI" recepticles needed at: ☒ Kitchen ☒ Bathroom(s) ☒ Exterior ☒ Garage

Remarks: ☒ Licensed electrician needed to inspect, repair and certify system

MARK 1
HOME INSPECTORS

Note: Read opposing page for further information, explanation and limitations.

Plumbing system

We can only comment on what we are able to see. We cannot report on what we cannot see due to pipes being underground, inside walls, in inaccessible areas, personal obstructions or otherwise.

Water lines

Galvanized water pipe rusts and corrodes from the inside out causing loss of water pressure. When corrosion and rust, becomes visible to the eye, it means that the pipe has no metal remaining at that spot on the pipe. Eventually the pipe begins leaking and will ultimately break. It is common to replace galvanized pipe with copper pipe which has a life expectancy of sixty (60) plus years. This can sometimes be done in two stages; (1) replace horizontal pipes and (2) replace vertical pipes later as needed.

Waste lines

During our inspection we make every effort to run as much water down the drains as necessary to detect any clogs or backup potential. We cannot detect root intervention problems or broken drain lines unless reasonable evidence is found at the time of the inspection. Any area where wet soil or other moisture exists may indicate the existence of water line seepage or drain line seepage underground. Accordingly, immediate steps should be taken to prevent further plumbing problems or structural settling.

Vent lines

We *do not* inspect drain vents for blockage.

Toilets

Toilets should be checked frequently to be sure they are tightly fastened to the floor. Loose toilets can leak at their base and cause damage to walls ceilings and floors.

Water treatment systems

We *do not* inspect or test water treatment systems.

PLUMBING SYSTEM   PAGE 5

A-Water Lines

Main line: ☒ Copper ☐ Galvanized ☐ PVC ☐ Other_____ Size: _1"_

Main valve: ☒ Appears dry & functional ☐ Leaking ☐ Corrosion visible

Location _FRONT_   **Pressure test:** Time of day _1015_ PSI _50 LBS_ top

Supply lines: ☒ Copper ☐ Galvanized ☐ Other _____

☒ Appear dry & functional ☐ Corrosion visible ☐ Active leak ☐ Evidence of previous leak

Exterior hose bibbs: ☒ Copper ☐ Galvanized ☐ PVC ☒ Functional ☐ Not fuctional

Volume test: ☒ Adequate ☐ Minor loss ☐ Significant loss

B-Drain Lines

Type: ☒ Cast iron ☒ ABS ☐ Galvanized ☐ Corrosion visible ☐ Other _____

☒ Drainage adequate ☐ Slow/stopped up   **Vent lines:** ☒ Adequate ☐ Other _____

☒ Appear dry & functional ☐ Evidence of leakage   **Exterior Clean-out:** ☒ Yes ☐ No

Water treatment system: ☐ Present ☒ None ☐ Hook-ups present

REMARKS: ☒ Licensed plumbing contractor needed to repair system

→ TUB DRAIN LEAK IN SUB AREA UNDER UNIT #2 - STANDING WATER

NOTE: Read opposing page for further information, explanation and limitations.

PLUMBING NOTES PER ROOM

☒ Bathroom # _2_ ☐ Kitchen # ___ ☐ Laundry Room # ___ ☐ Other _____ ☒ Repair Needed
Findings: _SINK FAUCET DRIPS, TOILET LOOSE ON FLOOR_

☐ Bathroom # ___ ☒ Kitchen # _1_ ☐ Laundry Room # ___ ☐ Other _____ ☒ Repair Needed
Findings: _DISPOSAL IS FROZEN, TOILET STICKS_

☐ Bathroom # ___ ☒ Kitchen # _4_ ☐ Laundry Room # ___ ☐ Other _____ ☒ Repair Needed
Findings: _LEFT (HOT) VALVE HANDLE MISSING UNDER SINK_

☐ Bathroom # ___ ☐ Kitchen # ___ ☐ Laundry Room # ___ ☐ Other _____ ☐ Repair Needed
Findings: _____

☐ Bathroom # ___ ☐ Kitchen # ___ ☐ Laundry Room # ___ ☐ Other _____ ☐ Repair Needed
Findings: _____

☐ Bathroom # ___ ☐ Kitchen # ___ ☐ Laundry Room # ___ ☐ Other _____ ☐ Repair Needed
Findings: _____

☐ Bathroom # ___ ☐ Kitchen # ___ ☐ Laundry Room # ___ ☐ Other _____ ☐ Repair Needed
Findings: _____

☐ Bathroom # ___ ☐ Kitchen # ___ ☐ Laundry Room # ___ ☐ Other _____ ☐ Repair Needed
Findings: _____

Water heater(s)

The average life expectancy of a water heater is from eight (8) to twelve (12) years. Draining the water heater and allowing settlement build-up to be drained off can extend life expectancy.

Safety codes require the water heater to be properly strapped for earthquake safety. A licensed contractor should be used to strap any water heater which is not properly strapped.

Pressure Relief Valves and accompanying drain pipe should be installed on each water heater. We do not test the Pressure Relief Valve.

Venting should be intact and extend above the roof line. We do not test for vent leaks or blockage, or for carbon monoxide leaks.

Water heater(s) in a utility area, such as laundry room, garage etc., or any other interior water heating unit(s) should be raised at least eighteen (18) inches off the floor to prevent potential combustion of flammable liquid spills by pilot lights. It is recommended that whenever possible, water heater(s) be moved from living space out to the exterior.

Heating unit(s)

Our inspection includes running the unit(s) when possible. We do not dismantle the unit(s). As a secondary inspection, we strongly urge the full inspection by The Gas Company prior to the close of escrow. This inspection is usually free and will uncover potential problems with areas of the unit that we do not inspect, such as heat exchangers and fire boxes. We do not inspect for proper ventilation, ventilation blockage or leaks, or carbon monoxide leaks.

If there is no proof of a recent service call performed on the heating unit within the last two (2) years, it is recommended that a full service of the unit(s) be performed by a licensed contractor prior to the close of the escrow.

It is common for older homes and buildings to have duct work and exhaust pipes that contain asbestos material. In this report we define the suspicious materials as *"asbestos-like"* material. To determine that asbestos content does exist a lab analysis of the suspicious material is required.

Air conditioning

Our inspection is limited to turning on the unit and determining that it runs. In all cases we recommend that a routine service call be performed to determine the condition and to check for adequate Freon levels. Running an air conditioner with a low level of Freon can severely damage the unit. We *do not* check Freon levels.

WATER HEATERS / HEATING & AIR CONDITIONING **PAGE 6**

WATER HEATERS

Water heater # 1 - Location _LAUNDRY ROOM_   Size: _30_ gallon   Approximate age _9_ years
☒ Gas ☐ Electric   **Pressure relief valve:** ☒ Present ☐ Not present ☐ Needed – _NO DIVERTER PIPE_
Vent: ☒ Intact ☐ Not intact   **Earthquake strap:** ☒ Yes ☐ No ☒ Improper – _NO MIDDLE STRAP_

Water heater # 2 - Location _LAUNDRY ROOM_   Size: _30_ gallon   Approximate age _12_ years
☒ Gas ☐ Electric   **Pressure relief valve:** ☒ Present ☐ Not present ☐ Needed – _NO DIVERTER PIPE_
Vent: ☒ Intact ☐ Not intact   **Earthquake strap:** ☒ Yes ☐ No ☐ Improper

Water heater # 3 - Location _LAUNDRY ROOM_   Size: _30_ gallon   Approximate age _4_ years
☒ Gas ☐ Electric   **Pressure relief valve:** ☒ Present ☐ Not present ☐ Needed
Vent: ☒ Intact ☐ Not intact   **Earthquake strap:** ☒ Yes ☐ No ☐ Improper

Water heater # 4 - Location _LAUNDRY ROOM_   Size: _30_ gallon   Approximate age _16_ years
☒ Gas ☐ Electric   **Pressure relief valve:** ☐ Present ☒ Not present ☒ Needed → _UNIT IS LEAKING_
Vent: ☒ Intact ☐ Not intact   **Earthquake strap:** ☐ Yes ☒ No ☐ Improper → _SUGGEST REPLACEMENT_

Remarks: ☒ Licensed contractor needed to perform service / repair and certify.
★ ALL UNITS SIT ON FLOOR – CONSIDER RAISING UNITS 18"
OFF FLOOR OR RELOCATION TO EXTERIOR.
NOTE: Read opposing page for further instruction, explanation and limitations.

HEATING & AIR CONDITIONING SYSTEM

A-Heating System:	Number of units _4_ (Electric wall heaters not included)
	Location: ☐ #___ Garage ☐ #___ Attic ☒ #_1-4_ interior closet ☐ #___ Other _____
	Type: ☐ #___ Floor Furnace ☐ #___ Wall Heater ☒ #_1-4_ Forced Air System ☐ #___ Radiant Heat ☐ #___ Gravity System ☐ #___ Other _____
	Approximate BTU rating # _1_ _50K_ # _2_ _50K_ # _3-4_ _50K_ ☒ Gas ☐ Electric
FLEX LINES NEEDED	**Gas line:** ☐ Flex ☒ Rigid **Electrical connection:** ☐ Conduit ☐ Wire _DAMAGED NEEDS REPLACED_
	Thermostat: ☒ Functional ☐ Non-functional ☐ Damaged ☐ Manual (on unit) ☒ Unit responded ☐ Unit did not respond ☐ Reason unknown ☐ Gas off
	Duct work: ☒ Appears intact ☐ Damaged ☐ Asbestos-like wrap on duct
	Vents: ☒ Appear intact ☐ Limited access prevents full evaluation
	☒ Gas Co. exam suggested ☒ Routine service call suggested ☐ Repair needed → _PRIOR TO CLOSE OF ESCROW_
B- Air Conditioning:	**Type:** ☐ Central ☐ Window mount ☐ Wall mount ☐ Roof mount Other _____
	Number of units ___ Location: _____
	☐ Tested ☐ Not test ☐ Responded ☐ Did not respond ☐ Routine service/repair needed

Remarks: ☐ Licensed contractor needed to perform routine service/ repair and certify system.

NOTE: Read opposing page for further instruction, explanation and limitations.

MARK 1 HOME INSPECTORS

Appliances

We will run the appliances whenever possible. We *do not* dismantle or represent that any unit runs properly. We simply determine that the unit is operational. We will report any obvious abnormalities.

Vents / fans

We recommend that all ovens and stoves be properly vented, preferably by a charcoal filter or exhaust fan to prevent unventilated cooking areas.

Garbage disposals

Many times garbage disposals will dry out and become stuck if not used. A tool exists that will assist in freeing the unit. In the event there is no power at the unit it may be restored by pressing the reset button on the bottom of the unit.

Occasionally, due to debris clogging the drain line water will flow out of the air vent which is usually located on top of the sink which is supposed to drain down into the garbage disposal. This can be corrected by removing the rubber hose on the unit and cleaning out debris caused from prematurely turning off the disposal unit prior to debris being washed away.

We *do not* dispose of food etc., to test the unit.

Trash compactor

We *do not* compact trash to test the unit.

Oven / stove / microwave

We *do not* cook on the units or test temperature accuracy. We simply report whether or not they operate.

Note: We do not inspect refrigerators, intercom systems, built-in blenders or can openers.

Units	GENERAL NOTES	PAGE 7

KITCHEN — DISPOSAL IS FROZEN - SPLICED CONNECTION.
Unit # 1 ✱ VERY CROWDED/DIRTY UNIT

Living room GOOD CONDITION

I CRACKED WINDOW

Bathroom #1 TOILET STICKS

Bathroom #2 _____

Bedroom #1 GOOD - 1 MISSING SCREEN

Bedroom #2 GOOD

Laundry Room GOOD

Water Heater SEE PAGE 6

Heater RESPONDED SEE PAGE 6

KITCHEN - GOOD
Unit # 2

Living room ROOF LEAK EVIDENT. BROKEN

WALL PLUG NORTH WALL

Bathroom #1 SINK DRIPS - TOILET

LOOSE ON FLOOR

Bathroom #2 _____

Bedroom #1 GOOD

Bedroom #2 GOOD

Laundry room GOOD

Water heater OLD UNIT - SEE PAGE 6

Heater SEE PAGE 6

Unit # 3 KITCHEN - ROOF LEAK EVIDENT. WIRE SPLICE AT DISPOSAL

Living room OK - GOOD

Bathroom #1 OK - GOOD

Bathroom #2 _____

UNIT - VERY CLEAN

Bedroom #1 OK - KNOB HOLE IN WALL

Bedroom #2 OK - GOOD

Laundry room GOOD

Water heater SEE PAGE 6

Heater SEE PAGE 6

Unit # 4 KITCHEN - VALVE HANDLE MISSING UNDER SINK

Living room GOOD - 1 MISSING SCREEN

KNOB HOLE IN WALL

Bathroom #1 GOOD - GROUT NEEDED

AROUND TUB. FIXTURE COVER MISSING

Bedroom #2 _____ ON LIGHT.

Bedroom #1 GOOD - MINOR PLASTER

CRACKS - NORMAL SETTLING

Bedroom #2 OK - GOOD

Laundry room GOOD - WATER HEATER LEAKS

Water heater SEE PAGE 6

Heater SEE PAGE 6

NOTE: Read opposing page for further instruction, explanation and limitations

GARAGE / ATTIC / GROUNDS — **PAGE**

GARAGE

A-Garage :

Size: □ Single □ Double □ Triple ☒ 4 car □ Tandem □ Attached ☒ Detached

Floor : ☒ Intact ☒ Cracking noted ☒ Minor □ Other _____

④ Garage Door : ☒ Wood □ Aluminum ☒ Swing □ Roll-up □ Other _____
☒ Operational □ Non-operational □ Other *BROKEN SPRING #3*

Garage door opener : □ Operational □ Non-operational □ Other _____
— *NONE*   Safety reverse : □ Yes □ No

Firedoor : □ Solid □ Hollow   Self closer : □ Functional □ Non-functional □ None

Exterior door : □ Solid □ Hollow □ Good condition □ Weathered/damaged

Window(s) : □ Appear operational □ Non-operational □ Other _____

ATTIC

B-Attic :

Rafters : *2x4* Joists : *2x8*

Insulation type : □ Blown □ Rolled □ Rock wool □ Fiberglass □ Cellulose ☒ None

Attic access location : *UNIT 2* _____ □ Limited access □ No Access

☒ Full view □ Limited view □ View obstructed _____

GROUNDS

C-Flatwork :

☒ Driveway ☒ Walkways □ Steps □ Patio

Condition : ☒ Normal Cracking □ Heavy cracking □ Buckling □ Trippers present
☒ Root lift □ Settling Describe : _____
FRONT WALK WAY

D-Fencing :

Type : □ Wood ☒ Block □ Brick □ Stucco □ Chain link □ Other _____

Condition : ☒ Over-all good □ Leaning ☒ Cracking *(minor)* □ Post rotting

Gates : ☒ Operational □ Need work ☒ Over-all functional

E-Retaining Walls:

Type : □ Concrete □ Block ☒ Rail tie □ Other _____

Condition : □ Over-all Normal □ Normal cracks □ Heavy cracks □ Bulging □ Leaning
□ Stable at present □ Unstable □ Repair needed

F-Decks & Stairs:

Type : □ Wood □ Metal □ Concrete/masonery □ Other _____

Condition : □ Good seal □ Cracking noted □ Deterioration noted □ Seal work needed

Railings : □ Sturdy □ Loose □ Inadequate □ Repair needed

Note : See termite report for condition of all wood

G-Sprinklers :

☒ Timers □ Anti-syphon ☒ Able to test □ Unable to test □ None present
□ Timers on □ Visible broken heads ☒ Maintainance suggested

Remarks:

MARK 1
HOME INSPECTORS

NOTES: Read opposing page for further information, explanation and limitations.

The *Unofficial Guide* Reader Questionnaire

If you would like to express your opinion about investing in real estate, or this guide, please complete this questionnaire and mail it to:

The Unofficial Guide™ Reader Questionnaire
Lifestyle Guides
Hungry Minds, Inc.
909 Third Ave.
New York, NY 10022

Gender: ___ M   ___ F

Age: ___ Under 30   ___ 31–40
___ 41–50   ___ Over 50

Education: ___ High school   ___ College
___ Graduate/Professional

What is your occupation?

_____

How did you hear about this guide?
___ Friend or relative
___ Newspaper, magazine, or Internet
___ Radio or TV
___ Recommended at bookstore
___ Recommended by librarian
___ Picked it up on my own
___ Familiar with the *Unofficial Guide*™ travel series

Did you go to the bookstore specifically for a book on investing in real estate?   Yes ___   No ___

Have you used any other *Unofficial Guides*™?
Yes ___   No ___

If "Yes," which ones?

_____
_____
_____

What other book(s) on investing in real estate have you purchased?

_____

_____

_____

Was this book:
___ more helpful than other(s)
___ less helpful than other(s)

Do you think this book was worth its price?
Yes ___   No ___

Did this book cover all topics related investing in real estate adequately?   Yes ___   No ___

Please explain your answer:

_____

_____

_____

Were there any specific sections in this book that were of particular help to you?   Yes ___   No ___

Please explain your answer:

_____

_____

_____

On a scale of 1 to 10, with 10 being the best rating, how would you rate this guide? ___

What other titles would you like to see published in the _Unofficial Guide_™ series?

_____

_____

_____

Are _Unofficial Guides_™ readily available in your area?   Yes ___   No ___

Other comments:

_____

_____

_____

Get the inside scoop...
with the *Unofficial Guides*™!

Health and Fitness

The Unofficial Guide to Alternative Medicine
ISBN: 0-02-862526-9

The Unofficial Guide to Coping with Menopause
ISBN: 0-02-862694-X

The Unofficial Guide to Dieting Safely
ISBN: 0-02-862521-8

The Unofficial Guide to Having a Baby
ISBN: 0-02-862695-8

The Unofficial Guide to Living with Diabetes
ISBN: 0-02-862919-1

The Unofficial Guide to Smart Nutrition
ISBN: 0-02-863589-2

The Unofficial Guide to Surviving Breast Cancer
ISBN: 0-02-863491-8

Career Planning

The Unofficial Guide to Acing the Interview
ISBN: 0-02-862924-8

The Unofficial Guide to Earning What You Deserve
ISBN: 0-02-862716-4

The Unofficial Guide to Hiring and Firing People
ISBN: 0-02-862523-4

Business and Personal Finance

The Unofficial Guide to Beating Debt
ISBN: 0-02-863337-7

The Unofficial Guide to Investing
ISBN: 0-02-862458-0

The Unofficial Guide to Investing in Mutual Funds
ISBN: 0-02-862920-5

The Unofficial Guide to Managing Your Personal Finances
ISBN: 0-02-862921-3

The Unofficial Guide to Marketing Your Business Online
ISBN: 0-7645-6268-1

The Unofficial Guide to Picking Stocks
ISBN: 0-7645-6202-9

The Unofficial Guide to Starting a Business Online
ISBN: 0-02-863340-7

The Unofficial Guide to Starting a Home-Based Business
ISBN: 0-7645-6151-0

The Unofficial Guide to Starting a Small Business
ISBN: 0-02-862525-0

Home

The Unofficial Guide to Buying a Home
ISBN: 0-02-862461-0

The Unofficial Guide to Buying a Home Online
ISBN: 0-02-863751-8

Family and Relationships

The Unofficial Guide to Childcare
0-02-862457-2

The Unofficial Guide to Divorce
0-02-862455-6

The Unofficial Guide to Eldercare
0-02-862456-4

The Unofficial Guide to Online Genealogy
0-02-863867-0

The Unofficial Guide to Planning Your Wedding
0-02-862459-9

Hobbies and Recreation

The Unofficial Guide to Casino Gambling
ISBN: 0-02-862917-5

The Unofficial Guide to eBay® and Online Auctions
ISBN: 0-02-863866-2

The Unofficial Guide to Finding Rare Antiques
0-02-862922-1

The Unofficial Guide to Selecting Wine
0-02-863668-6

All books in the *Unofficial Guide*™ series are available
at your local bookseller.